Effective IT Service Management

Rob Addy

Effective
IT Service
Management

To ITIL and Beyond!

With 50 Figures

 Springer

Rob Addy
www.effectiveitsm.com

Library of Congress Control Number: 2007929266

ACM Computing Classification: D.2.9, D.2.7, K.6.1, K.6.3, K.6.4, K.4.3

ISBN 978-3-540-73197-9 Springer Berlin Heidelberg New York

Springer is a part of Springer Science+Business Media
springer.com
© Springer-Verlag Berlin Heidelberg 2007

Typesetting: by the author
Production: Integra Software Services Pvt. Ltd., Puducherry, India
Cover Design: KünkelLopka, Heidelberg

Printed on acid-free paper   45/3180/Integra   SPIN   12267231   5 4 3 2 1

For Harry, Charlotte and Georgia
Thank you for reminding me of the
most powerful word in the world:
"Why?"

Preface

IT issues affect everyone... Whether it's a mix up at a government department delaying the payment of benefits/rebates or an air traffic control systems crash which causes inbound and outbound flights to be suspended at the nation's airports, IT errors can have significant consequences. Even when the results of such failures aren't life threatening they can have a massive financial impact upon the organisations concerned. Millions of dollars a year are lost due to IT problems. These losses accrue from waste, fines/penalties, decreases in productivity, the need to redo work that is lost and missed sales opportunities to name but a few.

Consider your daily routine – You're forced to skip breakfast because your 'Wheatie' flakes weren't delivered with your online grocery order as the order picking printout at the central depot got jammed in a printer. Your commute into work was even more hellish than normal due to a failure within the traffic signal control system. According to the news, the problem is due to the unexpected load the system is experiencing during rush hour. You arrive late, stressed and grumpy (probably due to hunger), this is compounded by having to walk up twelve flights of stairs to your desk because the main elevator control system needed a reboot. Out of breath, you attempt to begin your daily routine, unfortunately you are unable to check your email because a worm virus has infected your corporate email system causing it to melt down. The virus found its way into the network because a planned operating system patch was misapplied to one of the servers in the DMZ (whatever that is). Undeterred, you drag your aging underpowered laptop to the board room and plug in the LCD projector. For some inexplicable reason nothing happens... After several minutes plugging and unplugging the projector you scream for someone to get help. Several minutes (or maybe hours) later a man with a replacement bulb arrives and restores calm. The calm is short lived as some bright spark points out that the figures you ran for your important management meeting are wrong because the exchange rate metadata in the sales automation tool hasn't been updated. This problem soon becomes irrelevant as the video conference link with your remote sites is painfully slow due to network issues. It isn't even 10am and already IT has conspired to ruin your day, your career and your life...

Why oh why can't IT just work? To the best of your knowledge, these IT people get paid handsomely and yet they seem incapable of preventing even the most fundamental of issues... Surely they have systems in place to do this stuff for them? Operations, Sales or Manufacturing wouldn't be allowed to continue in such a shoddy manner! Something must be done! You're not exactly sure what that something is, but hey that's not your problem...

Put simply, IT Service Management (ITSM) is the group of processes and functions that oil the wheels of the IT machine. Without ITSM, every IT project and system would deteriorate over time until they fail. ITIL is the recognized best practice standard for ITSM. ITIL has been around since the late 1980s. And yet, many of today's IT problems have been around for just as long. Clearly to manage IT effectively organizations must go beyond the ITIL framework – This book is a practical guide to delivering and managing IT services in an effective and efficient manner by extending the ITIL approach to deliver proactive and pragmatic IT Service Management.

Depending upon industry sector ITSM related costs account for between 65 %-80 % of all IT expenditure. That's currently the equivalent of almost $300 billion per year worldwide (which is more than the GDP of Norway). Almost more than three quarters of every IT budget is spent keeping the application lights burning and the wheels of the IT machine turning. Most of this money goes on labour costs. There are more jobs within ITSM and related areas than in any other field within computing. And yet given this prevalence it is bizarre that so little is known about it. This book attempts redress the balance slightly by giving an honest unbiased view of the discipline, its objectives, major processes, and their benefits and shortcomings. IT is the single most pervasive discipline within the business world today. It touches and affects everything. Irrespective of their particular market sector and expertise, many organisations are completely reliant upon IT to enable them to get on with the business of doing business... Managing and mitigating IT risk is critical to the survival of every business. Success is an optional extra! Proactive IT Service Management can be thought of as risk management for IT – Can anyone afford to ignore it?

This book is a candid look into the relative merits of currently accepted wisdom regarding the provision of IT services using the principles of the IT Infrastructure Library (ITIL) guidance series. It describes IT Service Management processes related to Service Delivery and Service Support (as well as other non-ITIL areas), their objectives, shortcomings and how these issues can be addressed in real life situations. In addition to this, it delivers a workable definition of what exactly an 'IT Service' is and how it can be defined and used in practice. ITIL has been around for over 18 years and has been adopted by many large organisations as their primary mode of operation for IT delivery.

Its supporters and advocates claim that ITIL processes are the best and only way of managing IT delivery, especially IT changes effectively. And yet over the past decade, the IT analyst community have consistently stated that 80 % of all service impacting IT incidents are due to poorly managed change... If ITIL hasn't helped after being in place for almost twenty years surely the time has come to question whether or not it will ever be sufficiently 'fit for purpose' to be able to deliver upon its promises?

Rob Addy
January 2007

Contents

About this Book

Why this Book was Written

IT is the single most pervasive discipline within the business world today. It touches and affects everything. Irrespective of their particular market sector and expertise, organisations are completely reliant upon IT to enable them to get on with the business of doing business... Managing and mitigating IT risk is critical to the survival of every business. Success is an optional extra!

And yet given the criticality of the subject, it is amazing to see many IT shops still floundering in the dark ages with little or no focus upon proactive IT Service Management.

Who this Book is for ...

This book is aimed at three primary audiences:

- The business leader whose livelihood depends upon the availability of mission critical IT services (but maybe doesn't realise it yet)
- The IT Service Management professional responsible for keeping the IT lights burning
- The Computer Science student who is keen to find out how theoretical IT concepts are delivered, supported and maintained in the real world

The book is intended to enable business management to understand the importance of IT Service Management and to be confident enough to ask the right questions to ensure that the IT infrastructure underpinning their business is fit for purpose. By asking the pertinent questions, and demanding that their IT infrastructure is managed in professional manner, business leaders are uniquely placed to be able to significantly improve their bottom lines and reduce corporate inertia, allowing their organisations to react quicker and take advantage of new market opportunities.

Hopefully, the IT professionals reading this book will, for possibly the first time, have a reference guide and sounding board against which to validate, contrast and compare their own plans and ideas regarding IT Service Management and how best it can be implemented to improve the quality of IT provision within their business. The intention is not to provide all of the answers, or indeed to be right all the time, but instead to equip the reader to be able to ask the right questions and to feel confident enough to challenge conventional IT wisdom...

Whether they want to or not, many Computer Science graduates will find themselves coming into direct contact with IT Service Management processes when they join the industry. It is one of the aims of this book to make this meeting of minds as productive and painless as possible. Irrespective of their choice of role and discipline, ITSM will have a significant impact upon their working lives and as such it is useful to understand how these set of processes came into being and how they are intended to function.

What's in a Name?

This book could have had many titles but the top ten list of the ones that almost made it include:

- 101 Questions your CIO doesn't want to be asked
- Who wants to be average? Beyond ITSM best practice
- Everything you want to know about ITSM but were afraid to ask
- Better than best practice... ITIL is only the beginning
- Making IT work. The art of trouble free IT service management
- "The business says 'Yes' but the computer says 'No' " – Regaining control of the IT machine
- ITIL be alright on the night! Assuring IT Service quality using ITSM
- IT Service Management system failures (and how to avoid them)
- How to become CIO without really trying...
- Balancing the waterfall – ITSM best practice explained

Using this Book...

"Alice was beginning to get very tired of sitting by her sister on the bank, and of having nothing to do: once or twice she had peeped into the book her sister was reading, but it had no pictures or conversations in it, 'and what is the use of a book,' thought Alice 'without pictures or conversation?' "

Alice's Adventures in Wonderland, Lewis Carroll

This book has been carefully designed to fit handily underneath an unstable table leg or to help level up an uneven bookcase. In the unlikely event that you want to learn about IT Service Management, it has also been filled with information regarding the management of IT services and their efficient and effective provision for business benefit.

Based upon personal experience, direct observation and hundreds of conversations with the only real experts in the subject, i.e. those that do IT on a daily basis, it contains references to industry standards as well as definitions of practices that contradict currently accepted best practices. It is not for me, the author, to determine whether or not these contradictions represent new or improved best practices but instead I ask you to judge for yourself and make your own assessment. Only time will tell how this books content is received and adopted by the industry as a whole, if at all. But whether it is consigned to the dusty shelf of ridicule and anonymity or hailed as the definitive text on its subject – one thing is for sure, the experience of writing it has given me new insight and a new found respect for authors of all kinds.

Whatever your view, I invite you to follow me through the looking glass for a journey into the depths of ITSM, exploring the 'Why' as and 'How' as well as 'What' whilst trying to avoid getting stuck in too many unnecessary rabbit holes...

Why now?

Some people have asked why I haven't waited until version 3 of ITIL is released before publishing this work? Well, there are several reasons really... The publish date of ITIL refresh is not fixed, there is no guarantee that they will meet their deadline, and I wanted to ensure that any similarities between the revised ITIL text and this was purely coincidental. Also, why not? The scope of this book and its relatively small physical size mean that it will appeal to an audience very different from that of the official ITIL documentation.

Just like planning for marriage or children, I doubt there is ever a "right" time to do it – things could always be better, more convenient or more appropriate – but the important thing is why you're doing what you're doing. If you are convinced in your purpose then timing is largely irrelevant – at least I hope it is.

Additional Resources – the Ubiquitous Accompanying Website

No book would be complete these days without an accompanying website. This book may be incomplete in many ways, but not in this regard. The website www.effectiveitsm.com contains information regarding errors identified after going to press, example data sets, diagrams/flow charts etc.

About the Author

Rob Addy is an ITSM professional with over a decade of hands on experience in the field with both enterprise and medium sized organisations. During this time Rob has been fortunate to work for many of the biggest names in the industry in a variety of roles. From application development and support, to direct solution implementations, to product management and marketing, to consulting management and technical sales, Rob has gained insight into the ITSM world from a wide variety of angles. This 360 degree view of the market enables Rob to balance real life scenarios, customer requirements, best practice processes and technical solution capabilities and limitations to give a unique pragmatic approach to improving IT services using a combination of best practice and tried and tested experience. Prior to joining the IT industry, Rob worked as a Quality Manager within the risk management, service and manufacturing sectors where he oversaw and managed the process of gaining and maintaining certification to ISO 9000 on several occasions.

Disclaimer

The views and opinions expressed within this book are solely those of the author and should not be construed as being shared by his employers (past and present). Any similarities between examples cited within this book and real life companies/events is probably not accidental but the author reserves his right to change the names to protect the innocent as well as the guilty. Blah blah blah . . .

And so it Starts . . . An Introduction

Babbage was dead: to begin with. Turing was dead too. There is no doubt whatever about that. Old Babbage was as dead as a door-nail.

Mind! I don't mean to say that I know, of my own knowledge, what there is particularly dead about a door-nail. I might have been inclined, myself, to regard a coffin-nail as the deadest piece of ironmongery in the trade. But the wisdom of our ancestors is in the simile; and my unhallowed hands shall not disturb it, or the Country's done for. You will therefore permit me to repeat, emphatically, that Babbage was as dead as a door-nail.

But that, as they say, is another story . . .

The Birth of Computing

Today's computer owes its very existence to hypothetically clanking mechanical logic engines and the monolithic valve based decryption devices developed during the Second World War. These concepts were extended and enhanced over several decades to deliver what we know now as the micro processor and the personal computer. Geniuses such as Babbage and Turing went beyond the realms of conventional thinking to stretch the boundaries of what was possible in order to design and create machines that could emulate the logic based analytical behaviour of the human brain. It is somewhat ironic then perhaps that so many current IT issues are due to the inability of the eminently fallible user to get their head around the subtleties of logical procedural based systems . . .

Exponential Growth

In the late 70's and 80's computing came out from the gloomy shadows of the server room and began finding its way into the home and the office. This heightened visibility and the widely perceived untapped potential of IT led to the function being adopted, blindly in many cases, across pretty much the entire business world.

Rise of the Geek

Simple economic theory regarding supply and demand meant that skilled IT resources were now very scarce and had to be coveted and treated well if they were to stick around to feed the IT machine... And this is where many of the first wave of IT 'professionals' came from, from the ranks of the back office teams which loaded mountains of paper into the gigantic printers of yesteryear. One day you're stacking reams of paper, the next you're loading punch cards into an early not so super, super computer.

Welcome to the Human Race (Kind of)

As UK chat show host Mrs Merton once infamously asked Debbie McGee, the wife of magician Paul Daniels, "What first attracted you to the multi-millionaire Paul Daniels?". To paraphrase the Beatles, Money can't buy you love – but it sure can buy you a better quality of misery. As more and more money was thrown at IT, the discipline became more and more accepted as a career of its very own – no longer seen as an off shoot of the finance function, IT (egged on by those who held the keys to the computing kingdom) was standing on its own two feet proclaiming "Look at me Ma... Top of the world!"

Acceptance at any Cost

Over promising and under delivering was common place in the early days. Of course IT could do it. The computer was going to rule the world. IT was supposed to be a magic pill for every business problem and so numerous charlatans set up to sell the dream to the unwary. These impostors were almost indistinguishable from the real deal and consequently many organisations spent extortionate sums of money on systems which either failed to deliver their anticipated results or never made it into production at all...

The IT Bubble Bursts – Pop!

To quote Hugh Grant in Four Weddings and a Funeral, "Bugger! Bugger! Bugger! Bugger!". Just when it was all going so well, the world lets a little thing like profitability and underlying intrinsic value get in the way of the marauding IT industry. Many excellent IT professionals lost their livelihoods and their confidence in the crash. Many awful IT resources did too. The problem was that the dot com stigma tarnished both the competent and incompetent without prejudice... Only now are the green shoots of recovery beginning to emerge. It will probably never be the same again, which may be for the best as a healthy dose of realism would have probably averted the entire episode if it had been applied during the 1990's.

The Long Road to Recovery . . .

The first step on the road to recovery is to admit that there is a problem. Many within IT openly recognise that they need to improve the way in which they operate with their business peers. Those that do not will go the way of the dodo.

The average age of today's senior IT executive is somewhere in the region of mid to late forties. These are children of the 1960's who received their formal IT education in the mid to late 80's when high end computer processing power was equivalent to less than a modern day refrigerator. Is it really any wonder that things are as they are? To compound the issue, many senior IT executives do not come from a technical background and so rely upon marketing sound bytes from vendors and the like to inform and educate them with regard to what is practical and what should be expected.

IT has come an awfully long way since these early days; unfortunately a lot of IT Service Management process and procedure hasn't kept abreast of developments and is looking more than a little tired. Modern day ITSM best practice still has its roots firmly planted in the 70's and 80's. If things are to improve significantly then the industry must let go of its chequered past and look to the future whilst learning from the historic mistakes of more established industries such as manufacturing . . .

A Brief History of ITIL . . .

The Information Technology Infrastructure Library (ITIL) is a set of guidance developed by the United Kingdom's Office of Government Commerce (OGC). The guidance framework, published as a series of books, describe an integrated, process based, best practice approach to managing IT services. These books are a, non-proprietary, publicly available set of guidance for IT service management. So how did they come to exist in the first place? Well, the ITIL story is shrouded in mystery and the mists of time have done little to improve clarity to its origins, but here is a brief potted history of the first twenty or so years of ITIL.

The 1980s . . .

ITIL originally emerged in the mid to late 1980s. The CCTA (Central Computer and Telecoms Agency) was a major UK government department, with an IT budget of around £8 billion, which it was under severe political pressure to reduce significantly. The department decided that greater efficiency was one way to potentially reduce its costs. This focus upon process and efficiency, created a suitable environment for the development of ITIL as we know it.

It's ITIL Jim, but not as we Know it . . .

The earliest version of ITIL was originally called the Government Information Technology Infrastructure Management (GITIM). Obviously this was very different to the current ITIL framework we know today, but conceptually it was very similar, and primarily focused upon service support and delivery.

The 1990s . . .

During the 90s many large companies and government agencies throughout the UK and Europe, with particular penetration in the Netherlands, started to adopt the ITIL framework as the basis for their IT operations. The ITIL message was spreading quickly across the globe, and was rapidly becoming the de facto standard for IT service management by stealth.

Millennium . . .

The new millennium was a busy time for ITIL . . . The CCTA transformed into the Office for Government Commerce (OGC). In the same year, Microsoft used ITIL version 1 as the foundation upon which to develop their proprietary Microsoft Operations Framework (MOF). MOF takes the principles of ITIL and fills in some of the gaps in relations to routine operations, security management etc in what some might cynically say is a blatant attempt to shift more product. And to top it all, the British Standards Institution released BS15000 – legitimising ITIL once and for all.

2001 . . .

In 2001, following an extensive in depth review, version 2 of the ITIL framework was released. The new revision updated much of the text with more modern definitions, terminology and examples as well as significantly redeveloping the Service Support and Service Delivery books making them more concise and usable.

2002 . . .

The BS15000 service management standard is significantly revised and reissued to a waiting world.

2005 . . .

Consultation for a new release of ITIL itself is undertaken. BS15000 is placed under 'fast track' to become an ISO standard: ISO 20000.

2006 . . .

The 'ITIL refresh' process continues with the selection of authors for the core elements of the ITIL document set. The general direction and content has been determined and publication is due sometime in the first half of 2007.

1

ITIL – Holy Grail or Poisoned Chalice?

1.1 Introducing the Defendant

ITIL was born in 1987 to modest critical acclaim and spent its formative years as the preserve of large government and corporate IT departments with equally large budgets. Eighteen years after its creation ITIL is preparing, just as every other teenager/young adult does, to find its place in the world and make its presence felt. The prior publication of BS 15000, and its internationalization with the publication of ISO 20000, looks set to catapult this set of IT best practices into the mainstream. Love it or hate it, you certainly can't ignore it – ITIL is coming to an IT shop near you.

ITIL is now big business and is considered by some as the thing that will finally legitimize the IT function within the business world. Traditional references to nerdy back office geeks with beards and sandals have been replaced by talk of systematic incident management processes implemented by problem managers, solution engineers, change approvers and the like. The IT landscape is changing for sure, but is the brave new world of ITIL all that it is cracked up to be?

Before embarking on a project to embrace these standards you might be advised to take a few moments to consider whether or not they are right for your particular organization and specific business requirements.

1.2 What is ITIL?

Unless you have been living under a rock for the past couple of years you will know that ITIL is a documented set of processes designed to define how a company's IT functions can operate. It contains a series of statements defining the procedures, controls and resources that should be applied to a variety of IT related processes.

1.3 ISO 9000 – A Lesson for the IT Industry to Learn from...

The similarities between ITIL's latest incarnation as BS 15000 and the ISO 9000 family of standards for quality management are clear. This is hardly surprising since both sets of documents were drafted by the same standards organization. To put it simply, ITIL can be thought of ISO 9000 for the IT department.

Just as BS 5750 and latterly ISO 9000 attracted massive popular support within the business world during the 1980's and 1990's, ITIL looks ready to ride the wave of management popularity into the next decade. During its hey day ISO 9000 became an industry of its own with consultants advising on how to implement the standard, certification bodies auditing to see that the standard had been implemented and yet more consultants employed to rationalize the monolithic procedural manuals that were often created to gain certification so that they were usable. There were articles, training courses, text books, workshops, seminars and even government assistance programs dedicated to the implementation of the standard.

Despite all of this, ISO 9000 is infamous for failing to deliver upon its hype and has since been abandoned by many of its former supporters and advocates. The common response to critics of the standard from the industry gurus of the time went something along the lines of "There's nothing wrong with the standard – you must be implementing it wrong". This helpful advice fueled the market for further consultancy services even more and perpetuated what some consider to be one of the worst episodes in the arena of quality management.

Some brave organizations resisted the overwhelming market pressures to adopt the standard because they did not see sufficient benefits from it – many of these companies are still in business today and have suffered no long term effects from their decision not to ride the ISO 9000 gravy train.

1.4 The Case for ITIL

- **Structured approach** – There is no disputing the fact that ITIL covers all the major areas of interest that concern today's IT executive. It's structured and systematic approach mean that it will allow managers responsible for a chaotic IT organization to implement the various processes step be step without absolute confidence that they will have hit the major bases.
- **Good foundation upon which to build** – There is nothing in ITIL that is superfluous or unnecessary in the absence of a defined system. ITIL is an excellent starting point from which to build your IT service management system.

- *Analyst support/Easy ride for the CIO* – No-one is going to be criticized openly for deciding to implement ITIL. The press coverage and popular management appeal of it mean that it is the safe decision for any IT executive wishing to demonstrate that they are up to date with modern(ish) IT thinking.
- *Can be used to help prevent knowledge loss from the organization* – The documented procedures and requirements for documenting activities undertaken by the IT organization mean that should your key personnel decide to leave then they will leave less of a void than previously.
- *Prescriptive nature means that you don't have to think too much* – Many people don't like to think. Others claim that they don't have the time to think. And some prefer not to expose themselves by revealing that they can't think on their own. Either way ITIL will relieve you of the need to use your own thoughts and judgment when determining how you want to run your organization.
- *Allows for job specialization* – The demarcation of roles and responsibilities within ITIL will provide your HR department with many happy hours determining a whole series of role based job titles. These in turn may help you retain staff longer by offering them a defined career path through your organization.
- *Requires IT management to formally review all processes delivered by their teams* – When implementing ITIL, departmental managers will need to take time out to map their current operations to those flows defined in the framework. This in depth review can only serve to do good as it forces management to get down into the nuts and bolts of their business to reinforce their understanding of the issues facing their staff and the requirements of the business.
- *Encourages the use of flow charting techniques to map out business processes* – Visualisation of business processes is often the first step to process improvement. Having documented and defined the process graphically it becomes readily accessible to everyone within the organization and can the diagrams can become an invaluable troubleshooting and improvement tool.
- *Consistent usage of defined terminology across the industry promotes understanding and simplifies communication* – This is possibly the greatest benefit that ITIL brings to the industry. A common vocabulary allows us all to communicate more effectively and enables closer comparison of like with like than has ever been possible.
- *Traceability and accountability* – With structured systems come the ability to formally trace and review what was done about any particular incident or problem. Such audit trails are an invaluable aid to piecing together a picture of what transpired and allow even those not directly involved with a case to get up to speed quickly and contribute if appropriate.

- *Ambiguities and vagueness in definitions give you flexibility* – It should be remembered that ITIL is a loose framework of guidance notes and as such has sufficient holes to allow you to operate in many different ways whilst remaining in alignment with ITIL general direction.

1.5 The Case Against ITIL

- *Stifles creativity/innovation* – The very fact that ITIL lays down a framework of business processes means that those implementing do not have to go through the process development phase for themselves. Whilst this is undoubtedly a massive time saving it does also mean that those adopting the standard are locked into the overall direction of the ITIL model and will find it hard to do anything innovative or novel.
- *Food for consultants* – Just as the ISO 9000 phenomena created an industry of its very own, ITIL looks certain to do the same with countless companies already offering Certification, Compliance audits, BPR, Process consultancy and the like.
- *Diverts attention from real objectives/Becomes a goal in itself* – Implementing ITIL has become a job in itself for some IT executives. This misdirection of resources means that the improvement of services, reliability and user satisfaction can take a back seat.
- *Allows senior management to pay lip service to real issues "We're ITIL so we're alright"* – Being ITIL certified or implementing an ITIL certified system does not guarantee any level of system performance or achievement. It is dangerous to suggest that ITIL will fix all, or any, of the ills of your IT infrastructure. Only hard work and a systematic approach to problem resolution and subsequent prevention will do this.
- *Seen as a "Magic Pill"/"Silver bullet"* – Adding ITIL processes on top of a chaotic IT infrastructure is likely to make matters worse rather than better. The added burden of ITIL procedural requirements can make an overstretched IT operation lose its way and cause it to fail under the load.
- *Creates inertia/Can be used as an excuse for inactivity* – Formal procedures always bring some level of inertia into an organization. The need for everyone to be trained and the need for everyone to buy in to the new way of working is only one example of how ITIL could impact your operation. If you then throw into the mix the need for a procedural review body to oversee and approve any changes it is easy to see how you can spend more time on the paperwork than on what your actually supposed to be doing.
- *Lack of credible research into its effectiveness and value* – To date there has been no study into the implementation of ITIL on a large scale to identify and prove the benefits that its supporters claim. After sixteen plus years it is surprising that someone somewhere hasn't collected this data.

- **Doesn't promote a continuous improvement culture** – ISO 9000 was initially slated by many quality professional for its "consistency rules" approach. In subsequent revisions this was rectified somewhat with the addition of clauses relating to preventive action etc. Regrettably ITIL hasn't yet learnt from its quality focused relative and has very little to do with the systematic prevention of problems and incidents at this time. Even the areas of Error Control do not truly address what it is required to prevent something happening. Instead, they focus solely on root cause analysis with somewhat morbid fascination.
- **"Best practices" by definition mean that you are only average** – If everyone accepts something to be the best and adopts it wholeheartedly then everyone has the best, and the best then becomes only average. Unless organization continually review their processes and change them in order to achieve greater efficiencies, greater level of service or reduced costs then they will soon fall behind the marketplace and become less than average.
- **Devised by bureaucrats for bureaucrats** – ITIL was originally developed by government officials to allow government officials to manage IT projects more effectively than they had done previously. Whilst ITIL probably did do great things to improve the effectiveness of these institutions, it should be remembered that government is not, and is not likely to become, the performance standard against which modern business measures itself.
- **Creates arbitrary boundaries between functional groups** – The distinctions between problems and incidents highlighted within the ITIL framework do little to encourage cross departmental liaison and cooperation. There is a real danger that front line organizations will only focus on incident management and will not dedicate sufficient time and resources to problem resolution. Equally, second line organizations may feel justified in passing their customers to the first line rather than dealing with them directly with obvious detriment to customer service.
- **Blind faith on the part of some managers that ITIL processes are the best way of working** – The trade media has spent so much time extolling the virtues of ITIL that many IT executives have forgotten their usual scepticism. Managers that would never take the word of a vendor on its own are blindly following the pronouncements of a few industry luminaries as gospel.
- **Lack of detail in some areas/Over prescriptive in others** – The ITIL framework adds value in areas where it brings clarity to the unclear and definition to the chaotic. Unfortunately, some subject areas are covered in more detail and with more thought than others. This is the price to be paid by any document that has multiple authors contributing standalone chapters without a strong overriding editorial direction.
- **Fails to tie the provision of IT services back into the overall business goals and objectives** – Remember ITIL was born in government where the usual business rules don't always hold true. Sure, cost control

is important as is efficiency, but we should bear in mind that all government departments are constantly looking to increase their size and remit because with size and influence comes power.

- *Increased administrative burden* – Additional process steps and increasingly data hungry support systems can significantly increase the amount of reporting required of your employees. Don't be surprised if some of your staff resent this additional element to their duties and claim to have two jobs rather than one – the second being to write about what they do!

1.6 The Jury is Still Out . . .

It is not the intention of this book to answer the question "Is ITIL right for you?". This is something that only you can answer and even then only after you have conducted a careful review of the pros and cons as they apply to your organization. The following set of points are intended to act as a guide for readers when deciding on whether or not to go the ITIL route or not.

1. Make your own assessment
2. Don't believe the hype – Healthy scepticism is a good thing!
3. Use the framework as a starting point/foundation on which to build
4. Don't change for the sake of change – Know why you are changing and what you want to achieve from the change
5. Measure before, during and after any process change
6. Keep it simple – Please!
7. Don't be afraid to question the validity of the framework – Always, always ask why?
8. And remember to be better than average you will have to go beyond ITIL!

1.7 Closing Remarks and Verdict

Many solution vendors are jumping on the ITIL band wagon to add weight to their claims about their products and services. Until such time that ITIL has been proven in the field by legitimate research it would be wise to treat such statements as any other marketing sound byte.

The industry is already awash with people claiming to certify solutions and organizations against ITIL. The publication of ISO 20000 is likely to increase the number of parties involved in these activities and means that buyers should be increasingly careful to do appropriate due diligence on any 'expert' they are planning to engage.

Ultimately ITIL will probably be a good thing for everyone involved in the IT industry – it will require all IT professionals to raise their games to a reasonable level and may even help eradicate some of the more technology centric practices of the past.

ITIL won't change the world, but it might just make it a little less chaotic... Providing you implement it "correctly" for your own individual circumstances and treat it as the starting point of your ITSM journey and not the final destination.

BS 15000/ISO 20000 – Legitimising the ITSM Market . . .

The British Standards Institute and the International Organisation for Standardisation are responsible for the drafting and publication of many thousands of different standards covering everything from apples (ISO 1212 – Guidance on conditions for the cold storage of apples) to zinc (BS 2656 – Specification for zinc anodes, zinc oxide and zinc salts for electroplating).

With the publication of BS 15000 and its internationalised counterpart ISO 20000 IT Service Management has taken a giant lead towards acceptance and legitimacy. Both standards are based upon the ITIL documentation library and outline a system for the management of the IT function geared towards the provision of IT services. It should be noted that external certifications against these standards are available to enable organisations to demonstrate that they comply with the requirements of the standard. Whether or not they deliver excellent IT services is another matter entirely. Products cannot be certified against the standards and as such any vendor claims or implied claims should be treated as nothing more than marketing sound bites.

2.1 Are Standards a Good Thing?

Standards work best when they describe something in quantifiable terms that can be independently tested and verified. Standards define a definite output in unambiguous language to prevent miscommunications and misunderstandings. Common understanding allows different parties to deliver something in a standard manner. Standards enable standardisation. Standardisation aids the commoditisation of an item. Commoditisation allows different items that meet the standard to be used interchangeably i.e. standards improve the level of interoperability that can be realised. Interoperability reduces dependency upon any one specific vendor. Free market economics can then be applied to reduce the cost of standards based items. Reduced costs are a good thing. Therefore, standards are a good thing!

The above tongue in cheek analysis does hold true for some cases and indeed standards can be incredibly useful. However, within the IT industry standards compliance is not always consistent and just because something is purported to follow a specific set of standards does not necessarily mean that it does. Take for example the DOM standards laid down by the W3C committee governing HTML and JavaScript implementations within web browsers. Anyone who has had the pleasure of developing web content for multiple browser platforms knows that the organisations behind browser development often take dramatically different views of the meaning of the standard and implement significantly different approaches to satisfy its requirements.

Let us consider the mission of Apollo 13...

As the spacecraft was on its way to the Moon, at a distance of almost 200,000 miles from Earth, the number two oxygen tank in the Service Module exploded. This created a series of problems which were overcome thanks to the ingenuity of both the crew and the flight controllers in Houston. As well as working out how to return the crew safely to earth, they had to contend with the minor irritation of the Carbon Dioxide scrubbers in the Lunar Excursion Module (LEM) 'lifeboat'. The lithium hydroxide canisters available for the LEM's CO_2 scrubbers would not last long enough to get the crew home. Although the Command Module (CM) had an adequate supply of replacement canisters, they were the wrong shape to fit the LEM's receptacle; an adapter had to be fabricated from materials in the spacecraft. Mission Control devised a way to attach the CM canisters to the LEM system by using plastic bags, cardboard, and gaffer tape - all materials carried on board.

However, had the scrubber's design been consistent i.e. standardised across the LEM and the CM, then the potential for CO_2 poisoning would have been one less headache for NASA to deal with during the crisis in 1970.

3

Aligning IT with the Business

In recent times there has been much talk of the need to align the IT function with the business. The theory being that if the IT function is heading in the same direction as the business it can begin to actually help, rather than hinder, the business to meet its wider objectives. IT leaders and software vendors have seized upon this piece of 'wisdom' and have lavished many hundreds of hours and millions of marketing dollars upon the promotion of IT as a valuable business contributor rather than a necessary evil.

Such attempts are largely nothing more than window dressing to cover up for the fact that IT departments the world over are largely left to function in isolation with little or no impact upon business strategy. Instead the role of IT in even the most progressive organisations is to maintain the status quo and ensure that the business can proceed in the direction it already believes is appropriate. The investigation of new technology advances and their potential usage to further business objectives and/or open up new markets are left to the larger systems integrators, management consultancies, analyst community and self proclaimed industry gurus...

3.1 What Do We Mean by Alignment?

When pushed to explain what is meant by the term 'IT – Business Alignment', the market responds with clichéd sound bites regarding opening up positive channels of communication between senior IT management and key stakeholders within the business.

Through additional communication it is believed that common concerns will be identified sooner and that the IT function will be able to respond to changing business requirements faster. In reality such regular meetings do little to improve the way in which IT contributes to the organisation other than perhaps reducing the time lag between external business impacting events and the issuance of demands to the IT function to enable the business to respond effectively.

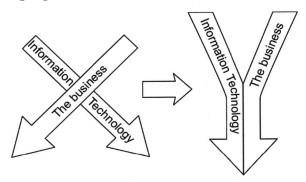

Fig. 3.1. Aligning IT with the business – Turning "X" into "Y"

ITIL goes one stage further to promote the setting up of regular dialogues between service providers and service consumers to thrash out requirements and concerns regarding delivery quality etc. The output of such conversations are intended to form Service Level Agreements (SLAs) which clearly define what the business expects of the IT function (and indeed what the IT function can expect from the business with regards to inputs and information etc) and the performance metrics in place to measure compliance against the agreed terms. Having had the mis-fortune to review many hundreds of such documents over the past decade, I can categorically state that I have never seen any such agreement that has been designed to improve and enhance the business's overall performance. Instead they are typically formalised sticks with which either party can beat the other in the event of a failure on the part of the other.

Another common approach to aligning IT with the business is to decentralise the IT function and embed small IT teams within local business units. Such an approach is based upon the premise that close physical proximity will breed a closer working relationship and that this will improve the level of understanding and cooperation on all sides. Regrettably, the reality is often less than beneficial as the inherent void between the IT function and the business becomes clearer for all to see...

A 2006 survey of IT directors and Finance directors showed that IT management don't trust their boardroom counterparts in charge of finance to manage offshore IT outsourcing contracts. By coincidence, the survey showed that Financial management don't trust their IT directors either.

It is perhaps no surprise that the survey found significant differences of opinion between these two factions. Finance directors are the old guard, protecting the company from the vagaries of the market and management fads. They see IT directors as the young upstarts, keen to squander the company's precious resources on the promise of untold gains. IT directors often have about the same standing with Finance directors in blue chip firms as rookie sales executives - they are tolerated because they are a necessity, nothing more.

But the differences in perception shown by the survey are quite stark. One per cent of finance directors thought IT directors should be trusted with responsibility for managing an outsourcing deal. Only 2 per cent of IT directors thought that their Finance colleagues should be given the job. Such a result clearly highlights the massive gulf between these two business critical functions, this may be due to the ghosts of one too many failed ERP implementations coming home to roost. One thing's for sure, aligning IT with the business will take much more than marketing sound bites and ambitious proclamations if it is to become a reality.

Such misalignments are invariably about trust or the lack of it. Trust has to be established between IT and the rest of the business. Because of IT's pervasive nature, the internet boom of the late 1990's, IT's chequered past and less than perfect track record there are many people with business that have had personal negative experiences with IT. If real change is to be made regarding the perception of IT within an organisation it will have to be done one person at a time. Unfortunately, building trust takes time and requires a concerted effort on the part of everyone concerned. Every tentative step forward must be built upon positive user experiences and underpinned by consistent service delivery. Positive examples from senior management help, but it is worth remembering that months of progress can be undermined by a single momentary loss of focus or thoughtless comment.

3.2 How Aligned are You?

Whatever the definition of IT – Business alignment in use, it is necessary to first understand where you are before a useful plan of action to get to any desired end state can be determined. The following list of questions will help identify how aligned your IT function is with your business... Unfortunately there are no hard and fast rules regarding what it takes for IT to become a business peer to the likes of the sales, operations, marketing, finance, production and HR functions. The following questions will help you to ascertain how much work there remains for IT to be considered a valuable contributor to the business:

- Does the most senior IT executive within the business report directly to the CEO?
- Does the CIO attend all board meetings? Are IT related issues routinely discussed at such meetings?
- Are IT related performance metrics included within monthly management reports?
- Where is the CIO's parking space in relation to other senior executives?
- Is corporate IT policy dictated by the in-flight magazines that the CxO level executives read whilst on the plane?
- Is IT seen as a provider of toys for the boys? Or is it recognised as a valuable business contributor?

- Does the IT function actively participate within routine business reviews?
- Are there regular interlock sessions between every aspect of the business and IT to ensure requirements and constraints are fully understood?
- Is IT actively involved within ongoing continuous improvement programs and/or business process re-engineering activity?
- Is the IT budget isolated or is it formally split across all business functions depending upon operational usage/need?
- Are business critical systems and services identified? Has their importance been communicated to everyone within the IT function? Could every member of the IT team tell you the financial impact (i.e. cost per hour or opportunity cost per hour) of each business critical IT service if it were to fail?
- Do IT initiatives originate from within the IT function or are they instigated from within the business itself?
- Does the business understand the technical constraints under which the IT function operate and any limiting factors (e.g. legacy applications on archaic unsupported platforms etc) that may prevent them from meeting the needs of the business in the short or medium term?
- Is IT seen as a tactical or strategic issue by senior management?
- Do senior executives in non-IT functions accept and openly recognise the contribution that IT makes to the areas under their control?
- Does everyone within the IT function understand the different roles, responsibilities and dependencies of other business functions and how they combine to deliver the value to customers?
- Can IT management articulate the value proposition of the business that they support? And can everyone within the IT function describe what it is that the business does? Would your front line help desk agents be comfortable giving a 1 minute elevator pitch about your organisation?
- Is there a formal 3–5 year plan for IT within the business? Is this plan reviewed and approved by the board? Is everyone within the business aware of this plan and its content?
- Do senior IT executives review the short and long term business plans of other business functions?
- Are IT representatives regularly invited to local departmental meetings?
- Is there a vehicle (newsletter, open forum etc) to communicate IT related information to the business? What level of readership/subscription is there?
- Is the IT section of the organisation's intranet accessed frequently?
- Does IT proactively approach business leaders and suggest ways in which IT could be leveraged more effectively in their areas?
- Are there formal user satisfaction surveys in place? How often are these metrics used within the day to day management of the IT function?
- When was the last time a member of the IT team was voted employee of the month/invited to attend an off site team building event for another department? Are IT employees eligible to win and/or attend corporate

recognition events? When was that last time that a member of IT was recognised in this way?

- Do IT work closely with the HR function to profile the IT related skills of the user base and develop generic training plans and technical pre-requisites/skills requirements for common roles within the organisation?
- Does the new-starter induction program include the IT function and how it contributes to the success of the business? Or is it just about getting the users laptop running and setting up their email account?
- Is there an IT suggestion box scheme or similar for the business to record improvement ideas? How often are these ideas reviewed/recognised/implemented?
- Do all IT staff follow the corporate dress code?
- Could every member of the IT team tell you the current stock price, who the major competitors are and where your business sits in relation to them in the marketplace?
- Could every member of staff name at least one member of the IT management team? Does everyone in the business know the IT helpdesk number/intranet site URL?

3.2.1 So How Did You Do?

Predominantly "Yes" – Congratulations! Your IT function is the exception that proves the rule... Either that, or you are a delusional fool that has forgotten to taken their medication and shouldn't be allowed to play with sharp objects. If you really are doing all these things already then you are far ahead of the curve in terms of the way that IT works with the business and are undoubtedly experiencing many benefits from such a close and symbiotic relationship.

50:50 Mix of "Yes" and "No" – Congratulations! You appear to be on well the way to joining the ranks of the wider business community and gaining acceptance as a valued contributor to the organisation. The questions will hopefully act as a guide and point of reference for future initiatives, allowing you to consolidate your position and make even greater strides forward.

Predominantly "No" – Congratulations! Honesty is a vital component for any trust based relationship to succeed. It appears that you have plenty to work on and I guess the biggest question is "Where do you start?".

3.2.2 The First Faltering Steps to IT Becoming Accepted as a Business Peer

Before embarking on a quest to become recognised as a valued contributor to the business, the IT function must first take a step back and take a long hard dispassionate look at itself. Fault lies on both side of the relationship, but it is essential to recognise and admit to ones own past misdemeanours before anything progress can be made. When setting out on this path, the following guiding principles may be helpful:

- Accept that many of your first advances will be ignored, refused or ridiculed – get over it and get on with the job in hand
- Smother your biggest critics with kindness and public displays of support and appreciation
- Invest time and resources in communicating success stories – but remember that the business is the star of the show, not IT!
- Find one or two early adopters within the business and do anything and everything possible to make them successful
- Always remember to focus on explaining the "Why?" rather than the "How?" or "What?" – No one really cares about the technology...

This is all very well but many of you will be asking for concrete examples, at least I hope you will, of things that can be done to improve the relationship between IT and the business...

3.3 10 Things You Can Start Today to Get the Ball Rolling...

"A journey of a thousand miles begins with a single step."

Confucious

The following suggestions may not seem particularly significant or ground breaking, and indeed they are not intended to be, but they represent IT's best opportunity to begin turning around a dysfunctional relationship that has been neglected on both sides for more than a decade. Do one today! Not tomorrow, but today. And you will have taken that all important first step...

1. Identify ways in which individual department or functional heads could quickly and painlessly reduce their current IT expenditure e.g. the rationalisation of blanket VPN access rights, disconnection of unnecessary leased lines, recycling of equipment for new starters etc. Submit proposals for potential cost reductions to the business for their approval before implementing the changes i.e. let them take the credit for the savings.
2. Develop a departmental action plan for every business area to address their top five IT issues. Sitting down with functional heads and working through their current IT related pains will help build links as well as identify areas for investigation and improvement activity. These pain lists should be published and regularly reviewed in light of progress and changes to business priorities.

3. Develop departmental standard configurations (both hardware and software) to minimise the provision of unnecessary hardware and software. Request that each functional area takes time to explain how it is currently using IT, the tools it uses and the rationale behind their use. By suggesting freeware viewers, open source options and cheaper alternatives to current software tools the IT function can help the business to begin reducing its software spend going forward. Hardware specifications are often driven by a need to "keep up with the Jones's" in other departments and have little to do with the actual needs of the business...

4. Perform an external website performance assessment and identify areas that could be improved. Pass findings and recommendations (expressed in lay persons terms such as the reduction in time needed to open pages etc) to the marketing function for them to evaluate.

5. Start a tip of the day/week bulletin i.e. "Did you know that..." posts, to highlight ways in which users can improve their use of existing systems and tools. Do not use email (a banner ad on the corporate intranet homepage would be better etc) for the transmission of this messaging and ensure that it is as relevant and interesting to the user population as possible. Common subject areas might include corporate system short cuts, tips regarding email and vmail usage, reminders about where to find templates, links to cool and/or useful sites on the intranet etc.

6. Work with the quality management and business transformation functions to identify working practices that could be enhanced by automation etc. Develop cost models for such projects to be included within business process improvement plans. Take care not to presume that IT is the answer for all of the world's ills – Process automation and technology has its place but is not a magic pill in itself.

7. Invite the heads of different functional areas within the business to come and present at your future team meetings (and if you don't have formal team meetings... start those too!). Ask them to give an overview of their department, what it is that they do, how they use IT, their biggest IT issues and how they believe IT could help them more in the future.

8. Develop a new technology road show to demonstrate how advances in IT could be of benefit to the business. The road show should be taken out into the field and delivered at team meetings etc to spark interest and raise awareness of how technology could be leveraged more effectively. Care must be taken to avoid becoming overly focused on technology and toys – the aim is to related technical advances to current business problems e.g. the use of software distribution tools to disseminate and distribute company documentation to remote employees over unreliable low bandwidth internet connections.

9. Post pictures of all (or examples of each job role for larger organisations) IT staff on the departmental intranet site and explain what each team member does and how that can help an end user. This will help to start

to personalise the function and move away from the perception of faceless voices at the end of a help line.

10. Lobby to have IT service related metrics included within the monthly and quarterly reporting packs that are sent to senior managers and the divisional and regional heads. Be sure to limit the report to a single side of a piece of paper and to make the information provided pertinent to the business performance e.g. Number of hours within the period where the external web site, order management system, sales automation tool etc were unavailable or performance had degraded to an unsuitable level. By raising visibility in this way it allows management to start asking questions (some of which will be difficult so be prepared for them) – which after all is the first part of creating a meaningful dialogue.

3.4 Is Alignment Good Enough?

There is an unspoken assumption within the IT world that aligning IT with the business is sufficient to demonstrate value and be a valued contributor to the organisation. However, I would question this assumption and point out that such an approach may well be selling the potential impact of IT upon the business short of what could be achieved.

If we in the IT function limit our aspirations to merely following the business then we forego the opportunity to help shape the business and set future strategic direction...IT has the potential to be a business leader, not just a supporting part. However, before IT is ready to take center stage it must first learn the management and business ropes in an understudy role to ensure that it is ready for the time when its big break comes.

3.5 Is Running IT as a Business Really the Same as Aligning IT with the Business?

No. The purpose of running a business is to make the maximum possible financial return for the stakeholders. The purpose of the IT function is to facilitate, enable and support the business.

4

What Keeps Your CxO up at Night?

The root causes of senior executive insomnia will be varied and may include the following; Eating cheese before bedtime? A shopaholic spouse with your credit card in their hand? The last espresso shot of the evening? The stock price? Worry? Change? Fear? Risk? The fear of the risks related to change?

Whatever the reasons, there is a fair chance that they will be symptomatic of an underlying fear. That fear will be based upon a perceived risk. And that risk needs to be addressed if they are to sleep soundly.

Risk . . .

Risk is everywhere. It cannot be seen, heard or smelt and yet we can all feel it (and in extreme cases, maybe even taste it). Fear, uncertainty and doubt (FUD) is a marketing term used to define a mechanism for making ones competitors seem less appealing to a prospect by introducing the perception of risk into their minds by posing unanswered questions or theoretical concerns regarding the rival. Risk by its very nature introduces and spreads FUD. Risk is everywhere and comes in many forms:

- Commercial risk
  - Losing customers, customer dissatisfaction, competitors
- Financial risk
  - Reduced revenues, uncontrolled spiralling costs, downward pressure on profit margins
- Operational risk
  - Productivity decreases, increases in waste, poor product/service quality, contamination
- Regulatory/Legal risk
  - Possibility of legal action, non-compliance, excessive bureaucratic burden
- Health and Safety/Environmental risk
  - Incidents, accidents and injuries

IT is everywhere

IT is the single most pervasive discipline in business today. IT is everywhere. From front of house visitor logging systems, to EPOS systems, to production line automation, to websites, to back office finance functions, IT impacts every single part of today's business. IT issues can have the potential to unleash a crippling effect upon every part of the business. IT failures can directly increase costs, reduce revenue, upset customers, prevent shipments leaving, affect product quality, impair your reputation and have countless other undesirable side effects in the process.

IT can be very scary

The abstract nature of IT and its complex language of jargon and techno babble do little to ingratiate it with those not in the know. Historically, a lack of understanding has always bred resentment and unease amongst those excluded from the game (be that by social class, race, knowledge or skills). Resentment and unease are the foundations of fear.

The effects of fear

The effects of fear are varied and many. Paranoia, Paralysis, Peeing ones pants, Pretending it's not happening and Posturing are all possible responses to fear. Organisations that are gripped by fear seldom make any real progress until the root causes of the fear are understood and addressed. It should be remembered that fear is not always a bad thing. Fear breeds a healthy respect that can help to focus the mind and may be used to rally the troops to deliver more than they believed themselves capable of. It is just a matter of recognising it and working with it, instead of against it.

Information technology can either mitigate or exacerbate the level of risk

IT can be used as a force for good or it can be used as a force for evil. This may be overstating the case a little but you get the gist. IT can significantly improve the level of control exerted over a process if applied in a structured and planned manner. Approval cycles, go/no go decision points, audit trails, data validation routines, electronic signature requests, defined authorisation levels, embedded business rules, process automation, management dashboards, Service Level Agreements, automated escalations/notifications etc can all significantly improve the level of control within a business process and force employees to comply with corporate policies without them needing to know the details. Conversely, free format scratch pad systems allow employees to make the process up as they go along and introduce significant opportunity for risk and abuse.

IT is a risk in itself

All of the above IT based process controls will come to nothing if the infrastructure upon which they rely is inherently risky. In order to enable IT to assist with the management of business risk, it must be managed in a controlled manner to ensure it performs as required. The systematic planning and implementation of fault tolerant architectures and the use of systems without single points of failure help to minimise the likelihood of major IT incidents and service outages. However, technical controls and hardware based solutions may not be enough to guarantee IT stability.

Managing IT risk is increasingly critical to the survival of every business

IT controls are nothing without the appropriate management system to monitor their implementation, validity and usage. Process and procedures are needed to oversee the IT environment as well as to continually assess the level of residual risk that is inherent in the complete 'system' of IT including the infrastructure, application portfolio, organisational structure, procedures, practices and people.

ITSM = Risk management for IT

Implementing IT Service Management processes can go some way to holistically managing the risks associated with IT.

5

Traditional IT Service Management Wisdom

5.1 Maturity Models and Waterfalls

Conventional wisdom states that IT issues are complex and can only be understood by technical experts, this means that IT needs to be managed as a series of interconnected technically focused linear processes that feed each other and allow the organization to resolve incidents, fix problems and implement changes. This belief has propagated itself throughout organizations to such an extent that no other function believes they have any role to play in IT management and is singly responsible for the organizational isolation that many IT departments face today. This isolation is a double edged sword, in good times when money was plentiful the IT function was often given a blank check and left to get on with it with little or no leadership or direction. Unfortunately, as the economic climate changes and money becomes scarce, IT functions have their budgets cut with little regard as to how it will impact the operation of the business and again are left to make business critical value judgments on their own...

There is an unquestioned belief in some quarters that incidents are fixed by workarounds, logged against known errors or resolved to the satisfaction of the user. Incident analysis then spawns problems which are to be investigated, classified and either logged as known errors or rectified by implementing an infrastructure change. Changes to the IT environment are planned and implemented in a structured manner to ensure that the desired result is achieved. Where multiple changes are required to be managed as part of a wider program, they are grouped together and managed as a release. All activity and components of the infrastructure of documented within a centralised database known as the Configuration Management database (CMDB) and this information is leveraged by the other processes.

IT functions are sometimes evaluated on a sliding scale of goodness depending upon their level of ITIL process implementation. This arbitrary scale was conceived by the analyst community as a means of comparing different

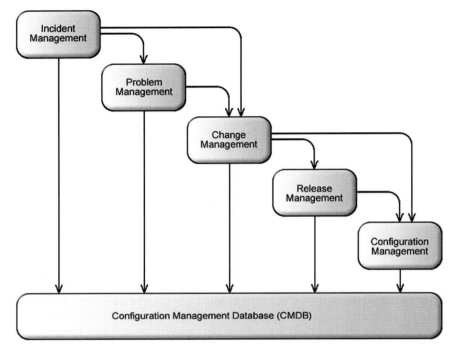

Fig. 5.1. Traditional ITIL Cascade or Waterfall

organizations against one another and has become a means of displaying progress to senior management who are keen to see how IT is improving.

The dreaded radar plot of ITIL maturity should strike fear into the heart of any manager keen to improve the level of service provided to the business...

5.2 Because Real Life doesn't Work That Way!

Unfortunately the purist view of the world only partially holds true.

Since 1999, The analyst community have been pushing a multi stage maturity model (the number of maturity stages you get depends on your particular analyst but as with all such information, you pays your money and you make your choice) against which many organisations have benchmarked themselves. These crude measures have little relevance to the real world as it is common for different departments (and indeed different functions within the same department) within an organisation to operate to different levels of maturity. Organisations typically target the areas most critical to them and often excel in one or two areas.

The focus of the maturity model also suggests that reactive capabilities are somehow less desirable and/or worthwhile than proactive or value based

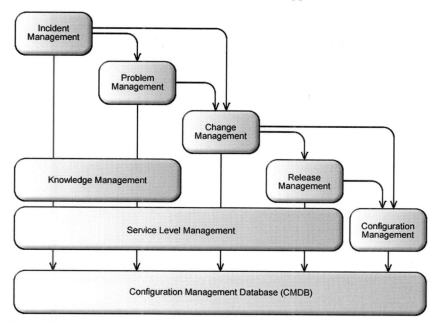

Fig. 5.2. Enhanced ITIL Waterfall with Service Level Management and Knowledge Management

processes. This simply isn't true. If an organisation is to grow and succeed it must be careful to balance the various needs of the business and take care to ensure it is aware of what is going on in the outside world and react accordingly.

5.3 A Balanced Approach to ITSM

The danger with ITSM maturity models and ITIL capability radar charts is that they can allow IT management to take their eye off the ball and focus on narrow metrics rather than the services for which they are responsible. As in all walks of life, it is necessary to take a balanced approach to something if one is to be successful. Too much focus upon any one area will always lead to sub-optimal performance overall.

The key to achieving balance is to identify and understand the contradictory nature of the things you are trying to manage. Strategic goals are often dramatically different to short term tactical actions, indeed it is not uncommon for tactical initiatives to introduce additional obstacles that must be overcome to reach long term strategic objectives. Sometimes it is necessary to introduce mid term pain to alleviate short term symptoms before reaching the final long term cure. To throw yet more clichés on to the barbie... Rome wasn't built in a day and you can't make an omelette without breaking eggs! I think you probably get the idea by now.

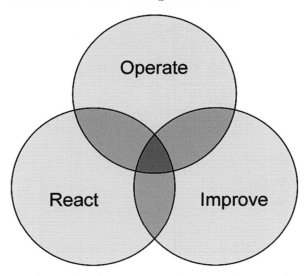

Fig. 5.3. A balanced approach to Service Management

With regards to IT Service Management, the key is to ensure the operational, reactive and proactive needs of the business have equal focus and importance. This will enable the IT function to handle life's little challenges, whilst keeping the lights on and in the mean time actively improving the way in which it delivers its services to the business.

The overlapping circles in the figure above can be thought of as a Venn diagram (AKA Set theory) outlining the inter-relationships between the reactive, improvement and operational disciplines. Where all three circles overlap is the success sweet spot which all organisations should be aiming for...

5.3.1 Operational Requirements

Operational needs are addressed by the day to day activities necessary to keep the IT machine ticking over. Such activities are sometimes known as routine operations or IT operations and represent the no glamour face of IT. Preventive maintenance activity is an established concept within non-IT operational areas e.g. production/manufacturing etc but is rarely considered as an IT discipline. This is most probably due to the "rip and replace" nature of today's IT hardware. The very first computers, such as those developed during World War Two, were massive valve based calculation engines and as such needed significant maintenance activity to ensure that they were operational. Valves were cleaned, tested and replaced on an ongoing basis. As hardware improved, the need for such physical maintenance activity diminished to a point where core components became modular black box elements that could be replaced upon failure. The truth of the matter is that all IT shops perform preventive maintenance activity upon their environments routinely but fail to make the link. Common prevention tasks within the IT space include:

- Patch application/Software upgrades
- Anti-virus updates
- Database re-indexing/statistic (re)calculation
- Data archiving/cleansing/duplicate removal
- File defragmentation
- Printer servicing
- Vulnerability testing
- Asset discovery sweeps/reconciliation runs
- Proactive cycling (Bouncing boxes)
- Preventive replacements
- Equipment cleaning

Routine maintenance activity remains the preserve of the IT Operations team and is often forgotten by other members of the IT fraternity let alone the rest of the business. How often are routine tasks incorporated into change management plans? Never? Rarely, at best. And yet, routine tasks such as database re-indexing or disk defragmentation can have a major impact upon available system resources and could negatively impact scheduled changes if they are run in parallel.

5.3.2 Reactive Capability

Unplanned events occur in a seemingly random manner and yet this 'randomness' enables us to statistically calculate anticipated incident rates with reasonable accuracy over a given period. The ability to be able to react to external or internal incidents is of paramount importance to any IT organization. When planning for the 'unknown' it is important to ensure that likely demand profiles are understood and that sufficient levels of resources are available to be able to handle the peaks as well as the troughs . . . Such a model requires a flexible staffing capability with the service delivery managers responsible for incident and request management processes being able to call upon their operational and improvement focused colleagues for support and assistance when required.

The ability to respond positively to unplanned events is an important measure of the capability of a service organization.

5.3.3 Improvement Focus

Any change to the status quo should be aimed at improving something (except for those rare cases where things have to get worse before they can get better). Continuous improvement is the only goal worth pursuing in a world where everything changes and standing still is tantamount to going backwards.

Proactive analysis of IT performance and the development of service improvement plans in response to identified opportunities is critically important if the IT function is to become a valued contributor to the business.

5.3.4 Overlaying Best Practice upon Our Balanced Approach

By combining the reactive, operational and improvement orientated process model with the traditional best practices waterfall we can begin to see a balanced approach to service management works in the real world. The merging of these two approaches allows organisations to take a pragmatic approach to service management whilst ensuring that they are aware of the need to maintain balance and activity in each of the three core areas.

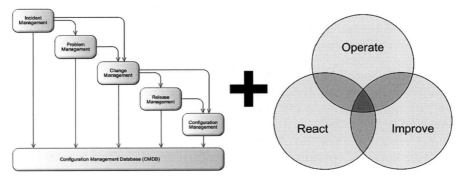

Fig. 5.4. Combining a balanced approach with best practice

You may note that the release management element of the best practice waterfall does not directly map to the Venn diagram segments. In reality this is because the similarities between change and release management are such that it makes sense, for the purposes of this diagram anyway, to treat them as one entity with slightly different characteristics.

The configuration management database (CMDB) does not participate within the balanced process model as it is a repository rather than a process. It does naturally participate as a repository and point of reference for all processes that leverage it however.

You can see that incident management is judged to be primarily a reactive discipline, change management is aimed at improvement and asset management is operationally focused. Where the model really begins to show its value is when we look at the interactions between reactive, improvement and operational goals i.e. the overlaps.

We see that request management is the bridge between the operational side of the business and the reactive element of the organisation. Requests are raised to address a defined business need and require attention and action to be completed.

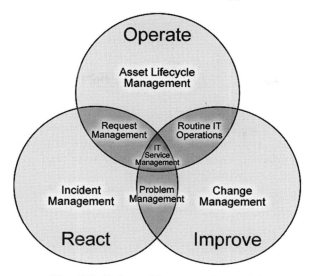

Fig. 5.5. Balanced best practice model

Preventive maintenance/Routine operations combine the day to day operational activities with the need to avoid outages and incidents i.e. to improve the level of service quality and reliability.

Problem management is a structured approach to the analysis of common issues (e.g. incidents, outages etc) with a view to determine what course of action is necessary to prevent recurrence. Where a valid action plan is determined then it needs to be implemented in a carefully controlled manner to ensure that it is completed appropriately and the desired result achieved i.e. problem management can be thought of as the bridge between incident and change management.

Where all of these best practices combine we see that true service management is achieved – this must remain the underlying goal of all forward looking organisations if they are to maintain their market position and grow in the future.

5.3.5 Service Definition – Part 1

We will define IT services in detail later on within this book, but for the purposes of this section lets consider a definition which compares a service with a traditional process diagram.

This basic definition of a service above shouldn't be contentious or surprising. It owes its existence to works of management and quality gurus, Deming, Crosby and Drucker, it simply shows that nothing comes from nothing and that for a desired outcome to be achieved consistently a combination of controls and resources need to be applied in a defined manner. We focus on three

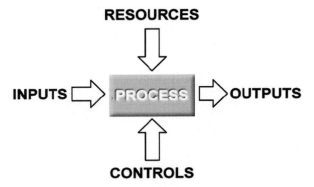

Fig. 5.6. Traditional process model

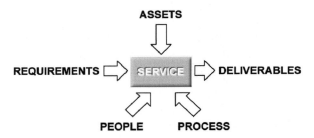

Fig. 5.7. Extending the process model into a service model

main areas of resource and control; people, processes and things. Each of these areas has their own particular requirements and needs to be managed in a specific way. Some services will be more people focused than thing focused and vice versa – the important thing to remember is that irrespective of the service being performed/delivered that all of these areas will be involved in some manner.

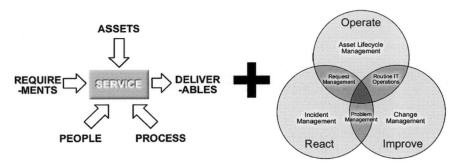

Fig. 5.8. Combining the service model with the balanced best practice model

Fig. 5.9. Balanced best practice process model

5.4 A Balanced Best Practice Process Model

So we have defined a balanced process model and a workable (for now) service definition... All that remains is for us to do now is to combine the two to determine an overall balanced service centric process approach to service management.

By combining the two models we are able to break the overall model into simpler disciplines that may be implemented in isolation or as part of a combined cross discipline project. There are advantages and disadvantages to both approaches, however the reality of the situation is likely to require a phased implementation approach as the majority of organisations will have pre-existing tools and processes in place which address some of these areas.

We identify asset centric processes, people centric processes and process centric processes...

6

Enough of the Management Fads, Marketing Hype and Analyst Bluster...

6.1 Does Anyone Really Do this Stuff?

Yes and No. IT Service Management processes and related practices can be found in many thousands of IT shops across the world. Not every organisation has implemented every discipline and not every implementation is in accordance with ITIL guidelines or the contents of this book. However, ITSM has become an accepted part of IT delivery, particularly within larger organisations where its structured approach and common vocabulary help ensure that IT has transitioned from the chaotic technology focused mess of the past into something slightly more useful.

6.1.1 What's in it for me? And by that, I of Course Mean you the Reader...

Perhaps, this is the most natural question in the world. And yet one which is often overlooked and ignored by local management and corporate HR organisations that often believe that the work is its own reward and after all "We are paying them for it aren't we?".

Promoting, implementing and managing IT Service Management processes can have a wide variety of impacts upon the individuals involved. The breadth and depth of these effects can range from the seemingly trivial to the blatantly significant and may include the following:

- Mutual respect with customers/users and peers
- Personal fulfilment/satisfaction
- A less repetitive and frustrating working day
- A quieter calmer lifestyle
- A fruitful and successful career
- The opportunity to leave your IT roots behind and branch out into different business roles
- World peace (OK, maybe this is a little ambitious)

Unfortunately the sad fact of the matter is that many people who work within the ITSM space have little or no enthusiasm for it. Maybe they have been worn down by years of oppressive management and the tirade of constant user complaints. Maybe they have succumbed to the self fulfilling prophecy that mistakes will always happen in IT. And maybe they are unable to get the jobs that they really want. Whatever their personal motivation, or lack thereof, it is the job of IT management to turn around these morale issues and provide an good working environment and room to grow for all concerned. ITSM, and in particular IT support, IT operations etc, is seen by some as a dead end job in a dull backwater of the larger IT pond – Nothing could be further from the truth. IT Service Management is the oil that lubricates the IT machine and without it no IT project would succeed in the long term. It is a shame that this fact is often ignored by those in senior management positions and the spoils of victory are often disproportionately allocated to the high profile, high visibility development and implementation project teams to the detriment of those that keep the wheels turning day in and day out.

Irrespective of why morale is low (if it is), it is essential for IT management to invest sufficient time and thought into making the back office functions feel appreciated, respected and valued within the wider IT organisation. Hopefully, this book will help the disenchanted and disillusioned rediscover their enthusiasm for the subject. The challenge for management is to help their people to find their own particular brand of ITSM fun and to enable them to practice it frequently.

6.2 Benefits of IT Service Management

The following section outlines areas where IT Service Management can deliver value to any business. From time to time we are all required by our masters to draft a business case or two to support our latest innovation, the bullet points and examples cited are intended to help readers articulate the value of their efforts as well as enabling them to prioritise which discipline/area is most appropriate to focus upon at any point in time. It should be remembered that all ITSM initiatives will require senior management commitment and support if they are to realise the benefits outlined below.

Implementing effective IT Service Management processes can:

- Improve efficiency
  - Increase productivity/operational efficiency/and encourage the efficient use of resources
  - Reduce resolution time/change implementation times
  - Improve the effectiveness of the IT function
  - Eliminate unnecessary/inefficient process steps
  - Stop wasted effort
  - Leverage unused capability (equipment and personnel)
  - Enable IT employees to manage their workloads more effectively

- Improve customer service
  - Improve the level of responsiveness to customer/user requests
  - Improve user satisfaction
  - Deliver improved access to IT products and services
  - Enable the IT function to demonstrate its value
- Improve system stability
  - Reduce incident volumes/unplanned outages/failed changes
  - Minimise the effects of business impacting events
  - Increase availability (service, hardware etc)
  - Increase the dynamicism of the IT function/infrastructure
  - Provide a solid foundation for prevention based initiatives
  - Improve the visibility of business processes
- Reduce costs
  - Promote the reassignment of under utilised resources (equipment and personnel)
  - Preventing unnecessary expenditure
  - Making the optimum purchasing decision
  - Avoiding penalties (Service Level related)
  - Avoiding penalties (Lease related)
  - Leveraging warranties
- Improve compliance and demonstrate corporate governance
  - Provide reliable and accurate performance metrics
  - Enable access to accurate real time data enables more effective management decision making
  - Clearly allocate IT costs to the users of the services – Improved accountability
  - Enforce best practice through systemised controls
  - Assure software licensing compliance
- Improve internal IT operations
  - Reduce staff attrition/Improvements in staff morale
  - Use best practices as the starting point for competitive advantage
  - Reduce call volumes – Call avoidance
  - Reduce call volumes – Logging of issues
  - Reduce call volumes – Preventing chase calls
  - Smooth peak call volume spikes

6.3 Details/Examples of ITSM Benefits

Increases in productivity/Improvements in operational efficiency/Efficient use of resources

Process automation and clearly defined roles and responsibilities can help lead to improvements in resource usage (increasing productivity and effectiveness).

When this is coupled with clearly defined task sequences and process models it can allow employees to plan their workload far more efficiently – working on what needs to be done, rather than responding to the latest crisis. Automation of routine tasks such as password reset and the installation of software on user PCs can also have a massive impact upon the productivity of the IT function.

Reductions in resolution time/change implementation times

Typically, chaotic or reactive service desks can gain significant benefit from utilising embedded knowledge management tools within their trouble ticketing solution. This sharing of corporate experience and knowledge can not only reduce resolution times but will also have a positive impact upon the first time fix rate.

Improved responsiveness to customer/user requests

Defined levels of service delivery allow IT groups to prioritise their workload more appropriately and can lead to a more consistent level of service for users. Having stabilised the delivery process, service managers can divert their attentions to refining and improving the underlying business processes to improve efficiency and responsiveness.

Reductions in incident volumes/unplanned outages/failed changes

An effective problem management process can identify the root causes of common incidents and projects/programmes can be initiated to rectify or eradicate the underlying causes and/or mitigate known contributory factors. Where service performance is analysed over time and trends identified this can be used to feed back into the organisations preventive maintenance or replacement schedule to minimise the risk of business impacting incidents and outages.

Minimising the effects of business impacting events

Process modelling and aligning business processes with the underlying IT infrastructure allows an organisation to clearly see the impact of events upon business operations and enables them to implement fall back plans and infrastructure redundancy to mitigate the effect of critical component failures.

Improving the effectiveness of the IT function

IT organisations are continually under pressure to reduce costs and deliver more and more services. These diverging and contradictory requirements mean that in order to continue to deliver to the business the IT function has to learn to work smarter as well as harder. ITSM processes enable IT teams to use the resources more effectively, eliminating unnecessary manual processes through automation and allows them to focus upon business critical problems that directly impact the operation of the business so that they can add real value to their organisation.

Elimination of unnecessary/inefficient process steps

Well thought out change management processes can reduce unnecessary process steps and delays for commonly requested services. The analysis of process design and work task make up associated with a specific change request will allow business managers to optimise service delivery rather than continue as they are at present simply because it has always been done this way. Data driven approaches and user configurable applications mean that as time goes by and delivery managers undergo process reviews and want to implement improvement initiatives, the supporting solutions can adapt and change to reinforce the business process they are implementing.

Stopping wasted effort

Something as simple as a central repository for service requests and incident reports can dramatically reduce the amount of duplicated effort wasted in an organisation. All members of the IT function can review the issues that have been raised and can prevent the logging of duplicate requests.

Reassigning under utilised resources (equipment and personnel)

Full end to end asset lifecycle management can save a large organisation thousands (if not millions) of dollars per year by avoiding unnecessary equipment purchases. The recycling and reuse of hardware within an organisation can on its own justify the investment in a management solution. It is not uncommon for large organisations to routinely purchase expensive IT equipment for every single new starter . . .

Leveraging unused capability (equipment and personnel)

All too often organisations spend money on equipment in one part of their business because they do not realise that they have spare capacity in another. This situation is often made worse by the hoarding mentality of some managers who jealously guard superfluous equipment 'just in case'. In order to encourage unused equipment to be returned to the centralised IT function, there must be some incentive to do so – otherwise unwanted kit remains in cupboards until it becomes to too old and antiquated to be used . . .

Increases in availability (service, hardware etc)

Consolidating routine maintenance tasks into predefined maintenance windows is one way in which proactive change management can be used to improve service availability. Also scheduling routine maintenance of service dependant equipment can also dramatically reduce the level of service unavailability i.e. scheduling a database upgrade to take place in parallel to an operating system patch for an application server can halve the necessary elapsed down time. Improved incident management processes and an effective problem management system can also contribute to shorter break-fix cycles meaning that unplanned outages are rectified sooner and the impact upon the business is minimised.

Improvements in user satisfaction

Greater visibility to the status of their requests allows end users to effectively manage their own expectations and can help to reduce the number of follow up or chase calls to the IT function. When this enhanced visibility is combined with an open declaration of agreed service level targets, there can be a real basis for improving the relationship between IT and the business. Proactive alerting and management of workloads allows the IT function to direct their limited resources most strategically and enables them to focus on the things that matter to the business most.

Reduction in staff attrition/Improvements in staff morale

Flexibility with task completion and an individual's workload can allow them to plan their time effectively and gives them the ability to service their customers as they wish. A lack of control and an inability within the management system toolset to enable employees to do their job right are often cited as the primary reasons for staff dissatisfaction – ITSM solutions that give local decision making capability to frontline staff and management help ensure that they are capable of delivering the level of service that the wish.

Increasing the dynamicism of the IT function/infrastructure

Equipment reuse and re-tasking means that the delay of a full procurement cycle can be eliminated for some change requests. This can considerably reduce the time required to implement changes (especially in the server arena where delivery and commissioning times can be many weeks).

Provision of reliable and accurate performance metrics

Much of the performance data used with management reporting can be generated automatically as the work is completed reducing the dependency upon individuals collating data and entering information manually. This can ensure that all departments are measured on a reliable and equal basis without the intervention of over zealous front line managers who are typically keen to ensure their functional area is depicted in the most favourable light possible.

Access to accurate real time data enables more effective management decision making

Real time metrics allow line managers at all levels to see a concise picture of the performance of their organisation and enable them to make fast and accurate decisions regarding prioritisation, staffing levels and the allocation of their limited resources.

Providing a solid foundation for prevention based initiatives

Before you can prevent any situation, you must first understand it fully. ITSM processes and management systems enable organisations to gather and collate data related to the multitude of influencing factors that affect and cause incidents to arise. Through careful analysis of this data, problem managers can creatively deduce root causes and put in place suitable control measures to ensure their effects are either eliminated or minimised.

Improving the visibility of business processes

Clarity of purpose is critical for any improvement initiative to succeed. Typically organisations do not have a clear and common understand of the processes they use to go about their daily business. ITSM solutions enable organisations to depict their business processes graphically and their dependencies in a readily accessible format so that sensible and useful discussions regarding the validity of the process, or otherwise, may be initiated. Only with this increased visibility can organisations re-engineer their procedures and practices to eliminate unnecessary process steps, remove black holes and bottlenecks and to improve the efficiency of their processes.

Delivering improved access to IT products and services

Many people within large organisations learn what they need to know about IT to get by from their colleagues. It is not uncommon for entire departments to be using their IT infrastructure sub-optimally because that is the way in which everyone in the department does it! A clearly defined service catalogue enables all users to see the wide array of products and services available to them from the IT function – This improved access to services can be used to spark their interest and begin getting them to leverage the power of IT to improve their daily work.

Clearly allocating IT costs to the users of the services – Improved accountability

All too often IT costs (including hardware, services and infrastructure charges) are allocated as a flat rate overhead to departmental functions rather than being distributed according to the level and value of usage consumed. This causes some functions to undervalue the contribution that IT makes to their operation and causes resentment in other areas that do not utilise the IT function as much. By accurately assigning costs incurred against individual cost centers it causes management to sit up and take notice of the amount they spend and the return on that spend that they receive. It is not uncommon for the overall IT spend to reduce significantly where functional costing is introduced as a result in management taking notice of the amount consumed and taking actions to eliminate waste and unnecessary expenditure e.g. Companies often find they are still paying for leased lines and network access to remote sites that are no longer staffed etc.

Enabling IT employees to manage their workloads more effectively

A concise work queue (on an individual or functional group level) allows people to clearly see what work is outstanding and allows them to plan their work accordingly. There is little as oppressive as running from one fire drill to another only to find that the issue in question is not urgent at all. By defining and classifying incident priorities clearly it allows IT staff to work through their workloads in accordance with the priority of the issue to the business.

Enforcing best practice through systemised controls

At their best, automated and assisted systems can be used to reinforce and systemise business processes and best practices. The use of pre-defined templates and data collection rules can be used to ensure that all the pertinent and necessary information required to process a request is captured exactly when it is required to eliminate the need to call users back to check or gather information omitted when the ticket was logged.

Cost reductions – preventing unnecessary expenditure

Equipment reuse, improving the visibility of IT costs, avoiding lease penalty payments for equipment non-return and the reclamation of software licenses can all contribute to dramatically reducing the level of IT expenditure required for an organisation to function. The removal of these unnecessary expenses enable IT functions to focus their limited budgets on improvement and replacement programmes which can significantly improve the level of service provided to the business.

Cost reductions – making the optimum purchasing decision

Providing line managers with pertinent information regarding equipment usage, fault history and warranty information can assist them to make the best possible decisions when considering whether or not to repair or replace faulty equipment. All too often equipment (typically printers etc) is repaired when it would be more economically viable to replace it without even wasting the effort of diagnosing the fault.

Cost reductions – avoiding penalties (Service Level related)

Service level management can be used to ensure that the IT function delivers its services to the level agreed with its customers. In the case of outsourcers, this can dramatically reduce the risk of incurring contractual penalties for poor or non-performance. Internal IT functions can use service level performance measures to visibly demonstrate their contribution to the business and ensure that their budgets are secured going forward.

Cost reductions – avoiding penalties (Lease related)

Effective IT asset management is critical in an environment where equipment is leased. Lease companies typically make their profits from penalising customers who fail to return equipment in its original condition. By carefully tracking equipment and having proactive processes in place to manage allocation, equipment changes (upgrades etc) and returns the level of exposure can be reduced significantly.

Cost reductions – leveraging warranties

It is not uncommon for IT support personnel to inadvertently junk broken equipment that is under the manufacturers warranty because they are unaware of the terms of the agreement. Repairs are also sometimes carried out upon equipment that is under warranty without contacting the vendor – this invariably invalidates any warranty in place and incurs additional cost to the organisation which should have been picked up by the supplier.

Software licensing compliance

Software license audits and usage monitoring tools can ensure a company is fully licensed and prevent it being scrutinised or fined for misused or license fraud. It can also prevent waste, by identifying those users that rarely or never used software that is installed on their computers – These licenses can then be redistributed (subject to the terms and conditions of the software vendors license agreement) to users that wish to use the software in question.

Using best practices as the starting point for competitive advantage

ITIL, BS15000, ISO20000 etc define the framework that an IT organisation should work within to be considered as implementing best practice. However, as more and more organisations adopt these standards the competitive advantage to be realised from doing so diminishes. It is therefore recommended that customers take such standards as the starting point from which they should move forward (utilising the adaptive and flexible nature of our products to enable them to do so) to go beyond best practice and start realising true competitive advantage from their IT infrastructures.

Reduction in call volumes – Call avoidance

Self help and self heal solutions enable end users to fix their own problems without having to interact directly with a service desk agent. It is important for the IT function to track the usage of such systems to identify any underlying trends (for further investigation as part of the problem management process) as well as enabling them to be able to demonstrate that the have added value to the organisation through the provision of these services.

Reduction in call volumes – Logging of Issues

Call volumes associated with the initial logging of requests can be significantly reduced where self service functionality is implemented. This pushes the work load associated with capturing the requester details and the nature of the request down to the user themselves. However it should be noted that, typically, it is necessary to offer users some form of incentive (reduced costs, improved service level etc) in order to get them to utilise a self help solution. It may also be possible to restrict the logging of certain types of issue/service request to a self service interface to force users to use the system.

Reduction in call volumes – Preventing chase calls

Such a system must also be implemented carefully to prevent it generating additional call volumes – it is not uncommon for a poorly implemented self service system to increase the number of call backs (chase calls) received as users desperately try to find out what 'Work in progress' means... In order to prevent this effect it is important that the self service solution provide a sufficient level of information regarding the current status of a request as well as some indication of when it will be updated and/or resolved.

Smoothing of peak call volume spikes

Self service interfaces equipped with a 'Please call me' button can be useful in reducing the peak volume of calls as users may (providing they have sufficient faith in the service organisation that their request will be followed up) decide to opt for a call later rather than wait in a queue to speak to someone.

Enabling the IT function to demonstrate its value

In order to be able to articulate their value to the organisation the IT function needs to have detailed information regarding their contribution to the business and the effectiveness of their operations. With outsourcing ever more common it is a priority for the IT function to be seen to be adding value in a cost effective manner. A highly visible and intuitive dashboard of IT performance coupled with a service orientated service catalogue for users to select from helps to ensure everyone is aware of the current status and what is available to them.

6.3.1 Quantitive and Qualative Benefits of ITSM

It is always difficult to put a financial value against the process improvements and efficiency gains outlined above. By using average pay rates and predicted time savings an estimation of the potential savings can be determined. However, shaving 10–20 seconds off of the time needed to log every incident, even if you are handling thousands of incidents per day, will rarely be bankable in terms of cold hard cash i.e. the theoretical savings will be absorbed elsewhere within the process somehow e.g. by employees taking more time on customer relationship building activities, improvements in the level of detail recorded against an incident, longer coffee breaks etc.

That is not to say that financial savings cannot be made from ITSM implementations. But a business case built around many many small incremental improvements is highly unlikely to deliver the anticipated return in comparison to an initiative which eliminates fewer cases of higher value waste. However, even improvements which are less likely to deliver financial benefits are still worthwhile when considered from a qualative point of view.

Take our example of shaving 20 seconds off of the time needed to report an incident –20 seconds does not seem significant until you place it into its proper context. Imagine a transatlantic telephone conversation in the days before high speed digital communications, the time lag between talking and being heard was little more than a second or two and yet it had the effect of making communication seem forced or contrived and led to people talking over each other with resultant misunderstandings and miscommunications. Consider a scenario where you would deliberately pause for 5 seconds before responding to each response from someone reporting an incident ... Now tell me that shaving 20 seconds off of the time needed to record an incident isn't beneficial.

6.3.2 Return on Investment (ROI)

Return on investment projections are often required as part of a business case to justify expenditure on ITSM related tools. All ROI calculations are based upon a series of assumptions which must be clearly defined as part of the exercise. Assumptions regarding the level of improvement to be realised should ideally be based upon actual real life data from other organisations that have already undergone similar processes.

Unfortunately, such data rarely exists and so assumptions will instead be based upon vendor statistics, analyst reports and estimations. The quality of the ROI projection will be directly proportional to the quality of the assumptions made and the data upon which the calculation is based. As with any house of cards, it only takes one card to fall to bring the whole lot down and require one to start all over again.

My advice is to avoid ROI projections completely, no one believes them anyway!

7

ITSM – A Definition

According to ITIL, IT Service Management is *concerned with the delivery and support of IT services that are appropriate to the business requirements of an organisation. ITIL provides a comprehensive, consistent and coherent set of best practice processes for IT Service Management, promoting a quality approach to achieving business effectiveness and efficiency in the use of information systems.*

7.1 Mmmmm . . . not the Most Useful Definition in the World

Let us suspend disbelief for a moment and make a massive assumption that we all have the same understanding of the term 'service'. If we have a common understanding of what an IT service is (and we will come to a definition and description of such a thing later in this book) then surely it would be easy to define what 'service management' is? Unfortunately, this is not as easy as many would believe – there are few, if any, universally agreed definitions within the service management space. Before we come to a definition, lets agree that the management of a service should be focused upon three main premises – what we need to do now, what we need to do if things go wrong and how we make things better in the long run . . .

By aligning (there's that word again!!) assets, people and processes to support the operational needs of the business we are ensuring that the service delivery function is contributing to success of the business and helping to drive the organisation forward. All too often, technical functions are omitted from corporate messaging and education programs meaning that they do not have a current understanding of the business landscape within which they operate. This can quickly lead to a disconnected organisation where the left hand is blissfully unaware that they are acting against the needs of the right hand.

Alignment is all very well but as everybody knows, things change. Unplanned events and external influences mean that any system must have a reactive capability to ensure it remains effective and focused. This closed loop feedback mechanism collates deviation and exception reports and manages them to completion ensuring that the system reacts appropriately and restores its level of service as soon as possible.

If an organisation is to maintain its market position, it must continually strive to improve all of its processes and procedures. Proactive problem management and change management processes are critical to ensure that organisations systematically improve – unless such practices are proceduralised and become part of the very core of the organisation there is a real danger that short term improvements can become undone as the programs and initiatives that implemented them finish.

Combining all of these elements, our definition of IT Service Management looks something like this:

"IT Service Management is the planned and controlled utilisation of IT assets (including systems, infrastructure and tools), people and processes to support the operational needs of the business as efficiently as possible whilst ensuring that the organisation has the ability to quickly and effectively react to unplanned events, changing circumstances and new business requirements as well as continuously evaluating its processes and performance in order to identify and implement opportunities for improvement."

7.2 So Much Talk of 'Management' but so Little Evidence of it . . .

It is somewhat amusing that every process area within ITIL is classed a separate management discipline. It is as if by adding the word 'management' to each discipline, the original authors believed that they were adding a veneer of legitimacy and credibility to raise the subjects above the throng of the IT function. The ITIL text is crammed full of references to the importance of management and managing issues effectively. And yet it is clear that commonly understood basics of management are neglected or ignored in so many areas. Defining good management practice is unfortunately beyond the scope of this book and the skill of its author, therefore we shall limit ourselves to briefly reiterating some conventional wisdom regarding management and its purpose. The role of management can be considered as a combination of the following functions:

- Leadership
- Definition of goals/objectives
- Development of strategic and tactical approaches to achieve short, medium and long term goals
- Identification of roles, responsibilities and functions
- Work planning, task design (in conjunction with those performing the work) and process development
- Selection of resources and assignment against tasks

- Motivation and coaching/mentoring of staff
- Facilitating employees to perform to the best of their ability
- Removal of factors that inhibit employees from doing their jobs to the best of their abilities
- Measurement of performance against objectives

Unfortunately, some IT managers have been promoted beyond their level of competence based upon past glories, time served or a wish to get them away from hands on situations where they can do harm ... It is not uncommon for middle managers within the IT function to have little or no formal management training and to lack the many of the 'soft skills' needed to effectively lead a team of individual contributors. Managing IT teams sometimes requires a delicate touch in order to be able to balance the ever changing needs of the business against the peculiarities of highly skilled technical resources. This is not to say that IT staff should be allowed to become demanding prima donnas but it is important to recognise that often the motivations and behaviours of the very best IT staff are more closely aligned to performing artistes than production line workers. It is important to remember that a good Java monkey or hard core DBA is worth their weight in gold and that they are in very short supply ...

Recording copious amounts of detail about something does not mean that you are managing it. It just means that the person following you will have an effective audit trail with which to follow your progress, or lack there of, and to review your untimely demise. The potential for improvement is inherent within every process, no matter how efficient or effective. All that is needed is for someone to identify the opportunity and to raise a call to action. Focused and concerted action, with pre-defined objectives for that action, is required if things are to actually improve. Improvement is the only goal worth coveting. Without improvement, things become stale and stagnant, and begin to fall behind in real terms as the rest of the world moves on. Improvement necessitates change. Else how can the improvement occur? Consequently, change is the manager's friend. However, change introduces risk to the business. Risk that needs to be controlled and minimised. Controls need to be effectively implemented, maintained and monitored. Reports and checklists will not do this on their own. People must be motivated to care about the tasks that need to be completed. In order to care, people need to understand the reasoning behind the work activity. A common understanding comes from the communication of information and a shared sense of purpose. Defining purpose is an explanation of "Why?". Knowing why something is important allows one to prioritise resources and sequence the work. Completing the work, generates value and enables new opportunities to be identified. Repeating this cycle continuously will ensure that efficiency, productivity and user satisfaction increase whilst costs, outages and incident rates decrease ... I.e. things will get better.

Which is surely the whole point of managing something in the first place?

8

The "Service" Part of ITSM...

8.1 What do we Mean by the Term "Service"?

If we are to have meaningful discussion regarding the subject of IT Service Management it is best to first gain a common understanding of the term 'service' since it appears to mean all things to all people. In order to reach a baseline definition lets first look at two points of reference; the dictionary and the ITIL documentation.

Dictionary definition

Despite checking over half a dozen different dictionaries from the most well known publishing houses in the world and numerous more dubious online repositories it has been impossible to determine a definitive definition, the word 'service' appears to have as many meanings as it does users. However, the following list of meanings appeared more frequently than anything else so we shall use them for now...
"Service" can be defined as:

- An act of help or assistance,
- An organised system of labour and material aids used to supply the needs of the customer,
- The supply, installation, or maintenance of goods carried out by a vendor,
- Commodity, such as banking, that is mainly intangible and usually consumed concurrently with its production,

ITIL definition

There is no formal definition of the term "service" within the ITIL V2 documentation. Even the guides for "Service Delivery" and "Service Support" fail to explain exactly what it is they are supposed to assist their readers delivering and supporting.

So should we get hung up on definitions? Probably not, but it is amusing that the ITIL framework fails to define the primary thing that it claims to be designed to underpin. Moving on from a definition of the term (which may or not fall out of the mix later), lets determine those elements that come together to form a service.

8.2 Components/Elements of a Service

"The whole is more than the sum of its parts."

Aristotle, Philosopher, 384 BC-322 BC

Service definitions should include reference to the wide variety of attributes and internal/external factors which come together to characterise what the nature of the service is and how it is delivered.

A service definition may include reference to the following subject areas:

- Users/Audience
- User Requirements/Expectations
- Deliverables
- Information/Input to be supplied by user
- Mechanisms for access/delivery
- Resources/Roles responsible for delivery
- Controls
- Contractual requirements
- Metrics
- Service Availability
- Service Capacity
- Service level requirements
- Security Requirements
- Cost Allocation/Charge backs

8.2.1 Users/Audience

Just as there is no murder without a victim, no foul without intent etc we can be safe to assume there is no service without a customer (or user). Whether or not the user population is aware of the service that they are consuming is largely irrelevant, think of that tree falling in the woods – does it make a sound? Who cares? Knowingly or not, anyone taking advantage of the output or capability of a service is a consumer of that service.

Service design must take account of the audience, or audiences, for which the service is intended. Some would also argue that the service should be capable of handling users for which it is not intended too... But we will leave that to one side for the moment.

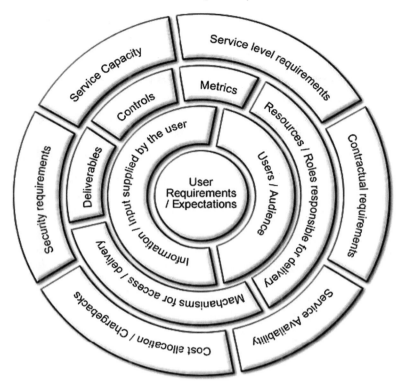

Fig. 8.1. Components of a Service

Volume of users

- How many people are likely to use the service?
- Are they likely to use the service regularly, intermittently, or sporadically?
- How long will they use the service for (at each usage)?
- What is the likely peak concurrent usage?

The answers to these questions will help define the operating capacity requirements of the service. After all, it is no use having a service that is incapable of satisfying the demand for it. Every service should have a predicted usage profile defined for it in order to enable those operating the service to determine if and when the day to day usage of the service goes outside of the original design boundaries.

Distribution of users

- Are the users geographically dispersed?
- Do the users operate in different time zones?
- Are the users clustered in multiple defined groups or are they more randomly spread?

User distribution will play a major role in service design, identifying whether it is necessary to provide local access points or a single centralised solution. The impact of time zones and how they affect service logic and flow will also need to be incorporated into the final service design.

Language requirements

- Do the users need to access the service in their local/native language?
- How many different languages need to be supported?
- What level of language skill is necessary to support the service i.e. conversational or technical?
- Is there a defined common language for the service?

Language requirements should not be underestimated. Forcing users to adopt a foreign language to access a service may significantly extend the time needed at each interaction point and will probably lead to an increase in misunderstandings and miscommunications. These, in turn, will increase the number of interaction touch points needed to deliver the service satisfactorily.

User profiles

- Are there easily identifiable sub sets of the user community with differing characteristics?
- What level of relevant skills and/or experience do the users have?
- Have the users received any training regarding the use of the service?
- Do any pre-requisites need to be completed by users before accessing the service?

Profiling users enables services to be tailored more closely to the specific needs of the individual without incurring massive costs associated with true bespoke service provision. It also enables those managing service delivery and service improvement initiatives to identify elements of the user population that could benefit from additional education and/or information.

8.2.2 User Requirements/Expectations

It can be said that user expectation is the measure against which service quality can be determined. The following equation shows the relationship between user satisfaction, service deliver and user expectation:

$$User\ satisfaction = Service\ delivery/User\ expectation$$

As you can see, the higher the user expectation, the better the service must perform for the user to remain satisfied. Service delivery professionals are required to balance this equation on a daily basis and employ a number of techniques to do so. Whether it is through under promising, over delivering or a combination of both it is imperative to ensure user satisfaction remains sufficiently high to avoid the pains associated with poor performance.

User requirements are typically formed in one of two ways, either directly by the formal definition of user needs or indirectly by experiences of comparable services received elsewhere.

Defined requirements

- Is the user need clearly defined in plain unambiguous language?
- Is the requirement defined in terms of inputs and outputs?
- Do the requirements compliment one another and avoid conflicting messages?
- Is it clear what the user expectation upon the service function is?
- Were the user community involved with the generation of the defined requirements?
- Are the requirements published and accessible to the user community?
- Are the requirements regularly reviewed and appropriate changes made with appropriate consensus?
- Is there a formal mechanism for users to suggest changes to services?

If the answer to any of the above questions is 'no' then the service may have a problem with user satisfaction due to unclear, conflicting or out of date requirements.

Inferred/Implicit requirements

It is a tragedy of modern life that we are all too often measured against criteria we know nothing of, by people who know nothing about us and do not understand why we are the way that we are. People use and experience countless services on a daily basis and their expectation levels are sometimes set by the performance (positive or negative) of the last service provider they interacted with. Resolve their PC problem in under 10 minutes after they have spent the past hour trying to get their bank to change their phone number on their account and you are a hero, do it after they have arranged for their home telephone service to be transferred to another provider in a 1 minute call and you are a slovenly villain eating into their day! Such are the joys of implicit and inferred user requirements...

8.2.3 Deliverables

It is important not to become too focused upon physical deliverables when talking about IT services. There are many different kinds of services and some will have more obvious deliverables than others. The important thing to remember is that the purpose of the service is to fulfil the defined needs or requirements. How this is achieved will vary from organisation to organisation, but there cannot be a service without a defined requirement and users who want this requirement to be satisfied.

- Are the service deliverables understood and documented?
- Do the deliverables satisfy the service driving requirements?
- Are the deliverables tangible or intangible?
- How can service delivery be measured objectively?
- Does the service have multiple deliverables associated with it?

Tangible and intangible

Service outputs may be tangible or intangible e.g. a ticket closure notification for a resolved incident or the fact that a specific network segment has been available for use for the past x business hours. The former is tangible, and indeed could be made physical if it were to be printed out, whereas the latter is a measure of something that 'was' and may or may not be 'as is' at this very instant.

Irrespective of what the actual service deliverable is, it must be verifiable i.e. there must be a mechanism available to determine whether or not the deliverable has been delivered. Without such a mechanism it is impossible to determine service delivery is complete (where such a concept exists) or that the service is available...

A single service with many different deliverables...

Some services by their very nature support multiple outcomes. Such services have processes inherent within them to determine specific user requirements and to put in place the appropriate series of actions, resources and deliverables to satisfy the initiating user requirement. Services such as Desktop support, New equipment provisioning etc enable users with different requests to be handled by a common process to meet their specific request. E.g. users requesting a new monitor would be handled in exactly the same way as users requesting some additional software to be installed. The end points are significantly different but the journey to get to there follow basically the same route. The same can be said of user reporting drastically different IT incidents, compare a user that is unable to print to one that has accidentally deleted an important file. The process to resolve these two incidents is common i.e. discovery, investigation, remedial action, confirmation, closure etc but the end results are very different.

In such services it is common to categorise incoming requests for assistance to enable those delivering the service to be able to quickly and easily identify the specific need in order to be able to deliver as efficiently as possible. The service definition may outline the types of request supported and how these may be identified (by request categorisation for example).

8.2.4 Information/Input to be Supplied by User

In order for a service to be delivered it may be necessary to capture specific information from the service user. In such cases the mechanism for collecting and recording this input data may vary but the following series of questions will hold true.

- Are the input information requirements for the user clearly defined?
- Can the user be reasonably expected to have or know the required information?
- If not, how will the user be expected to find out the required information?
- How will this information be verified and/or validated?
- At what point throughout the service lifecycle/process will the information be required?
- Can the information collection element of the service be split into sections in order to minimise the time needed to log a request initially?
- Can all of the information be collected initially to minimise the need to go back to the user for additional data points?

The success or failure of the service may well depend upon the quality of the data provided by the user themselves. In such cases it is imperative that the user is made aware of this dependency and asked to check that the recorded information matches with their understanding.

8.2.5 Mechanisms for Access/Delivery

Core to the service design is the method by which the user accesses, receives or initiates the service itself. Technology is such that there are usually multiple options available to users regarding how they access services and interact with the service organisation. The list below shows the most common methods used to interact with a service/support organisation:

- Self service
  - Web portal
  - Chat/Instant Messaging
  - Interactive Voice Response (IVR)
- Telephone
- Written request
  - Email
  - Letter
  - Fax
- In person
  - Walk in
  - Surgery/clinic
  - During a site visit
  - Whist doing the rounds
- Unconscious usage

When defining communication mechanisms for a service it is important to consider the following factors:

- Is the service simple enough to be requested without the assistance of someone involved with its provision?
- Does the service require specific information that can only be transferred diagrammatically i.e. voice contact would not be appropriate or useful?
- Does the timeline associated with the provision of the service require immediate feedback?

Irrespective of the method employed it is essential that service delivery is consistent. This does not however mean that the service must be the same across all of the above communication mechanisms, it is likely that an organisation will want to defer users to less costly methods of interaction where ever possible and may provide incentives (e.g. improved service levels or reduced costs for some types of interaction) to encourage usage of cheaper methods such as self service.

8.2.6 Resources/Roles Responsible for Delivery

In order to deliver a service it is usually necessary to use some form of resources. Even highly automated services require some form of resource, whether that be electricity to power the machines or people to process the requests/handle exceptions. In process-speak, resources are anything that is required to fulfil a process that are not changed by doing so . . . Obviously there will sometimes be accidents/damage as well as associated wear and tear, increased stress levels etc but fundamentally resources are reusable items that are utilised to facilitate service delivery without undergoing significant change.

Personnel

When identifying the personnel/staffing requirements of a service it is better to define the service's requirements in terms of roles and/or skill levels and qualifications/certifications rather than naming specific individuals. The following questions will help determine the service's resourcing requirements:

- Are users likely to interact directly with service deliverers?
- Is there a need for internally focused experts to support the front line service deliverers?
- What skills, experience and knowledge is needed to deliver the service?
- Are formal qualifications and/or certifications required?
- What additional skills, experience and knowledge is needed to support those delivering the service?
- What personality traits are best suited to perform the role?
- Does the service require multiple contacts with differently skilled personnel?
- Should the service delivery team include subject matter experts?
- How will silos of knowledge be avoided?

- What will the escalation route be in the result of the service deliverer being unable to satisfy a user request?
- What is the ultimate end point for user issues i.e. with whom does the buck finally stop?

After determining the type of person, or persons, needed to deliver and support the service the next task is to determine how many resources of each identified type are required... When deciding upon the service delivery team profile the following questions may be useful to identify the optimum size and make up of the team:

- What is the predicted productivity of the personnel types i.e. what ratios of 1st to 2nd to 3rd line staff etc are valid?
- Given peak anticipated service load and acceptable lead times (defined within service level agreements etc) what is the maximum load staffing level?
- Based upon service usage distribution what should the staffing profile be?

Tools/Equipment

Many IT services rely upon tools and equipment to deliver them. These systems and solutions may be physical assets in their own right e.g. servers, network routers, switches etc or may be logical assets such as software applications e.g. help desk ticketing systems, financial systems etc. Irrespective of what tools are used in the support and delivery of a service the following questions will help define the specifics of what is required:

- What equipment is needed to deliver the service?
- What capacity of equipment is needed to satisfy predicted demand?
- What level of equipment redundancy and fault tolerance is needed?
- Are there any pre-requisites needed to deploy the equipment?
- What tools are required to deliver the service?
- Are specific tools required? Are the requirements of the tools understood and defined? And can tools to satisfy these requirements be purchased off the shelf?
- Are there any specific tools or equipment needed to monitor and/or support the service?

Tool and equipment selection is a skill in its own right and beyond the remit of this book, however the high level process of defining requirements, identifying potential options and conducting fitness for purpose tests before complete cost benefit analysis to determine what to purchase should be familiar to anyone required to perform this function.

Controls

A control can be thought of as any rule or business logic that determines how the service is to be delivered. Controls can be defined and documented or they can be inferred by common practice. Ideally all controls should be clearly defined and documented and available to all persons consuming and delivering the service to ensure they are aware of the parameters within which everyone should be operating. In reality, controls are usually consigned to a dusty manual on an equally dusty shelf... But that doesn't mean that is how it should be.

Policies and procedures

Policies are intended to outline high level direction and purpose of the service. Procedures are supposed to fill in the gaps regarding the physical implementation or manifestation of the service on earth. Unfortunately many policy documents are third or fourth generation edits written in management speak and bear no relation to the original intent behind them. The only thing worse than a poorly written policy document is a poorly written mission statement! Mission statements are the stuff of urban legend and deserve consigning to the bowels of the earth for their de-motivational effects and ability to confuse and create misunderstandings between service users and service deliverers alike.

Policy documents should be brief, direct and to the point. The following questions will help identify whether the policy statement in question will be useful or not:

- Does the policy clearly describe what the service is?
- Is it clear why the service exists i.e. what is the purpose of the service?
- Does the policy avoid using jargon or overly emotive/descriptive language?
- Is it clear from the policy how the success or otherwise of the service will be determined?
- Can the policy be read and understood by a small child?

Procedural information should extend the policy document expanding upon how the service is provided/supported and how key service related model transactions are to be addressed.

Transaction models can be thought of as defined interaction flows for anticipated needs (e.g. subscribing to or requesting the service, using the service, cancelling the service, determining service status, reporting service issues, troubleshooting the service, providing feedback (positive and negative) etc) regarding the service. The following questions will help ensure that procedural documentation is relevant and useful:

- Have transaction models been created for all of the potential interaction types associated with the service?
- Do the transaction models avoid excessive steps and possible black holes?
- Are the procedural flows clear and easily understood?
- Are written instructions clear, concise and unambiguous?
- Are actors and their roles clearly defined within the procedures?
- Are key deliverables and milestones documented?
- Is the procedure demonstrable i.e. can it be audited against?

Legislation

Legal frameworks and local regulations differ dramatically the world over, typically legislation exists to protect the privacy rights of the individual and the intellectual property rights of an organisation. It is essential that any service involving the use, storage or transmission of sensitive data be designed from the outset to comply with the legal requirements in place. Procedures and policies regarding data retention, data security, rights to access and update etc will all need to be reviewed and implemented as appropriate. The following questions may help identify if there are specific legal controls that need to be implemented if the delivered service is not to fall foul of the law:

- Does the service involve the use of potentially sensitive data? How will sensitive information be adequately protected in order to comply with the law?
- Are there legal requirements regarding the length of time that auditable records must be retained? i.e. How does this impact archiving and online retrieval of data?
- Does the service span multiple regions with different legal requirements? Has the service been designed to satisfy the most rigorous requirements?
- Do service users need to be informed of any statutory notices (e.g. right to access data and/or amend personal information etc)? When do users need to be informed (i.e. initially upon subscription or at every transaction point etc)?

8.2.7 Contractual Requirements

Contract terms and conditions are often used to formally communicate requirements and responsibilities for service delivery. Unfortunately, the involvement of legal and purchasing professionals and their particular dialects/languages may mean that the intended meaning is lost and that the customer signs up for something dramatically different to that what the service provider believed they were offering.

- Are contract terms clear and understandable?
- Is the service defined in terms of measurable deliverables?
- Is service quality (and how it will be measured) defined?
- Are responsibilities for delivery and service quality reporting defined?
- Is the process for handling contractual disputes documented?

Penalty charges

Nothing focuses the mind quite like the possibility that the money you have earned through the diligent provision of valuable IT services could be ripped away from your clutches due to poor performance or non-compliance with previously agreed penalty clauses. Punitive penalties are common place within the IT outsourcing market place and can significantly affect the profitability, or indeed very survival, of the service provider.

- Are incidents or performance levels that incur penalties clearly defined?
- Is the way non-performance is measured clearly understood?
- Are the penalties time boxed or can they accumulate indefinitely?
- Are service level periods defined? Are these based upon fixed periods or a rolling window of performance?
- Are penalties limited by an upper threshold?
- Are payment terms for penalties defined?
- Are there any arbitration processes described in case of disputes over penalties?

It is essential that those responsible for the delivery of the service are involved in the review of the contractual penalties being agreed. It is all too easy for a sales team to get carried away and sign up for a contract within which it is impossible to meet the defined performance requirements. Hard won experience of operational reality is needed to be able to review such clauses and to determine whether it is viable for the organisation to take on the business and make a profit.

8.2.8 Metrics

Believers in 'management by the numbers' are obsessed with the collection of performance related metrics and can be inclined to base all operational decisions upon their short and long term effects upon the numbers. Whilst this approach can deliver significant returns when used to good effect, it is also possible that such a style could alienate or demoralise a workforce if the agreed metrics are considered unrealistic and unachievable. Another tendency for organisations which are too overtly focused on metrics is that a culture of cheating may develop where employees are so concerned with making their numbers that they let other elements of their role slip and in extreme cases may perform contrary to the business objectives in order to meet their measured targets.

For example, if a frontline agent is measured solely upon the number of calls they answer then they can improve their statistical performance by a wide variety of means including; rushing callers, being rude and abrupt, transferring calls before attempting to resolve the callers issue, dropping calls (i.e. hanging up on callers accidentally on purpose).

Another common problem with metrics is that organisations sometimes go over the top and devise hundreds of different measures to effectively monitor the same thing. Care must be taken to devise only enough measurements to give customers, service delivery groups and management the information that the need. 'Need' is the keyword here, nice-to-haves and archaic metrics to enable bogus historic comparisons are all well and good but should be left to the statisticians and kept away from those who should be focused upon the here and now. When devising service related metrics the following questions should be used to evaluate each potential data point:

- Does this metric tell me how the service is performing right now? Note: If it does, then historical analysis of the same data point will tell you how you performed in the past ...
- Does the metric tell me how the service is likely to perform in the immediate future?
- What benefit to the business does this metric provide? i.e. would the service fail if I didn't know the value of this metric?

Assuming that you do manage to avoid the statistics trap, it is essential that all service related metrics are carefully designed to ensure that they give a true and fair picture of the performance of the service and the people responsible for delivering it.

Definition of service measurements

Given that we want to ensure service related metrics are focused and help with the operation and ongoing development of the service, it is important to ensure that the following areas are covered by sufficient and suitable metrics in order to allow the business to manage the service effectively:

- Usage
- Capacity
- Backlog
- Quality
- Financial Cost
- Profitability
- Risk

These seven core areas need to be addressed if useful analysis and comparison of different services can be undertaken.

Usage Metrics

Typically these are time based measurements of volume and elapsed duration. The number of times a service has been used, the time taken to deliver the service etc. This type of metric is most common as it is usually the easiest to calculate (or at least people perceive it to be the easiest to calculate). Automated systems count service requests within a given period, starting and stopping the clock accordingly to measure how long the service was in use. Usage metrics are typically sliced and diced according to request categorisation and the like in order to enable management to see how the service usage is distributed across different parameters.

Usage metrics should also be useful in predicting future demand, assuming that service usage is predictable and upcoming external events are known about and can be correlated against similar historic events i.e. knowing that a mass mailing to all customers is going to happen next Monday is only of use if one understands the effects that a similar mailing campaign had upon service usage in the past.

Unfortunately many organisations never go beyond these types of metrics and kid themselves that they know what's going simply because they have a wad of pie charts and graphs to go through on a regular basis.

Capacity Metrics

Knowing how much capacity you have available within the system to handle additional workload is critical if you are to maintain service levels to within agreed limits. Capacity can be measured in a variety of ways depending upon the nature of the service in question. It may be related to the number of man hours scheduled to be available/online at a specific point in future, it could be the total processing power available to a specific application, it could be the amount of free disk space available within a disk array, whatever the measure, it should give those running the service an understanding of how much they have left in the tank in order to enable them to refuel in time for a planned long journey or to handle an unpredicted diversion without getting stuck on the side of the road.

Backlog/Work in progress

Knowing what is coming down the line (Usage Metrics) and knowing what you have left in the tank (Capacity Metrics) is not sufficient to give you a definitive view as to whether you will make it to your destination. In order to be sure, a service manager needs to understand the amount of work that is currently in progress, its status and the expected time to completion. Think of this as the big caravan that is being towed by the service team – too much backlog will use up all of the available capacity and prevent the service from delivering, too little and the service delivery teams may not be as productive as they should be and resource utilisation levels may suffer.

Quality related metrics

Few things are talked about more and understood less than quality. Where quality is thought of as the relative goodness of something then there will always be differences of opinion. Subjective measures are of little use to a service management team trying to ensure that every customer has a good experience when using their service. Instead, service quality must be broken down into a number of distinct measurable characteristics that can be monitored and improved upon if the overall level of service quality is to be maintained and/or improved. Examples of service quality related metrics include:

- Percentage of tickets that require rework/re-opening i.e. cases where they weren't closed out to the satisfaction of the requester initially.
- End to end response times for key user actions within a distributed corporate application – measured across various geographical regions to ensure consistent service delivery from the underlying network infrastructure.

- Number of interactions necessary to close out a request – people typically like to have their issues dealt with the minimum of fuss and passing back and forth
- Availability of service – excluding periods where the service was available but system performance was outside of the agreed performance envelope.
- Percentage of incidents that are resolved (and accepted as resolved by the requester) within the defined service level
- Number of rejected or aborted attempts to access the service within a given period

The key to determining useful quality focused metrics for a particular service is to place yourself in the position of the service user and ask the following questions:

- Why am I using the service?
- What am I hoping to achieve?
- What could happen to prevent me achieving my goal(s)?
- Can these events be measured?
- What would irritate me about the service if it happened?
- How can that irritation be expressed as cold hard facts?

You will note that we haven't discussed satisfaction surveys as part of this section on quality related metrics . . . Whilst surveying the user population for their feedback and comments regarding their experience using a service is a valuable tool – it does not necessarily help drive or improve operational behaviour.

Financial Cost metrics

Money is the lifeblood of any business and it is only fitting that if IT is to be taken seriously as a legitimate business discipline that it be financially accountable. Cost tracking and allocation is a routine part of business, it allows senior management and internal service subscribers to have visibility of financial exposure, and variance against previously agreed budgets. When defining cost based metrics it is important to ensure that charge out rates, exchange rates, materials uplift percentages etc are sourced from the Finance department in order to ensure that everyone accepts the results as fair and accurate.

It is not uncommon for businesses to under report the costs associated with IT service failures because they typically only account for actual time spent working on the resolution and do not include the indirect costs of failure. Indirect failure costs include;

- lost transactions/opportunity cost – service requests that would have been submitted during the outage that will never be raised as the moment or need has passed

- data corruption related costs – the costs of analysing systems for corrupted data, identifying dubious data points and rectifying corrupted datasets
- costs associated with data loss – assuming that the data can be retrieved then these costs would cover its retrieval (including the manual re-keying of data if the original source is available)
- non-productive time of users – the cost associate with having users of the service sitting there twiddling their thumbs waiting for the service to be reinstated
- re-work costs – the costs associated with service users redoing work that was either lost or corrupted beyond repair by the service failure
- service reinstatement costs – enterprise applications are rarely able to be turned on and off at the flick of a switch and it is sometimes necessary to restart such services in a structured manner which may lead to the service performing at a degraded level for an interim period whilst caches are reloaded, database indexes recalculated, sessions reinstated etc

Some of the above cost elements will be easier to identify and calculate than others. In reality, it will not always be possible to gather these values with 100 % accuracy, this in itself is not a major problem as the sums associated with even 50 or 60 % of these indirect costs will be sufficient to focus the minds of even the most IT agnostic executive...

Profitability

By understanding which services cost the most to deliver an IT function can set its chargeback or cross charge rates to an appropriate level to ensure that the appropriate margin is made. Internally facing IT organisations may not be overly concerned with turning a profit but they will want to ensure that their financial cost to the business is understood and can be demonstrated to senior management in order for them to understand which areas of the organisation are placing the largest drain on IT resources.

Not all services will make a profit, in fact it may be impossible for certain activities to ever make a positive return. However, these should be balanced out by other services within the IT portfolio which do make a positive contribution. By funding less popular or more expensive services with others, the IT function can ensure its service portfolio covers all of the needs of the business.

Risk

Risk is the hardest service metric of all to measure due to its subjective nature and the lack of quantifiable metrics upon which to base a calculation. Risk is often thought of as the likelihood that harm will befall the organisation. Within a service metric this generic concept is not too useful, instead we shall consider risk as the likelihood that the service will fail or be degraded to impact users. Risk may be affected by technical, personnel and exterior factors. Any combination of threats in these categories can combine to give the overall level of risk that the service delivery team believes exists at any point in time. The purpose of the risk measurement is to ensure that the business understands which services are more likely to cause issues in the short term. In an ideal, world management would review the controls underpinning at risk services and determine appropriate action plans to mitigate the risk.

Method of collection/calculation

Metrics should wherever possible be transparent (i.e. it should be clear how the values are calculated) in order to ensure that their audience clearly understands what the figures before them actually mean. It is all too easy to fall into the trap of being overly sceptical, after all we have all heard the phrase "lies, damn lies and statistics", and if we are to have faith in service related numbers then they must understand how they were calculated and from where the original data upon which they are based was gathered.

- Is the data collection methodology clearly understood? Is the capture of raw data automated or does it involve manual data input? Can the data be contaminated in anyway? Is the raw data subject to any human interpretation e.g. relative value judgements of goodness etc?
- Can the integrity of raw data be guaranteed? How? Remembering that given the right motivation, everybody cheats... What procedures and controls are in place to ensure data accuracy?
- Are the formulae for metric calculation open for inspection? Have the formulae been reviewed and approved?
- Is the metric based upon any assumptions? Are these assumptions documented and provided with the metric? Have the assumptions been reviewed and validated by the relevant parties?
- Is the metric calculated using external data e.g. exchange rates, pay rates, material costs etc? How were these external data points captured? When were these external values updated last? Are we sure that these values are valid and/or reasonable?

Reporting requirements

There are many ways of displaying data in order to aid usability and improve understanding, reports should be designed with a specific purpose, use and intended audience in mind and laid out to reflect these requirements.

Frequency of collection and reporting

When determining the frequency of data collection it is important to ensure that data is collected sufficiently regularly to enable the business to make accurate and up to date decisions based upon the information to hand. Different metrics will have different collection requirements and as such it is inefficient to delay some measurements and over collect others in order to meet an arbitrary schedule.

Benefit vs. burden

Even the most automated data collection and measurement systems will have some level of manual intervention required (even if this is limited to having to delete the hundreds of automated reports from your email inbox every morning). The key is to define reporting schedules to meet the operational needs of the business without creating unnecessary work for those involved in the preparation of such content.

8.2.9 Service Availability

The service availability definition describes when the service can be accessed. These rules may hold true across the board or there may be specific restrictions relating to individuals, user groups, methods of service access and times of the week, month or quarter etc. It is essential that the times when the service is available are clearly defined and understood by all service users/subscribers in order to ensure that non-availability related issues are limited to outages and the like rather than misunderstandings. When defining the availability profile for the service it is important to consider and address the following areas:

- Hours of use/operation – The times when the service is available and/or supported, ensuring that it is clear which time zone the defined times are within.
- Level of service – It may be appropriate to operated restricted services at some times of the day, week, month etc. Any such assumptions and corresponding downgraded service levels must be defined.
- Seasonal variations – changes to the availability profile based upon known resource limitations and/or demand fluctuations based upon historic seasonal behaviour e.g. holiday periods
- National holidays – Pre-defined dates where service cover may be withdrawn completely or a limited level of service provided
- Defined maintenance windows – Periods where preventive maintenance tasks may be performed without negatively impacting availability metrics.

8.2.10 Service Capacity

Every service must be designed with a target capacity in mind in order to enable optimum staffing levels and hardware/infrastructure sizing to be calculated.

These defined capacity requirements can be expressed in a variety of terms including:

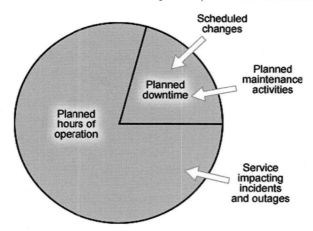

Fig. 8.2. Service availability and its components

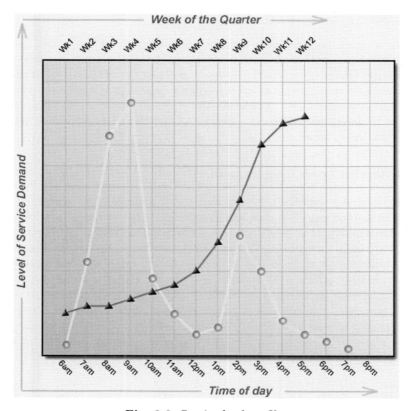

Fig. 8.3. Service load profiles

- Transactional load
  - Volume of service requests submitted within a defined period
  - Volume of service updates completed within a defined period
  - Volume of service queries responded to within a defined period
- Concurrent availability
  - Number of concurrent user connections
  - Number of manned phone lines available to take calls
  - Number of transactions that can be processed simultaneously
- Physical capacity
  - Number of records that can be held i.e. Disk space

Each capacity measure will typically be specified for three scenarios:

- Peak load requirements
- Normal use
- Out of hours

Service quality vs. service capacity

It is worth remembering that in circumstances where a service is used beyond its designed capacity there may be degradation in the level of service delivered. The end user effects of such performance impairment can be difficult to predict accurately and response times etc invariably extend in a non-linear fashion. The use of automated load generation and stress testing tools and procedures is useful to determine the service characteristics when the service is pushed beyond its design envelope.

8.2.11 Service Level Requirements

Service Level Agreements are supposed to be defined in consultation with those who use the service and should identify key service related metrics which determine whether or not the service is performing as required. Unfortunately ITIL's lofty aims to promote continuous service improvement by defining a set of baseline metrics upon which to build have been somewhat misapplied in practice and SLAs are more often used as weapons to abuse the service organisation with. In essence, service level requirements should cover the key areas of a service and allow service deliverers and users to have a common understanding of how well, or otherwise, the service is being delivered.

There are several main categories of service level metrics used to monitor service level performance, including:

- Service delivery metrics
- Acceptable levels of disruption
- Service quality metrics

Service delivery (Time based measures)

Rightly or wrongly, time based metrics are by far the most common type of service level measures in use today. One of the reasons for this is that they are often simpler to capture, calculate and analyse than other types of service delivery parameters. The key to developing meaningful time based metrics is to be sure to carefully define exactly what it is that is being measured. All too often, SLAs purporting to measure, resolution time, response time, time to fix etc do nothing of the sort... In order to be sure that the service delivery metric is actually measuring the element of the overall service delivery that you are interested in, it is important to define the following:

- Start and Stop trigger points – i.e. the points within the service timeline when the SLA should be started and stopped. These may be defined in terms of ticket submission and/or update, specific status/state transitions, ticket related conditions etc. It is also worth noting that there may be multiple start and/or stop triggers that may come into play at different times during the ticket lifecycle and in different scenarios.
- Exceptional circumstances ('Stop the clock' criteria) – The business rules governing the circumstances where the ticket can be considered outside of the scope of the SLA need to be carefully defined and will typically include; authority necessary to suspend an SLA, ticket conditions necessary to be in place for the ticket to be considered for exclusion and how the SLA will be (re)calculated when the clock is restarted.

Acceptable levels of disruption

It could be argued that there is no such thing as an acceptable level of disruption for business critical services. Some would say that by setting such a level, this sends out a message to the service delivery organisation which becomes a self fulfilling prophecy. On the other hand, it has to be recognised IT services have not yet reached a level where 100 % reliability and availability are the norm. Irrespective of your personal view, service level agreements defining acceptable performance limits do exist, particularly in outsourcing environments, examples include:

- Service availability i.e. the proportion of time when a service should be available that is actually is
- Maximum number of service impacting incidents permitted per period
- Permitted time to fully restore a service following a failure
- Average time between service impacting events i.e. MTBF (Mean time between failures)

Service quality metrics

Defining service quality in terms of goodness does nothing to improve the end user experience. It is necessary to determine specific, measurable, achievable, realistic and time based objectives (i.e. SMART) for service delivery. If an overall service quality metric is needed then it should be based upon multiple data points related to the overall service. Management and customers may require a banded approach (e.g. traffic lights with green, amber and red values) to give a quick view of the general health of a service. In such instances the bands need to be carefully defined and these definitions need to be made available to users so that they can understand what the high level value really means.

When measuring service 'quality' and the degradation of that 'quality' over time it is important to keep consistent definitions and to use the same algorithm for the calculation of the service quality value...

"Measurements" of service quality which may be combined to calculate the overall metric include:

- Response times – end to end measures for key user transactions measured from various locations within the IT environment (thereby identifying network related issues as well as system problems).
- Deliverables – the percentage of successfully completed transactions within a given period.
- Data quality – the number of data quality issues identified within a given period.

8.2.12 Security Requirements

Service security is often an area which is overlooked or left until last. And yet it is one of the biggest areas of potential risk to any organisation. In today's on demand one click economy, it is possible to commit the resources of an organisation faster and more anonymously than ever before. Providers of IT services need to be sure that they are conducting the necessary level of authentication and validation of user data prior to providing service access in order to protect themselves, their customers and their employees from identity theft and online fraud.

Entitlement checks to access service

Whether service entitlement is governed by unique service references/account codes or via individual passwords, Security tags etc, it is important to ensure that the process for administering user accounts and login credentials is as robust and secure as possible. The following questions should be considered whenever defining the entitlement policy of a service:

- How can users demonstrate that they are entitled to access the service?
- How can it be verified that users are who they say that they are?
- Has the entitlement verification process been designed to prevent service desk personnel having unnecessary access to confidential user data?
- Are the entitlement checks sufficiently rigorous to deter system abuse whilst not being too onerous for legitimate users?

- Is multi-element security required? i.e. smart cards, key fobs, biometrics etc.

Service security enforcement

In an ideal world, user validation and access rights security would be sufficient to enforce the desired service security model. However, in light of the ever increasing sophistication of the security risks facing business, it is vital to supplement such measures with additional controls and procedures designed to minimise the impact of a security breach.

- Has vulnerability testing/probing been completed? Have all recommendations arising from such activities been implemented?
- Are trusted data sources, domains, IP ranges etc identified and enforced?
- Is the system continuously monitored to identify the first signs of a potential intruder e.g. uncharacteristic downloads, excessive database load from unqualified queries etc?
- Are there plans in place to deal with denial of service attacks?
- Has routine security testing been scheduled to monitor the continued effectiveness of controls?

Encryption (Information transfer e.g. SSL etc and database level)

Encryption can be applied at the message and database level at varying levels of complexity. The important thing to remember is that you rarely, if ever, get something for nothing. Enhancing the level of encryption applied to transaction traffic or at the database layer will always have a corresponding negative impact on overall system performance. Therefore it is important not to over specify the level of encryption required, to prevent hardware costs spiralling out of control to support the increased processing overhead.

Row level security/Data segregation/segmentation

Row level locking, as it is sometimes called, can be applied at the business logic or database layer of an n tier application stack. The purpose of such data security is to ensure that users only have access to view and edit (subject to access permissions) data related to them. Such capabilities are particularly important within outsourcing contracts and it may be necessary to have duplicate systems running on separate/isolated hardware infrastructures in order to satisfy certain customers with specific data security concerns.

8.2.13 Cost Allocation/Charge Backs

Cost allocation and paying for services received has always been a part of outsourcing arrangements. In recent times, IT has been under increased pressure to demonstrate a return on the massive investment that organisations have made in technology. It is therefore becoming increasingly common for charge backs and cost allocations to be implemented within internal IT functions as a means of demonstrating value and return.

All IT overheads as well as the costs of every element of work and every piece of infrastructure/equipment/asset associated with IT related services are cross-charged against pre-defined cost centres. This transparent and granular approach to cost control allows business users to clearly understand the costs associated with providing services, costs incurred supporting those services, the cost of implementing specific changes and how those costs are calculated. This increased visibility of the financial impact of IT can be fed into the decision making process to ensure that an organization makes the most appropriate choices based upon the actual facts rather than gut feel or instinct.

Charging models

Vast arrays of different charging models are in use within IT organisations today and include the following methodologies:

- Pay per use/flat fee per ticket
- Subscription models
  - Initial subscription charge and ongoing fees
    - Departmental subscription
    - User based
- Service volume based pricing
  - E.g. Physical disk space used, Network bandwidth consumed etc
- Time and materials
  - Call out fee and time and materials
    - Typically the first hour of labour is included within the call out fee
  - Rate card (based upon skills, location or time of day etc)
  - Uplift percentages
- Service charge
  - Flat fees for access
  - Banded fee structures
    - Bulk usage discounts

When determining the appropriate model, or combination of models, to be used for a particular service it is important to select methodologies which are easy to calculate and explain to the end user community in order to ensure that transparency is maintained.

8.3 Service Definition

8.3.1 How the Service is Defined

Service design is often a rather unstructured and iterative process where a workable service definition is stumbled upon over time after numerous conflicts and misalignments between the service delivery team and their customers. Intermediaries such as departmental heads, sales executives and relationship managers can either be a massive help to the process or a terrible hindrance. If the definition process is to be efficient then it should be treated as any other business project with defined phases, check points and deliverables. The major steps to creating a service definition are as follows:

- Requirements capture
- Capability assessment
- Story boards, scenarios and flow diagrams
- Review of existing documentation/processes
- Drafts, reviews and pilots
- Sizing and Implementation planning

8.3.2 Requirements Capture - The Difference Between Requirements and Specifications

When I was a naïve green product manager, my engineering colleagues were constantly frustrated by my inability to define user requirements without including my personal suggestions regarding a specific implementation approach. Rather than say "The users want X" I fell into the trap of saying "The product needs to do Y" ... Now, my previous field and development experience did mean that my suggested implementation approaches were at least feasible, but I initially misunderstood this element of the product manager's role. By defining the "How?" rather than the "What?" or the "Why?", I subconsciously limited the creative scope of the development team and tried to enforce my own particular view of the world upon the products under my governorship. Thankfully, I eventually learnt from my mistakes – Hopefully this confession will help you to avoid this fundamental error in the first place.

8.3.3 Capability Assessment

The purpose of the capability assessment phase is for the service organisation to take a step back and evaluate whether it believes itself capable of fulfilling the defined requirements of the service on a consistent basis. Self-delusion is common during such exercises and so it is important to take a dispassionate view if trouble is to be avoided downstream. Just because an organisation is incapable of delivering a specific service today does not mean that it won't be very capable tomorrow. The aim of the assessment is to perform a gap analysis to identify the required skills, staffing levels, procedures, supporting systems and infrastructure needed to deliver the service effectively. The following questions are aimed at focusing the mind of the service design team to ensure that service agreements are not entered into without first considering the likelihood of successfully delivering the service requested:

- Can the requirements be satisfied using existing resources, skills and tools? How will this increased demand be handled without negatively impacting other services? What level of staffing is required based upon projected service demand?
- What level of investment is required to be able to deliver the required service? What is the lead time between investment and achieving the relevant level of capability i.e. procurement timelines, implementation timescales etc?
- Is it practical to deliver the service in-house or would it be better to outsource the requirement?

8.3.4 Story Boards, Scenarios and Flow Diagrams

A picture is worth many thousands of words. Nowhere is this truism more true than in the arena of IT service definition. To be frank, if you can't flowchart or represent the service delivery process graphically, you can't deliver it. Anyone who says otherwise is kidding themselves and you. Process charts, diagrams, swim lane flows etc are all excellent communication media and help to gain/reinforce a common understanding as to what is being described and designed. Never skip the process flow phase of the service definition process. If you do, it will come back to haunt you many times over.

8.3.5 Review of Existing Documentation/Processes

Knowing what you already have can help reduce rework and save time, providing it is used as a basis for the design rather than a blueprint. There is little or no point in redesigning the service to be a clone of its predecessor.

8.3.6 Drafts, Reviews and Pilots

Foster a culture that allows and encourages mistakes again and again. The very best services and products don't happen over night – they take time! And lots of it. Test your theories and ideas frequently to ensure you remain on track and gain user buy in to the process.

8.3.7 Sizing and Implementation Planning

Having determined what it is that you want to deliver, who it is that is going to use it and what the related transactional flows are – you are at last in a position to start estimating the resources necessary to facilitate, deliver and support the service. It is important to remember the predicted usage volume and profiles at this point and ensure that the service design has sufficient latitude to be scaled up or down in the event of these predictions falling wide of the mark in either direction.

8.3.8 Who should Participate?

If a valid and useful service definition is to be delivered it is important, no essential, to ensure that the appropriate personnel are involved at the appropriate point of the process. It is important to maintain a core group of people throughout the process to ensure consistency and continuity; however this central team should be supplemented along the way to gain different perspectives and technical insights as required. The following groups should be involved:

- Service delivery teams – to give a pragmatic practical view on how the service can, could and should be delivered and supported
- Focus groups of users – to give a view on exactly what it is that is required, why they want it, what's important to them and what is irrelevant
- Market intelligence/Competitive analysis – by casting an eye outside, service delivery organisations can avoid some of the mistakes of the past and ensure they are moving in the right direction to remain competitive in the marketplace
- Sales executives – there is no point defining a fantastic service if it can't be sold, good sales execs inherently have a feel for what works and what doesn't, leverage this innate skill to ensure your service offering has user appeal
- Technologists – these guys and girls know the nuts and bolts of the underlying solution, its infrastructure requirements and how they all play together, essential for the detailed design element of the process
- Long haired freaky people – Never underestimate the need for innovation. Long hair is obviously an optional extra, but try to include at least one person who is a little 'out there'... Such individuals can be infuriating as they unpick a weeks worth of work with a single 'silly' question, but better to do it now then when in production!

8.3.9 Review Cycles

Every service definition should include details of when the service will be formally evaluated, who will perform the review and the methodology to be used to conduct the review.

8.3.10 Process/Procedures to Change a Service Definition

It is essential that the service definition be a living thing that can react to changing circumstances and new business requirements. Unless the service adapts to meet the needs of the organisation it serves, it will quickly become outdated and irrelevant.

- Improvement suggestion scheme
- Periodic service reviews

- Bundling multiple service changes into releases
- Review and Approval process
- Communicating the change

8.3.11 Disputes

Every service will experience customer dissatisfaction at some point. Whether this unhappiness is due to the level of service delivery falling below agreed thresholds or the expectations of the customer being different to that what is being delivered is largely immaterial. Disputes should be handled in an open, transparent and fair manner. Moreover, they must be seen to be dealt with effectively and fairly if the process is to remain credible.

The process for handling disputes should cover the following subject areas and should be made publicly available where possible:

- Format of the dispute submission – i.e. the minimum level of detail necessary for a dispute to be logged/raised
- Makeup of the review panel – i.e. information regarding who will review disputes and their responsibilities, may include details of the makeup of the review panel and the function of panel members etc.
- Timetable for the process – i.e. defined timelines for the process, schedule of review board meetings (if relevant) and target timescales for reparation in the event of a dispute being upheld
- Right of appeal and the appeals process – i.e. what options are open to the person raising the dispute in the event of them being unhappy with the initial response/findings.

9

Defining Meaningful IT Services

There is no right or wrong way to define IT services. Different organisations will have different preferences and approaches to how IT services should be defined. Currently there is relatively little formal guidance available related to the definition of IT services and even within progressive organisations it is sometimes left to individual service team leaders to define the way in which they describe how their team services their customers and/or user base. In an ideal world, all IT services (and potentially other business services delivered by other support functions such as Finance, Facilities and HR etc) within an organisation should follow a consistent format in order to enable the business to readily compare apples with apples and to easily understand what to expect in return for the costs they incur.

9.1 Common Service Models

The following basic methods, used in combination, may be useful in defining a full catalogue of IT services:

- Functional/Technical based
- System/Application based
- Business orientated models
- Support centric services
- Ongoing subscriptions
- One off transaction based services
- Role based models

9.1.1 Traditional Functional or Technical Based Models

The service is defined in terms of the functional role responsible for delivering the service and/or the technical description of the primary components of the service itself. Such a model assumes that the people working with the service definition are aware of what the various teams do and how they fit together to deliver an end to end service experience for the end user. Examples of services based around technical disciplines would include:

- Networks
- Database
- IT Operations

9.1.2 Systems Based Models

The service is represented in terms of the system or application that the end user sees and uses. Whilst highly visible and easily understood by end users, such definitions sometimes fail to encapsulate the full scale of the service supplied.

- Email
- ERP access
- Sales Automation

9.1.3 Business Oriented Service Models

Perhaps one of the trickiest service groups to define adequately is that of business process support services. Such services require a truly cross discipline approach to service delivery which is alien to many IT functions. The provision of a single business service may require contributions from a wide variety of IT functions from security and networking, to applications, to databases to end user support etc. Indeed, a single service may utilise numerous IT systems throughout the process flow and may touch upon countless elements of the IT infrastructure. The following list outlines some of the underlying systems which go to support common business processes:

- Monthly payroll run
  - ERP system, Payroll system, BACS transfer, Printers (where payslip printing remains in-house)
- Close of financial quarter
  - ERP system, Accounts Payable, Accounts Receivable, Order Management system, Sales Force Automation solution
- Online shop
  - External web site, Order Management system, Credit Card payment authorisation gateway, ERP system, CRM system etc

9.1.4 Separating the Service from the Support (or Vice Versa)

Sometimes it may be appropriate to treat the support of a specific IT capability as a service in itself.

- Workstation support – Generic service covering the support of user hardware, network connectivity and core software applications
- Mobile user support – Covering areas such as modem setup, communications configuration, connectivity issues, VPN access problem diagnosis etc
- Specialist application support – The provision of technical support for non-core applications

9.1.5 Ongoing Usage/Subliminal Services

These are the services that the users do not recognise that they use and yet without them they wouldn't be able to do anything at all. Often thought of as the cost of admission to the IT environment, subliminal services may include the core networking infrastructure and communications setup as well as basic security and storage items.

- Data storage and file space management – Service defining a user's file server space, backup/archiving of stored data and provision of tools and assistance regarding associated data retrieval procedures
- Systems access and security – Network login administration, Provision of authentication systems (e.g. smart cards, RSA tags etc), Password management (including resets), Antivirus update provision, Infection cleansing etc

9.1.6 Transactional Services

Services which are used occasionally to fulfil a specific business need.

- Hardware provisioning – Service to cover the sourcing, procurement, commissioning, transportation and installation of physical items of IT equipment
- Software provisioning – Handling requests for new software, the service covers the sourcing, procurement and installation of software tools and applications
- IMAC – Installations, moves and changes. The historic bedrock of the change management discipline.

9.1.7 Role Based Service Models

Role based service models are typically bundles of other IT services that are required to perform a specific job function. The two examples below show some of the IT services that people within different job roles may need to subscribe to in order to operate effectively:

- Sales Executive
  - ○ Systems access and security
  - ○ Workstation support
  - ○ Mobile User support
  - ○ Siebel access
- CAD Manager
  - ○ Systems access and security
  - ○ Workstation support
  - ○ Specialist application support
  - ○ Data storage and file space management
  - ○ Document Management system access

9.2 What's in a Name?

Given that the service name is probably the first and last exposure that some users will have to a particular offering from the IT function, it is important to ensure that the service name and description are clear enough to enable users to fully understand what is on offer and how it could benefit them. Consider it as the newspaper headline designed to entice the casual reader browsing the publication to read the detailed in depth article that follows.

9.3 Differences Between Internal and External Facing Services

In general external facing services involve the payment of a fee to access or use the service (directly or indirectly) whereas internal services involve the allocation of a cost (directly or indirectly). Apart from this minor differentiation, they are pretty much the same and building arbitrarily different processes, infrastructures and procedures does little to improve either side of the fence. IT should treat its users as customers and its customers as users – both sets of people form their client base, and therefore the reason for existence, of the service organisation...

9.4 Service – a Definition

A service can be defined as:

"A defined capability or set of deliverables aimed at satisfying a defined requirement, using resources (people, things and tools) and following a defined delivery process."

Simple really!

The IT Service Catalogue/Service Portfolio

What is it? Do I need one? And if so, why?

The service catalogue is a repository and/or tool to house the collection of service definitions defined between the business and the IT function.

The IT service catalogue is often represented as a menu of options from which users are entitled to pick services and equipment that they wish to receive. Such an analogy only partially holds true as there will always be services that users will need to be subscribed to, whether or not they realise it. If we consider the service catalogue as a portfolio of all of the possible services available from the IT function then we can defined some elements as mandatory and others as optional. Similar service offerings should be grouped and each service group may have mutually exclusive options, or selection rules, associated with it. For example, a service representing the provision, maintenance and support of a desktop PC may have a variety of options (typically relating to hardware specification and the software bundle supplied for instance) of which the user may only subscribe to one selection. This is not to say that they user is limited to using this default software bundle only, it is likely that there would be a service related to the provision, maintenance and support of non-standard software that could be subscribed to in addition to the basic package.

Given the breadth of IT services available today it is likely that larger organisations will require a dedicated system specifically to manage the thousands of entitlement requests and updates they receive weekly and to maintain each user's service subscription profile accurately. Maintaining accurate profiles of user entitlement is essential if the business wants to allocate IT related costs according to usage.

The objectives of the service catalogue/service portfolio may be described as follows:

- To enable individuals within the business to understand what services are available to them
- To facilitate the selection of services by individuals and/or groups
- To enable service delivery groups to understand what specific individuals and/or groups are actually entitled to access, use and receive

There are many ways in which an individual's personal service portfolio selections can be managed and administered, ranging from the use complex rules based sales configuration engines to encode business dependencies and approval processes to relatively simple manual paper based systems. Irrespective of the mechanism used it is advisable to group similar service options together to improve the ease of selection and the application of business rules. Service selection groups will typically have the following high level business rules applied to them:

- Mandatory service selection – all users must subscribe to this service (or all services within the group where there is more than one) irrespective of user profile, location and role etc. An example of this type of service would be the provision of network access, an LDAP profile and password maintenance. Note: It is likely that automated service catalogue solutions would add such services to an individual's personal portfolio without any manual intervention.

- Mandatory unique selection i.e. mutually exclusive – all users must subscribe to one, and only one, of the services within the service group. An example of this type of service would be the amount of personal file space provided on the corporate file server (Naturally the service would probably also include the backup and restoration of data stored on the file space in the event of the data being lost (although this may be a separately costed item based upon transaction frequency i.e. a fixed charge back fee per restore etc). Typically we would expect everyone to have space allocated but there may be different options allowing more or less disk space based on role and projected usage etc.
- Mandatory choice selection – all users must subscribe to at least one of the services within the service group. An example of this type of service might be the choice of base hardware and software configuration discussed earlier.
- Optional unique selection – users may decide whether they wish to subscribe to one, and only one, of the services within the service group. An example of this type of service might cover the provision and support of mobile computing devices, where users may be given the choice of a variety of PDAs and Handheld computing options.
- Optional selection – users may decide to subscribe to none, one, or more than one of the services within the group. This sort of service grouping would be used to administer the subscription to services such as the non-standard software requests mentioned previously.

Within a single service selection it is possible that there would be a variety of mandatory and optional service options that the user, or the person requesting the service on their behalf, must/may select from.

An individual's service profile (or subscription list) would be built up by selecting those services and options necessary to fulfil their role within the organisation. In reality it is likely that generic role based templates would be devised in order to simplify the administration of new starters and employee transfers.

10.1 Entitlement

In the past, internal IT functions rarely checked to see if an individual requesting assistance was entitled to use the service related to their inquiry. There was an assumption that if they were asking for it, then they needed it. Such an approach led to waste and unnecessary expenditure being incurred as people saw what others within the organisation were doing with IT and wanted it a piece of the action too. Outsourcing and the need for internal IT functions to account for IT expenses has meant that this free and easy approach is no longer practical or acceptable.

Individual service portfolios allow the front line teams to determine exactly what somebody is entitled to and the processes to be adopted to fulfil their request. For example, It would not be uncommon for different approval processes to be in place for individuals from different parts of an organisation that are requesting the same thing. Where someone is not entitled to a particular service or item, then procedures need to be in place to determine how the request should be dealt with. Depending upon the nature of the request, the costs associated with fulfilling the request, and the policy of the user's business unit, the following actions may be appropriate:

- Decline the request and direct the requester to take the issue up with their line manager
- Suggest alternative services that may meet the needs of the user that they are entitled to
- Refer such a request back up the food chain for an ad hoc approval from the requester's management for this specific request
- Create a subscription change request to grant access to the service on an ongoing basis to the user and start the approval process running
- Approve the request (providing it is within a defined number of 'free' uses of the service) and pass details of the request to IT management for them to negotiate an approved/authorised service definition with the relevant business owners at their next interlock session

10.2 More than a Dusty Folder on the Shelf!

Service definitions must be more than a paperwork exercise if they are to be any real benefit to the business. They need to be a working set of definitions and requirements that underpin the operation, if they are to be of any significant benefit. In an ideal world the service catalogue would be tightly integrated with all of the tools used to manage ITSM related processes. Every ITIL discipline would leverage the catalogue to determine what and how the service should be delivered as well as the agreed performance objectives that should be aimed for. Unfortunately we don't yet live in an ideal world and so in a spirit of compromise and realism the following hierarchy of service cataloguing options may be used to determine how best to incorporate service information into your current ITSM landscape:

- Paper based service documentation
- Definitions posted up on the corporate intranet
- Historic performance metrics published along side service definitions
- Real time (or as near to it as practical) approximations of current status
- Service definitions embedded within service delivery tools to automatically inform and enforce service subscriptions etc
- Subscription aware self service interfaces which guide the user to select only those items for which they are entitled

10.3 Common Problems with Service Catalogues/Service Definitions

The following list outlines some of the common issues identified with service catalogues and service definitions:

- Too many services defined – excessive management overhead
- Too few services defined – insufficient detail
- Remain a theoretical exercise – lack of practical implementation
- Excessive use of technical language/jargon
- Overly focused on tools rather than capabilities or business needs (i.e. more 'what' than 'why')
- Insufficient consultation with interested parties
- Lack of understanding of IT services within the business

Having defined exactly what we are to deliver and to whom, let's now see how we assure that service delivery to ensure that we meet our commitments...

11

ITSM Disciplines Explained

Fig. 11.1. The IT Service Management ecosystem with supporting processes

The following section goes into the various ITSM processes in depth. Each discipline is initially defined at a high level before addressing the following subject areas in depth:

- Process objectives – A definition of the purpose(s) of the process i.e. the "why?". This section will outline the primary reasons for performing the actions associated with the process in terms of their potential benefit to the business.
- Common issues – A listing of the most common technical, process and business issues that are inherent within the ITSM process under discussion. These problem lists have been collated from many real life situations and largely represent a worse case scenario – in practice it is unlikely that any organisation would suffer from every issue listed simultaneously.
- Process flow(s) – A series of process flows that describe the general way in which the process functions, the key milestones and decision points.
- Key players – A description of the various roles/actors that are involved in the ITSM process and their particular requirements/focus.
- Process metrics – Example measurements that are often used to monitor the effectiveness of the ITSM process and the services/infrastructure that it supports.

Self Service

In today's on demand world customers and users expect to be able the information and services they want, when they want. Using conventional service delivery mechanisms such as 24 hour contact centres is an expensive way of meeting this expectation. Web based self service interfaces have evolved to give a lower cost alternative to a fully manned option and can be used effectively as part of a wider service management solution. However, unless implemented effectively, self service solutions can generate more call traffic and lead to user/customer dissatisfaction by providing poor levels of ticket related information and not updating status reports regularly enough to meet the needs of modern information hungry consumers.

Self service portals enable service and support organizations to provide their users and customers with the highest level of service all of the time. Periodic automated updates and event driven business logic are often used to update tickets with real time status reports, ensuring that requesters and affected individuals have the information they require without feeling the need to contact the support organization directly for status reports on current status, work progress, expected timelines for resolution etc.

12.1 Objectives of Self Service

Self-Service functionality is intended to:

- Reduce the amount of time taken to enter incidents and requests for service
- Avoid data entry related issues by getting users to enter the details of their requests themselves
- Provide access to corporate knowledge repositories to end users and customers
- Enable users to diagnose their own issues and implement their own workarounds/fixes
- Empower users to order their own hardware software and IT related services (subject to appropriate approval cycles and access permissions)
- Receive real time updates from the user community, preventing you working on issues and requests that are already resolved or no longer relevant/required
- Reduce the number of follow up or chase calls received by providing users with online access to real time status information regarding their requests, incidents and purchase requisitions
- Seamlessly embed your IT service management self service portal within your corporate intranet/customer extranet infrastructure

12.2 Common Issues

Common issues with self service include:

- Low levels of self service usage
- Increases in follow-up/chase calls due to vague status information etc
- Out of date or erroneous information being displayed
- Inappropriate content/comments being shared with the user base

- Lack of integration with the rest of IT support organisation
- User dissatisfaction at being asked all the same questions again and again
- Poor traceability of self help usage
- User frustration at not being able to find a solution, request assistance etc

12.3 Elements of a Self Service System

Modern self service solutions have come a long way since the earliest static fire and forget web based solutions. Today's self service solution provides a rich interactive user experience consisting of some, or all, of the following elements:

- Bulletin boards/Broadcast information provision
- Context sensitive personalised content
- Service subscription interface
- Request logging and tracking
  - New requests, updates, status reports, closure etc
- FAQs, Solutions database, knowledgebase
- Satisfaction surveys
- Suggestion box
- Self healing capabilities
  - Diagnostic tools, Patch/Fix downloads etc
- Self service requisitions
  - Software downloads
- Call me back...
- Training portal links

12.3.1 Bulletin Boards/Broadcast Information Provision

A forum to publish announcements that may interest, impact or affect a cross section of the user community in an attempt to pre-emptively provide information which the users may want or need thereby reducing inbound call volumes. Typically announcements will describe major changes, planned system outages, ongoing major incident status etc. Sadly, bulletin boards are often ignored by the user population. This disaffection may be due to many factors including; stale content, difficulty accessing the data, delays between events and information updates, poorly targeted messaging (overly specific or overly general), volume of content (too much or too little) etc.

12.3.2 Context Sensitive Personalised Content

Personalisation "technologies" were all the rage within CRM applications a few years back and they have since found their way into some ITSM application suites. Basically, the purpose of the functionality is to give users only the information they need when the need it. This is typically done via a series of content type subscriptions based upon one or more characteristics of the individual in conjunction with ongoing campaigns and issues within the IT environment. Content may be restricted according to many criteria including:

- Department/Function/Job role
- Physical location
- Service subscriptions
- Equipment used/owned
- Incident/request history
- Current issues

The content may be delivered to the user in a variety of ways e.g. specific portlets within the self service interface or portal, targeted email messages, banner advertisements, recommended results within knowledge base searches etc.

12.3.3 Service Subscription Interface

The service subscription interface provides a mechanism for users to opt in and out of specific services. It may automatically process the request behind the scenes (for services not requiring approvals) or it may raise a service request for later processing. The interface may also provide users with information regarding the costs of services they use (including usage based cost models e.g. file space etc).

12.3.4 Request Logging and Tracking

The core of the self service application is the ability for users to be able to record issues (service requests and incidents), to update them and to check their status when they wish. It is essential, if unnecessary chase and clarification calls are to be avoided, that the support team update tickets with clear comments and status information promptly and set the end users expectation as to when the next update will be made.

12.3.5 FAQs, Solutions Database, Knowledgebase etc

In order to avoid the need for the user to raise an incident report or service request, they are encouraged (and in some implementations they are actually forced) to check the corporate knowledge repository for an answer before logging a ticket. Occasionally, a user will actually find an entry that addresses their particular need. And in such cases the fact that the user's requirement has been satisfied by a knowledgebase entry should be recorded to allow the knowledge management team to understand which content is useful. This is all pretty straight forward and predictable. However the real business requirement is to understand what it is that the user was looking at that did not help them before they raised their incident. Which knowledge base entries were reviewed and discarded by the user? What terms did they use to conduct their search(es)? Maybe they found the answer to their problem but didn't understand it? It is the answers to these are the questions that would be truly helpful to help avoid calls to the service desk.

12.3.6 Satisfaction Surveys

The self service interface often includes a mechanism for users to provide feedback regarding the level of service they have received. This is often done via a series of multiple choice questions where the user is asked to rate the performance of the service delivery team and/or the quality of their experience on a numerical scale. Such surveys can be useful to take a crude measure of the general feeling of the customer population however management must not be overly focused on these metrics to the detriment of everything else.

12.3.7 Suggestion Box

The user base is an often untapped source of incredibly valuable improvement suggestions and enhancement requests with which the organisation can improve its usage of IT. Ideally, suggestions should be able to be submitted anonymously, if the user prefers to, but where the user does provide their details then they should be thanked for their input by senior IT management and kept up to date with how the suggestion is received and implemented if appropriate. In order to generate interest in the suggestion scheme it may be useful to hold a monthly prize draw for all suggestions as well as publicising those suggestions which are adopted in in-house newsletters etc.

12.3.8 Self Healing Capabilities

Online diagnostic tools are still relatively new, but they are slowly becoming more widespread and can be used to interrogate client machine settings against the corporate standard and to reset the configuration to the corporate 'factory' settings if required. In addition to diagnostics, some organisations may permit users to access and download/apply patches, scripts or fixes. By giving the user the keys to the medicine cabinet, IT organisations are enabling them to heal themselves but they also have the opportunity to misdiagnose themselves and potentially cause harm by taking the wrong treatment for their current illness. In order to mitigate this self harm option, IT organisations need to spend considerable time and thought when planning such scripts/patches to ensure that the relevant checks are put in place within the fix logic to prevent them overwriting something inadvertently etc and make them as benign as possible.

12.3.9 Self Service Requisitions/Software Downloads

No internal or external support site would be complete without a download area. Users are able to decide which items they want and to install them for themselves. Typically, such distribution mechanisms are used for non-critical add-ons, updates, small utilities etc. It is common for the use of such areas to be completely unregulated with no tracking of who is accessing the download area and what they are using it for.

12.3.10 Call me Back . . .

In order to help smooth inbound calling patterns, support teams may provide self service users with the capability of requesting a call back. Such mechanisms may enable the user to specify a time slot and the general topic of discussion (in order to ensure that a suitably skilled member of staff is assigned to the call) or they may just place call back requested in a sequential queue that is dealt with on a first come, first served basis when there are lulls in the inbound call loading.

12.3.11 Training Portal Links

IT illiteracy is one of the primary causes of user requests. Users that don't know how to use their IT equipment and software tools are less effective and more prone to errors and mistakes that cause system down time and losses of productivity. The general level of IT awareness and skill within many organisations is pitifully low. And yet, given this background, it is amazing to see how little proactive IT related education is provided. More often than not, IT training is nothing more than a line item within an annual performance review (and then only for the lower ranking employees). It is not that individuals don't want to learn and improve. It is that the environments within which they work don't value, support and facilitate IT education as a worthy goal. It is also true to say that you can take a horse to water but you can't make them drink. For everyone that would like to learn more, there is someone who is happy with their current level of IT ignorance. By providing easy access to a wide range of focused IT education, the support function can go some way to helping to change the user mind set, helping them to see the value and relevance of IT skills.

12.4 Usability is Key

It is not the intention of this section to be a guide to computer system usability; this is a diverse and surprisingly complex subject that affects everyone who uses computers. There are numerous excellent sources for such information on the subject, many of which are referenced at the Usability Professionals Association website which can be found at www.upassoc.org.

When designing a self service interface, as with any system, it is essential to get inside the mind set of the user population to understand what they want, need and expect. Self service portals are more usability critical than other systems for a variety of reasons. The following factors need to be considered when modelling the worst case self service user scenario:

- Low frequency (hopefully) of use
  - The user is unfamiliar
- Limited time for the transaction (almost definitely)
  - The user is impatient
- IT illiteracy/poor skill levels (maybe)
  - The user is confused
- Unhappy about needing to use the system in the first place
  - The user is disgruntled

Is it any wonder then that users are often confused, irritated and annoyed by self service interfaces to the point where they abandon them in disgust...

12.5 The "I Want..." Box

The most elegant user interface of all time was developed in ancient Egypt in around 3000 BC. It enabled the capture of text and graphical information in an intuitive and tactile manner which has yet to be equalled with all of the power of today's technology. A simple piece of paper and a pencil or pen is the usability paradigm that all self service systems must aspire to. The electronic equivalent would be a single text box with a single button. The user would enter details of what it is that they want or need and hit the button, only to await a response. Now this would be fine if the user provided all the information that the support organisation needed in order to be able to deal with the request. However, users are rarely that giving and such a system would invariably mean that the first person to person contact between the user and the service function would be to clarify requirements and capture additional pertinent information. Or so it was...

The advent of Natural Language Processing (NLP) technology has meant that systems can interrogate free format text and interpret the meaning and intention behind it. Advanced NLP systems may also extract pertinent data points from within the body of text and use them appropriately to assist with the automated processing of the request. At the very least, such systems can request additional context sensitive data from the user at the point of data entry in order to minimise the need to initiate contact to merely capture information or clarify what it is that the user requires. Unfortunately, such technologies are still relatively expensive and may be beyond the reach of many organisations. However, this will change over time and their use is likely to increase in the areas of self service and front-line request processing.

12.6 Shifting the User Mind Set

Studies show that the service costs associated with handling requests raised via a self service solution are significantly lower than those that are called into the service desk directly. In order to reduce service delivery costs it is therefore necessary to increase the level of usage of self service solutions. Organisations may choose to do this through the use of a combination of the stick and the carrot.

Incentives for users to encourage them to use self service solutions may include:

- Improved service levels
- Reduced costs
- Increased choice/selection

Whereas, users may be discouraged from using direct, labour intensive channels by:

- Restricted access to other channels of communication
  - Reducing the hours of the day when the phone lines are staffed etc.
- Charge premiums for person to person requests

12.7 Is Self Service Always Appropriate?

There is an unquestioned belief in some sections of the IT community that it is always better for users to report their own issues and attempt to resolve them themselves rather than contact the service desk directly. The theory being that it is cheaper for users to spend time helping themselves than to have people waiting at the end of a help line to assist them. This assumes that the costs associated with the help desk personnel is greater than the costs associated with the loss of productivity incurred when a user attempts to help themselves. Expensive resources e.g. investment bankers, lawyers, accountants, senior executives etc will invariably telephone the help desk rather than use a self service system. At a push, they may get their secretaries or administrators to use the self service interface on their behalf but even this is pushing credibility to the extreme.

The sad fact of the matter is that self service systems are primarily seen by many senior IT managers as an easy means of reducing their costs of delivering service to their lower value customers and/or employees i.e. its good enough for them but not for us etc. Until this mindset changes, the self service user experience will always be a bit of an after thought.

Interaction Management

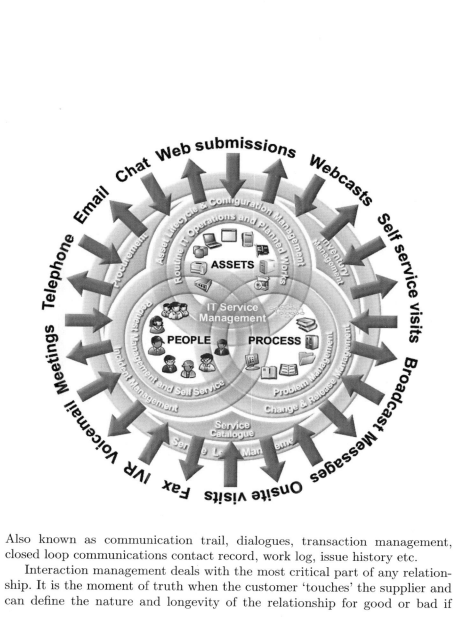

Also known as communication trail, dialogues, transaction management, closed loop communications contact record, work log, issue history etc.

Interaction management deals with the most critical part of any relationship. It is the moment of truth when the customer 'touches' the supplier and can define the nature and longevity of the relationship for good or bad if not handled appropriately. Unless every interaction is treated with the appropriate seriousness and commitment then customer satisfaction can be negatively impacted and the entire customer-supplier relationship may be placed in jeopardy. It is after all where the wheels touch the road that determines not only the speed and direction (which ultimately determine the success or failure) of any given transaction.

Interaction management is seldom, if ever, treated as a standalone discipline and is typically consumed within the request, incident and change management processes with varying degrees of success. It is not suggested that the function should be broken out as a standalone entity, but instead it is highlighted here to ensure that it is practiced consistently across all service management disciplines. Unless all user – system interactions are proactively managed in a consistent way throughout the organisation, users will be unsure of the level of responsiveness to expect from specific service functions and are likely to either become dissatisfied or to generate additional workload by calling to progress chase and/or get status updates.

13.1 Process Objectives

The interaction management process should be focused upon the following core objectives:

- Effective routing and processing of inbound and outbound communications
- Provision of interaction information to all persons working with a contact to ensure service consistency etc

13.1.1 Effective Routing and Processing of Inbound and Outbound Communications

The primary purpose of the process is to effectively handle and route inbound and outbound communications to ensure that the relevant parties receive the information they need, when they need it, in order to enable the associated/dependent processes flow smoothly and without delay.

13.1.2 Provision of Interaction Information to all Persons Working with a Contact to Ensure Service Consistency etc

All too often within organisations, the left hand doesn't know what the right hand is doing. Such disconnects cause duplicated and wasted effort as well as damaging the customer's perception of the level of professionalism of the organisation in general. In order to ensure everyone is on the same page and that users are given consistent and accurate information it is important for everyone working on a particular case (be it an incident report, problem investigation or change request etc) be up to speed with the latest developments and to have a holistic view of the ongoing and historic communication chains related to the issue in hand.

Types of interactions that should be governed by the process include:

- Telephone calls (Inbound and outbound)
- Email messages (Inbound and outbound)
- Walk in/Face-to-face discussions
- Web site visits (Intranet and extranet)
- Site attendances/visits
- Web requests/submissions
- Chat sessions
- Voicemail (including associated IVR captured data)
- Meetings (Either physical or virtual (Conference calls/Web based collaborative sessions etc))
  - Including actions points and/or verbal commitments
- Outbound mailings/notifications
  - Marketing material/promotions
  - Bills/Statements
  - Product/Service announcements
  - Status reports related to ongoing tickets etc
- Satisfaction survey requests/completed surveys

More often than not services are designed around email and telephone communication channels only and may fail catastrophically when attempting to handle other forms of interaction.

13.2 Common Issues

Common issues include:

- Volume of interactions is increasing faster than capacity to handle/manage them
- Details of interactions being lost which result in incomplete audit trails for the issues, incidents and changes etc that are related to them
- Failure to respond to inbound interactions in a timely manner
- Over-reliance on impersonal communication mediums
- Quality/Usefulness of automated responses
- Pressures to minimise contact time and frequency
- Mis-understandings/Miscommunications
- Not all interaction types are treated with the same level of importance
- Mis-routing of interactions
- Language difficulties
- Cultural differences
- Misrepresentation of the content of an interaction within the historic record i.e. biased views of a communication exchange based upon personal opinion etc.

13.3 Process Flow

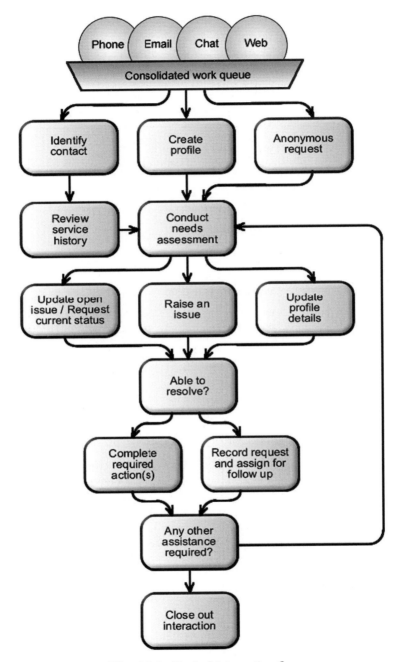

Fig. 13.1. Typical interaction flow

13.4 Key Players

Caller/Visitor/User/Customer – The people without whom there would be no service function at all.

Anyone with a phone, email account or a role that gives customers access to them – Everyone within the organisation should be aware of how to handle misdirected calls or direct approaches to ensure that the user experience is professional, courteous and efficient.

Call handling agents/Service representatives – Irrespective of which channel is used to communicate with the service function, the front line staff are critical to the quality of each interaction and should be treated as such.

Field personnel – Remote personnel are just as likely, if not more so, as office based staff to engage users in discussion. The outcomes of such interactions need to be tracked and recorded to ensure commitments are kept and that the rest of the business is aware of what has been agreed.

13.5 Process Metrics

Volumes of interactions by channel

Percentage of inbound interactions that are responded to within predefined objectives

Percentage of inbound interactions that are 'dealt with' at the first point of contact

Request Management

Also known as call handling, request handling, record/log and forward, call forwarding, request processing etc

Often used in conjunction with a web based portals to give users a shopping cart to load up with services from a predefined catalogue of options

Request management processes are common within organisations that have consolidated their frontline support organisations into a one stop shop for assistance (i.e. a consolidated service desk). The purpose of the request management process is to accurately determine the user requirements, gather any and all appropriate data points related to their identified need and to forward all of this information on to relevant specialist group for further action. It is not uncommon for such front line services to also attempt to resolve common and/or simple issues or information requests at the first point of contact. It is also important that the front line support organisation is informed of the current workload and capacity of the supporting functions as it is useful if they are able to set user expectation appropriately regarding an anticipated time for response or resolution. This simple action can avoid countless follow up calls and much user dissatisfaction if practiced diligently and accurately.

14.1 Process Objectives

The request management process should be focused upon the following core objectives:

- Efficient handling of requests for service(s)/assistance
- Accurate routing of requests to the relevant people/groups
- Provision of closed loop feedback (e.g. status updates/information to requesters)

14.1.1 Efficient Handling of Requests for Service(s)/Assistance

It could be argued that organisations implementing request management processes are adding an additional unnecessary layer of support personnel between the end users/customers and the service delivery teams. However, in large organisations with highly specialised back office functions it is impractical to expect end users to have sufficient knowledge or understanding of the underlying organisational structure and functional roles/responsibilities – in such cases the addition of a single point of contact, or one stop shop, for assistance can significantly improve the overall efficiency of the business as time is not wasted hunting for the right person to help when there is a problem.

14.1.2 Accurate Routing of Requests to the Relevant People/Groups

Such efficiency gains are only practical if the request handling function accurately routes issues to the relevant skill centres within the business. In order to facilitate this objective, request handling personnel need to have a good basic understanding of the business and the issues it commonly faces as well as being trained in high level diagnostic techniques so as to be able to confidently identify the most probable type of issue being reported and pass it to the appropriate function for further investigation and resolution.

14.1.3 Provision of Closed Loop Feedback (e.g. Status Updates/Information to Requesters)

In some cases, the request handling team may be the only person to person contact that the requester experiences. Irrespective of whether this is the case or not, the request management process should be designed to provide regular status updates regarding the progress of issues and enable the originator of the request to update the details as appropriate.

14.2 Common Issues

Common issues with Request Management include:

- Extended delivery times
- Lack of visibility of request status
- Unnecessarily high levels of follow up/chase calls
- Incorrect routing of requests
- Multiple contacts required to capture all required information
- Errors capturing request details/data

14.3 Process Flow

Fig. 14.1. High level request handling process

14.4 Key Players

Requester – Someone who is requesting something for themselves or on behalf of someone else.

Recipient/Beneficiary – The person who is to receive the benefit of the output of the request process.

Service/Support Agent – Front line personnel responsible for handling requests, reviewing the requirements and taking the appropriate actions, be that to action the request themselves or to refer it on to another group or individual.

Service Delivery Manager – Management role with responsibility for the request management process and/or the services that are related to the requests being raised.

14.5 Process Metrics

Percentage of requests that are reassigned between functional groups due to incorrect initial routing

Percentage of requests that did not initially contain all of the necessary information required by the delivery teams i.e. the proportion of requests which had to be clarified with the requester

14.6 What is the Difference Between a Service Request and an Incident?

Let us consult the trusty dictionary once more:

"Request – to express a desire for, esp. politely; ask for or demand"

"Incident – a distinct or definite occurrence"

Which comes first the incident or the request? Well if the person discovering the incident, requests assistance rather than logging an incident then maybe the request will precede the incident. Alternatively, an incident may be reported and then multiple requests may be received as a result of its impact. But to be honest, does it really matter providing all requests and incidents are dealt with effectively?

It will not always be appropriate to separate requests from incidents. In some organisations the lines will be sufficiently blurred to make the distinction academic. Organisations that are implementing a true cross discipline consolidated service desk incorporating the first line support capabilities of the Facilities, HR, Finance (typically to handle payroll related issues etc) and IT functions may gain significant benefit from extracting the request management layer as a distinct process in order to clearly delineate between the one stop support shop and the 2nd line service desks within the specific functions.

14.6.1 Requests as a Type of Incident

In order to simplify the arbitrary labelling of requests and incidents many organisations use a 'ticket type' attribute within their incident management system to differentiate between true incidents i.e. user/service impacting events, requests, questions and complaints. The selection of ticket type may be automated and based upon the categorisation of the ticket or it may be manually selected. Such an approach enables management reports to include or exclude requests from incidents and vice versa. The benefits of such an approach are that front line agents have only one interface to use and therefore are more likely to choose the correct one! However, such an approach will also have its downsides as a typical incident management interface may be overly complicated for service personnel who predominantly handle less technical requests such as those related to facilities etc.

14.7 Common Request Types

But what do we actually mean by the term 'requests'? Within an IT context, requests may come in a variety of forms, some of which are outlined below:

- Questions i.e. requests for information
  - When? What? Who? Why?
- Support requests i.e. requests for technical assistance
  - How do I . . . ? Can you tell me how. . . ?
- Complaints i.e. a request for reparation, explanation and/or apology or combination of all three
- Subscription requests i.e. requests for services
  - Service enrolment/Subscriptions
  - Subscription changes
  - Cancellation of subscription
- Profile updates e.g. Personal information changes etc
- Equipment requisitions
  - Low value items e.g. Replacement mice, keyboards, computer bags, telephone headsets, USB memory sticks etc
  - High value items e.g. Laptops, screens, PDAs, mobile phones etc
- Consumable requisitions
  - Printer toner/ink cartridges, screen wipes, network cables, blank CDs etc
- Resource bookings i.e. requests for Meeting rooms, LCD projectors, loan equipment etc
  - Availability checks
  - Bookings/Reservations
  - Cancellations/Booking amendments

Some of you reading this list may consider some of the above items to be 'changes', and indeed in some organisations such requests are handled as part of the change management process. It largely depends upon the level of granularity used to filter inputs to the change process as well as the level of control the business wishes to exert over a specific type of user requirement.

14.8 Request Management and the Change Management Process

The request management process shares as many similarities with the change management process as it does with the incident management process. It may be necessary to implement approval processes for certain types of request to ensure that sufficient levels of financial control are exerted. Requests may require a series of actions, or tasks, to be completed by various groups to fulfil their stated requirement e.g. a simple meeting room booking request may require Reception to place the attendees names on a welcome board and prepare visitor passes, Facilities to arrange the furniture and provide suitable refreshments, IT to provide a LCD projector and ensure internet connectivity is available and the Telecommunications team to set up a video conference call. All of these discrete tasks need to be coordinated to ensure that the request is satisfied fully.

Perhaps the most far reaching service requests are those that hail the arrival of a new starter to the organisation. There is often hundreds of finite tasks associated with someone joining a company which range from the provision of hardware (e.g. laptop, PDA and mobile telephone), the installation of software (e.g. office automation suites, sales tools etc), the granting of system access (e.g. network logins, application accounts etc) to less obvious tasks such as desk allocation, business card printing, issuing of security pass etc.

14.8.1 Request Management Sub-processes

Request management consist of the following process flows:

- Identification/Data capture
- Routing
- Processing
- Closure

14.9 Triage

"the practice of sorting causalities in battle or disaster into categories of priority for treatment"

The word 'triage' originates from the French word 'trier', which means "to sort". According to many historians, modern day triage owes much of its origins to Dominique Jean Larrey, a famous French field surgeon in Napoleon's army. Larrey devised a simple method that could be taught to non-medical field personnel in order to enable them to quickly evaluate and classify the wounded in battle. Using triage the troops could prioritise casualties and evacuate those requiring the most urgent medical attention whilst the battle was in progress with no regard to rank.

Within an IT context 'triage' is used to describe the formal classification of requests and incidents based upon priority etc. By definition, triage is performed by the front line support staff and it is therefore essential that the techniques and procedures used to sort incoming issues is simple and easy to understand as it will often be performed by relatively inexperienced and unskilled personnel.

- Is the requester able to continue to work without their request being dealt with?
- Does the requester want to change something?
- Is something broken/not working?
- Is the request a question?
- Does the requester want to get something that they haven't already got?

14.10 Scripting

14.10.1 VBscript, Javascript, Python, Perl etc?

No. "Scripting" is a term borrowed from the contact centre and customer relationship management (CRM) arenas to describe a tool, or functionality, aimed at walking a service agent and caller through a telephone conversation in a structured and consistent manner.

The script can be thought of as a predefined road map of phrases, statements and questions to guide the agent when talking with a user. The script path usually contains branches to allow the agent to react to user input/responses and may or may not end with a proposed solution for the caller's issue.

14.10.2 Why Script?

Scripting was originally introduced in high volume call center environments to enable relatively unskilled staff deliver a consistent level of service. The use of scripts has had somewhat of a bad press in recent times and many people object to their use. However scripting engines can be a very good training aide and can help to implement process change in a fast paced environment. Scripting helps to:

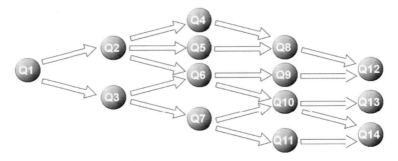

Fig. 14.2. Diagram of script path (including branching at conditional nodes)

- Ensure a consistent approach
- Minimise agent training requirements
- Adapt to changing requirements quicker i.e. just publish a revised script
- Capture information is a structured manner
- Reduce the number of call backs needed to clarify reported data

14.10.3 But that's not what you're Supposed to Say!

Unfortunately scripting interfaces are also subject to misuse and abuse and their implementation can sometimes lead to more problems than they solve. The key to good scripting is "Less is more". Scripting should be used sparingly if it is to be effective and should only be deployed in response to legitimate business concerns and/or requirements rather than being applied as the default for every interaction with the end user.

Common issues with scripting include:

- User resentment for being treated like an idiot
- Inability to exit the carriage before the train comes to a stop
- Irrelevant/Inappropriate questions
- Insufficient branching options
- Too much granularity/Too high level

Incident Management

Also known as Break/Fix, Issue Management, Trouble Ticketing, Case Management, Remedial Action and Corrective Action

ITIL definition of an incident:

Any event, not part of the standard operation of a service, that causes, or may cause, an interruption to, or a reduction in, the quality and/or level of service provided.

Incident management is the high profile public face of the IT organisation to its user base. It is the first port of call in times of trouble and because of this often assumes negative connotations in the minds of its users and those providing the function. The sporadic and unpredictable nature of end user contact means that effective relationships and trust are difficult to forge. Despite all this, it is the incident management function (commonly known as the help desk or service desk) that are the unsung heroes of the IT service management space. For it is their role to resolve and/or fix incidents that are raised by the user base as quickly as possible, so that the user community can get on with the business of doing the business, whatever that may be . . . .

A more useful definition of incident management might be:

"Getting systems and people up and running again when something goes wrong."

15.1 Process Objectives

The incident management process should be focused upon the following core objectives:

- Rapid restoration of service to the agreed predefined level
- Minimising overall disruption to the business
- Implementation of permanent fixes/workarounds
- First time fixes/resolutions (minimising the number of interactions needed to resolve an incident)
- Minimising the number of incidents that need to re-opened

15.1.1 Rapid Restoration of Service to the Agreed Predefined Level

By definition, incidents are symptomatic of a failure within the service provision and/or its usage. In order to get the user productive as quickly as possible the primary goal of the incident management process must be the restoration of the service to level delivered immediately before the incident occurred. This primary directive allows for the application of temporary workarounds in order to return the system to the status quo until such time that a permanent remedy can be implemented.

15.1.2 Minimising Overall Disruption to the Business

According to Mr Spock, "The needs of the many outweigh the needs of the few" and this may indeed be true at times of immense self sacrifice as seen in Star Trek II: The Wrath of Khan. However, within an ITIL and ITSM context, the needs of the business often outweigh the needs of the users (be they an individual or a group). The incident management process should be designed to continuously evaluate the pool of open issues and prioritise them according to the particular needs of the business at any point in time.

15.1.3 Implementation of Permanent Fixes in Preference to Workarounds

It is always better and more efficient to do something correctly the first time than to have go back and do it properly at a later date. Wherever possible the incident management process should attempt to eliminate and/or fix issues rather than provide short term workarounds which will require further remedial action to be undertaken at a later date.

15.1.4 First Time Fixes/Resolutions (Minimising the Number of Interactions Needed to Resolve an Incident)

If you think about what you want and hope for when you call a service desk for assistance I am sure that you will agree that most people would wish to be treated courteously and professionally by someone with the necessary skills, experience and support structure to enable them to resolve your issue as quickly as possible with the minimum amount of fuss. Since the longer an issue drags on, the more interactions, user involvement and hassle it causes, it is therefore preferable to resolve an incident at the first point of contact whenever possible.

15.1.5 Minimising the Number of Incidents that Need to be Re-opened

Incidents that need to be re-opened are really incidents that shouldn't have been closed in the first place. When reducing the number of re-opened cases it is important to understand why they needed to be revisited. Was it because the service desk wanted, or needed, to close them out in order to make their performance metrics look better than they should be? i.e. Were they cheating? Or was it because the incident had more far reaching implications than initially understood? Or perhaps, it was because a temporary workaround wasn't removed and replaced with a permanent fix? Whatever the reason for re-opening an incident, it is important to minimise the frequency of such events if service quality and user satisfaction are to be maintained.

15.2 Common Issues

Common Incident Management issues include:

- Extended resolution times
- Inconsistent service delivery/approach to resolution
- Incomplete fixes/Incidents needing to be re-opened
- Too many touch points required to resolve an issue
- Inefficient trouble shooting procedures
- Poor visibility of impact of incidents upon the business
- Routing errors/Multiple re-assignments

- Inappropriate prioritization of incidents
- Inefficient workload management
- Poor communication of outages and their impact
- Lack of a closed loop process i.e. no formal closure
- Continuously re-inventing the wheel
- Ineffective use of knowledge repositories
- Poor categorisation/classification of incidents
- Buck passing between functional/implementation groups
- Lack of visibility of incident status
- Temporary workarounds being left in place as permanent fixes
- Unnecessarily high levels of follow up/chase calls
- Availability of Help Desk staff
- Skill levels of Help Desk staff
- Single incident management process irrespective of nature and scope of incident e.g. Critical service impacting incidents treated in the same way as a user that has forgotten their password.

15.3 Process Flow

Fig. 15.1. High level overview of the incident management process

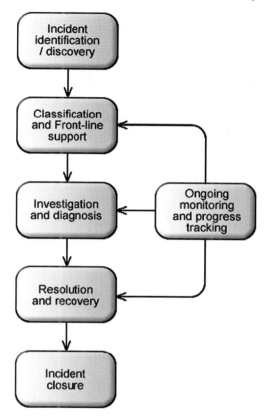

Fig. 15.2. The ITIL approach to incident management

Incident management sub-processes include:

- Incident investigation/analysis
- Resolution
- Incident closure

15.4 Key Players

Requester – The person contacting the service desk to report an incident and/or request assistance for themselves or on behalf of others.

Affected/Impacted User(s) – Any person, or persons, that are being negatively affected by the issue at the heart of the request.

Service/Support Agent – Service delivery personnel tasked with the handling of incident reports, their diagnosis and resolution.

Implementation Group(s) – Specialist technical teams that are responsible for investigating technical issues beyond the remit or understanding of the service agents. Implementation groups may also be involved in the application of workarounds and the implementation of fixes etc.

Incident Manager – Individual with responsibility for overseeing the incident management process and communicating its status and effectiveness to the business (including service delivery managers responsible for services that are impacted)

Service Delivery Manager – Individual with management responsibility for a portfolio of services delivered by the IT function to the user base. Involved in service design, costing, delivery management and reporting in order to ensure that the needs of the business are fully understood and satisfied by the service offerings under their control.

15.5 Process Metrics

Traditional measures	Improvement focused metrics
Total numbers of Incidents	Distribution of incidents by time of day, day of week and day of month/quarter
Mean elapsed time to achieve Incident resolution or circumvention, broken down by impact code	
Percentage of Incidents handled within agreed response time (Incident response-time targets may be specified in SLAs, for example, by impact code)	
Average cost per Incident	Financial impact of incident to the business i.e. direct costs associated with handling and resolving the incident + costs associated with the loss of productivity of impacted users, rework due to data loss, opportunity cost of system unavailability etc.
Percentage of Incidents closed by the Service Desk without reference to other levels of support	Number of re-assignments (within functional teams and between functional groups)
Incidents processed per Service Desk workstation	
Number and percentage of Incidents resolved remotely, without the need for a visit.	

15.5.1 Graphical Representations of Performance Data – Bringing the Figures to Life

It is often useful to represent data graphically to aid user understanding and make it similar to compare separate datasets against one another. The following example is used to give incident managers an immediate picture of the current status of their overall workload, as it clearly depicts incidents that have been in the system for extended periods and the current position within the incident management process.

The swim lane diagram below allows anyone viewing a specific incident record to quickly see how the incident progressed and which groups were involved at any point in time.

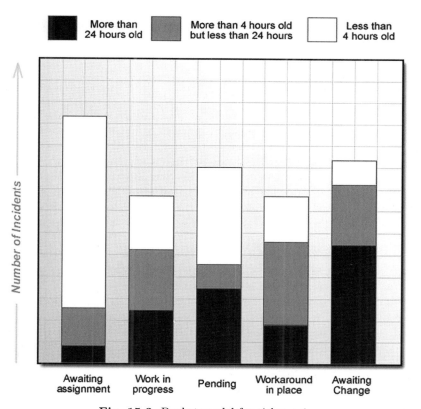

Fig. 15.3. Bucket model for ticket aging

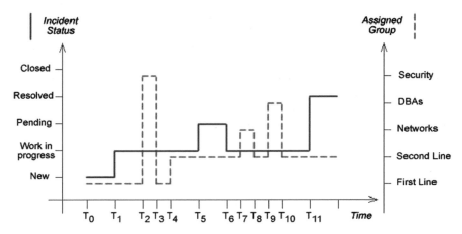

Fig. 15.4. Swim lane time line diagrams for assignment and status changes

15.6 Categorisation

15.6.1 Categorisation Types

The way in which incidents are categorised can dramatically affect the effectiveness and usefulness of the incident tracking solution. The problem with the majority of commercially available solutions available today is that they attempt to use a single categorisation structure for multiple purposes with little thought as to the consequences of this decision and how best to structure categorisation data given this inherent limitation of their application. To make matters worse, many vendors restrict categorisation models yet further by enforcing mandatory limits on the breadth and depth of the categorisation model.

There are many ways in which incidents can be classified and there are no right or wrong answers. The fact of the matter is, if a categorisation model works for you and gives you all of the information you need, allows the desired level of system automation to be implemented etc, then it is a good model.

For organisations struggling to work with unwieldy or overly simplistic structures, then it is a good idea to go back to basics and develop a structure that reflects the needs of the business and the desired capabilities of the incident management process. The following list outlines some of the most common forms of incident categorisation model in use today:

- Symptom based categorisation
- Affected CI categorisation
- Combined Asset and Symptom categorisation hierarchy
- Service related categorisation
- Functional/Departmental based categorisation structure
- Root cause based categorisation structure

Symptom Based Categorisation

Incidents are categorised by the way in which the user requesting assistance describes the symptoms they are experiencing e.g. "It's making a funny noise". This model is typically complemented by also identifying within the incident record which specific asset (or asset type/class in the absence of detailed asset information) is affected and/or displaying the reported symptom(s). Due to it's direct correlation to what the requester is experiencing this model is often the simplest for end users to report accurately.

Affected CI Categorisation

Asset type is selected from a hierarchical structure of asset descriptions ranging from generic terminology (e.g. printer), through a series of more granular descriptions (e.g. inkjet, laser or dot matrix (yes they still exist)). It is not uncommon for organisations to include manufacturer and model information within such a structure, the relative merits of this are discussed later. The nature of the incident is often consigned to the free text description field which can lead to helpful phrases such as "broken" and "not working". Unfortunately such categorisation structures can be overly technical if developed in isolation by the IT function and as such may not be used to best effect by the user and front line service agents.

Combined Asset and Symptom Categorisation Hierarchy

By far the most common approach is to combine asset class information and symptomatic details in a single categorisation structure. This can cause an initial meta data collection overhead but does facilitate a reasonably structured approach to incident classification upon system users. Regrettably, the most common side effect of combining both of the aforementioned methods is to generate a massively diverse structure with many hundreds of end nodes which do not generate usable trend data for ongoing analysis to identify candidates for preventive action.

Service Related Categorisation

By focusing the categorisation model on the services provided by the IT function, the system can be used to help embed and communicate the concept of a service catalogue and the associated service deliverables throughout the organisation. Typically such a categorisation model would start with a layer outlining the high level service structures and would then drill down to specific deliverables and/or characteristics of the service. An approach such as this can be confusing to end users who may have little or no exposure to the IT service catalogue and defined services provided by the IT function.

Functional/Departmental Based Categorisation Structure

Embedding technical group names and functional areas/titles within a front-line facing categorisation structure is not an uncommon practice, but it is one which causes confusion and almost guarantees that tickets will be misdirected and require reassignment as a matter of routine. This approach assumes that the people categorising an incident (see later for when this occurs) know whom should deal with the issue at hand, such an assumption requires that this person also therefore knows exactly what the problem is as well as who is the best group to fix it . . . In reality this is rarely the case for anything more than routine issues and consequently such an approach is not recommended.

Root Cause Based Categorisation Structure

It is usually almost impossible to know the root cause or causes of an incident at the time of logging an incident and yet some organisations attempt to do so (placing enormous faith in the divine predictive capabilities of their help desk operatives). Such an approach is usually a result of a rigid help desk application which will not facilitate more than one categorisation structure to be applied against an incident – this system limitation is then compounded by the desire to implement preventive action (which requires the collection of structured root cause data) and a disjointed mess is the only likely result.

15.6.2 When to Categorise

The above section outlined various methods of categorisation that can be applied to incident records. However, knowing how you wish to categorise incidents is only half the story. It is also important to determine when to categorise incidents so that valid comparisons of how the IT function handled an incident can be made. It is recommended that incidents be categorised a several points during their lifecycle so that sufficient focused data can be collected to perform meaningful trend analysis for preventive action initiatives. The following milestones within the ticket lifecycle are suggested:

- Reported categorisation
- First line/Initial categorisation
- Closure categorisation
- Root cause(s) categorisation

Reported Categorisation

Upon submission via self service interface, the end user would be asked to determine the nature of the problem they are facing. Such a categorisation model will undoubtedly be simpler than that expected from a front line help desk agent however it should be sufficient to enable automated assignment/routing

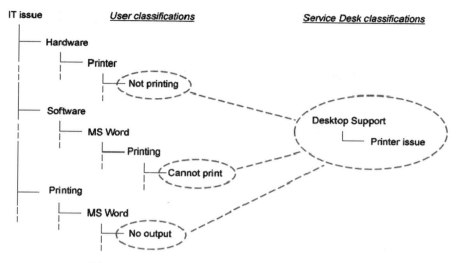

Fig. 15.5. Multiple routes to a common end point

of the incident wherever possible. The use of a simple incident classification selector (incorporating multiple routes to diverse end points that correlate back to a single categorisation node) is recommended to assist the user with the completion of this data point.

In situations where an organisation is using Natural Language Processing (NLP) technology to review and automatically categorise inbound incidents, it is recommended that such input be treated as a reported categorisation, thereby enabling first line support to review and validate the success of the artificial intelligence system. Any alterations to the categorisation made by the first line agent should then be fed back to the NLP solution in order to enable it to learn and improve the accuracy of its selections in future.

First Line/Initial Categorisation

This is the categorisation assigned against the incident record the first time it is manually touched by the IT function. The frontline agent will use the information provided within the self service request in conjunction with information gathered by discussing the incident with the requester to determine the nature of the issue and/or the configuration items affected.

Closure Categorisation

This categorisation point and data is not to be confused with closure code. The closure categorisation is intended to record the actual incident classification as determined by the person(s) that investigated and resolved the issue. Such a categorisation can then be compared with the initial categorisation to give a measure of the effectiveness of the front line's high level diagnosis skills and the accuracy of the classifications.

Root Cause(s) Categorisation

Specific incident types (usually identified by the initial or closure categorisations) may require additional data to be collected regarding the root cause, or causes, that contributed to the incident. Such categorisation data should entered by the person that resolved the incident and should be based upon their knowledge of the actual problem, the factors that gave rise to the problem being identified as an incident and the circumstances within which the incident arose. This data is critical to allow similar incidents to be analysed to determine if there is any common themes of consistent influencing factors that should be addressed by preventive action.

15.6.3 Reason for Categorization

The categorisation of incidents is a critical part of the incident handling process as it is the one piece of data that is routinely used to determine how the incident is handled, who handles it and what the service delivery objectives are. In addition to these uses categorisation is the cornerstone of all management reporting and is often the most visible way in which the IT function represents itself to the business. Categorisation data is used for a wide variety of purposes within the IT service management system including:

- Reporting
  - Management information
  - Trend analysis
  - Activity reports
- System automation
  - Routing/Automatic assignment
  - Prioritisation
  - Informational alerts/prompts
  - Assisted data capture/Scripting
  - Diagnostic scripts/Q&A flows
- Service Level Agreements
  - Application of specific SLAs
- Process identification/selection

As you can see from the listing above, the vast array of system uses of categorisation data often mean that the resultant categorisation model is a combination of various classification methods that compromise each others integrity delivering a less than optimal solution. In order to reduce the level of compromise it is advisable to have multiple categorisation data points associated with the incident record and to use the appropriate categorisation structure for the relevant data point.

15.6.4 Common Categorisation Mistakes

Given the importance of incident categorisation to the wider incident management process it is surprising that it is often overlooked by management as nothing more than a piece of meta data, with responsibility for its creation and update delegated to relatively inexperienced members of staff. This abdication of responsibility can lead to a variety of problems down the line including:

- Using categorizations to try to track too many things
  - Equipment manufacturer detail as part of structure
  - Model details as part of structure
- Overly complex categorisation models
- Too many levels of categorisation
- Non-intuitive terminology/language e.g. Acronyms and jargon
- Too many category choices at any particular level
- Requiring users to categorise incidents to the final level of detail
- Excessively similar options
- Overly abbreviated categorisation options
- Arbitrarily forcing all categorisations to have the same number of levels/ tiers

Using Categorizations to Try to Track too Many Things

The trouble with trying to cover every conceivable base and angle is that there is a real danger that you will fail to cover any of them properly. Categorisation hierarchies that include multiple parameters are often very deep and users may have difficulty backtracking when they make mistakes.

Overly Complex Categorisation Models

Complex categorisation models introduce may problems to the process which go far beyond the initial selection of the appropriate category. Adding complexity to the classification of incidents automatically increases the complexity and management overhead associated with the creation of SLAs, Management reports, automatic assignment rules etc. Before devising a complex n dimensional array of incident classification it is as well to remember how such classifications structures are used and the likely effects of the design.

Non-intuitive Terminology/Language e.g. Acronyms and Jargon

The use of jargon and acronyms is often a direct result of system limitations dictating the maximum number of characters a menu drop down can contain. Whatever the reasons for it, the use of acronyms etc should be avoided as they are often confusing to end users and may result in the incident being incorrectly categorized by individuals who have a different understanding of a specific TLA (Three letter acronym) of FLA (Four letter acronym).

Too Many Category Choices at any Particular Level

Best practice dictates that multi-level menus should never have more than ten to twelve options to choose from at any level. Users typically find it hard to navigate and use menu systems that require excessive scrolling and eye movement to see all of the choices before them. It is usually preferable therefore to group selections into groups and have an additional level of menu to navigate than to force users to work with excessively long lists of choices.

**Requiring Users to Categorise Incidents to the Final
Level of Detail**

Systems that require users to navigate to, and enforce a mandatory selection from, the end node of a classification tree are responsible for more incident misclassifications than any other categorisation related issue. Many users will not be comfortable categorising an incident to the nth level of detail and will be forced into making an educated guess at best and a random stab in the dark at worst. Ideally, solutions will enable users to stop classifying an incident at the level of detail with which they feel most comfortable.

Excessively Similar Options

Choice is not always a good thing. Giving users too many similar choices can leave them bewildered and confused. More often than not, when faced with overly similar options the average user will pick either the first or last item on the list without considering the subtle nuances that those who created the categorisation structure were hoping to identify.

**Arbitrarily Forcing all Categorisations to Have the Same Number
of Levels/Tiers**

We have all seen systems where classification options have been duplicated at various parts of the classification tree. The dreaded "Other, other, other" or "Misc, misc, misc" classifications have been used extensively in help desk systems for years as a means to try and compensate for this system failure. Such categorisations do nothing to improve the understanding of the importance of accurate incident classification and merely go to show how little understanding the solution vendors have regarding how their tools are expected to be used in the real world.

15.7 Prioritisation

Not every high priority issue is important! Naturally it is important to somebody, else it wouldn't have been prioritised as 'high', but the level of importance of a specific issue affecting a specific service, impacting a specific subset of users at a specific time is far more complex than randomly selecting a value from a drop down box . . .

Incident priority should be determined through the evaluation of a number of factors including:

- Number of people affected (sometimes referred to as the scope)
- Severity of incident impact
  - (i.e. is it stopping the user(s) from working completely?)
- Risk to business operations
- Business priority of the user(s) affected
  - Role based priorities
  - VIPs
- Business priority of the services impacted/affected
- Time sensitivity (Sometimes referred to as urgency)
- Operational schedule
- Calendar sensitivity
- Previously agreed contractual terms

Number of People Affected (Sometimes Referred to as the Scope)

Obviously an incident affecting multiple similar users will have a higher priority than that affecting a single user of the same profile. Where many systems and/or processes fall down is that they treat all users as equal and would rank an incident affecting a hundred salespeople as more important than a similar incident affecting a single personal assistant – Now, it is not for us to say here whether or not the needs of an entire sales team outweigh the needs of their administrator, but it is important to recognise that when looking at the number of user affected it is essential to be sure to compare apples with apples.

Severity of Incident Impact i.e. Incident Type/Categorisation

Not all incidents prevent a user from continuing to work productively. Work patterns and job functions may mean that the affected user(s) can get on with alternative tasks while they wait for the incident to be resolved. Also the incident may not prevent the user working but may impair their productivity e.g. a central business application that is running slowly does not prevent the user base working but it does reduce their effectiveness and the value that they can add to the business.

Risk to Business Operations

Some incidents may not directly have a negative effect upon the business immediately but they may have the potential to significantly affect the business if left unchecked in the short term. A classic example of this would be a user reporting strange behaviour on their PC, these symptoms may be indicative of a virus infection and as such would merit immediate action to try and isolate the potentially infected machine from the network as soon as possible in order to prevent the virus spreading throughout the organisation.

Business Priority of the User(s) Affected

It is a fact of life that some groups of users are perceived by management to be more critical to the success of the business than others. Naturally all users will play a role in the overall working of the business, but the business will rank and prioritise the order in which users should be dealt with cases where all other factors are equal.

Business Priority of the Services Impacted/Affected

Some IT services will be more important to the business than others. An external facing online ordering system will always out rank an internal HR solution. Typically, services will be prioritised based upon the revenue risked if they are unavailable i.e. their opportunity cost, as well as the amount of money wasted by having employees unproductively waiting for the service to be restored i.e. the failure cost.

Time Sensitivity (Sometimes Referred to as Urgency)

So you may be wondering why the time at which the incident is reported have any bearing upon its priority? Consider a ticket raised regarding an issue affecting a user PC at 4:30pm in the afternoon . . . If the user is due to finish for the day at five then there is little point in pulling out all the stops to get them back up and running before the close of business. Providing the issue is resolved before the next morning then the user (and consequently the business) will be happy. Time sensitivity is sometimes referred to as 'Urgency' within ITIL and ITSM solution sets, unfortunately such a name causes users and agents to misapply and misuse such a data point with everyone asserting that their particular incident is very urgent indeed.

Operational Schedule

Let us now consider the above scenario again but imagine a different user that has just started their evening shift and has another 7.5 hours to work. Naturally the priority of an incident impacting this user would be higher than that of the previous user. The priority of an individual issue should be dependant upon its impact upon the business. Operational hours and shift patterns can have a significant effect upon how a particular incident is prioritised.

Calendar Sensitivity

Throughout the week, month, quarter and year - business priorities change depending upon external influences, scheduled events and unplanned incidents. Incidents impacting business critical services that occur during periods when those services are needed most should be treated as a higher priority than they would normally. For example, incidents affecting a payroll system only begin to become critical in the run up to a payment run.

Previously Agreed Contractual Terms

Where contract terms and penalties have been defined, it is likely that these will have a significant impact upon the way that incidents are prioritised.

15.7.1 Why Prioritise?

Let's take a look at the dictionary definition first and see how this can help:
    "Prioritise – to arrange (items to be attended to) in order of their relative importance"
    Right then, in an ideal world we will use the relative priority of an incident in a work queue to schedule our work and ensure that the most important issues are dealt with first. Unfortunately we seldom live in an ideal world and system limitations are often such that once a priority is set for an incident it is not changed again. This one off approach to prioritisation means that incidents which start off seemingly unimportant are treated this way to their conclusion irrespective of whether or not external events conspire to make the apparently routine something far more critical. Even when their priority is increased manually, the majority of ITSM solutions fail to take appropriate actions (such as applying more stringent SLAs, escalating to specialist teams, notifying key individuals etc) automatically.

15.7.2 Common Problems with Incident Prioritisation

When done appropriately, incident prioritisation can significantly improve the way in which incidents are assigned and the order in which they are tackled. However, prioritisation is not without its potential pitfalls, some of which are listed below:

- Over prioritisation of less significant tickets
- Under prioritisation of important tickets
- Arbitrary use of default priorities
- Changing ticket priorities throughout the ticket lifecycle
- Use of internal and external priorities

Over Prioritisation of Less Significant Tickets

By diverting limited IT resources to deal with tickets that have had their priority artificially raised there is a real danger that other incidents (that are more deserving of immediate attention) may be left in a work queue and have an increased detrimental impact upon the business.

Under Prioritisation of Important Tickets

Similarly, tickets which have not been recognised as significant may languish in a group or individuals work queue whilst they get on with resolving less critical incidents that they mistakenly believe take precedence.

Arbitrary Use of Default Priorities

Default priorities are usually tied to the categorisation or classification of the incident record. As can be seen from earlier within this section, the nature of the incident is only one of many factors that should go to form the overall priority of the incident. By relying on system defined default priorities the service desk may inadvertently incurring additional business risk, or instead be inefficiently over delivering for some minor incidents, depending upon individual incident circumstances.

Changing Ticket Priorities Throughout the Ticket Lifecycle

The only constant in life is that everything changes. As circumstances change, business priorities may alter and incident priority should be upgraded or downgraded throughout the incident lifecycle to reflect the current importance of the incident to the organisation. Unfortunately, most incident management processes, and the tools that support them, are incapable of responding to changing circumstances in real time. This can lead to incidents being treated inappropriately and additional risk or inefficiency being incurred.

Use of Internal and External Priorities

Nothing is more likely to cause confusion and resentment within the user community than the discovery that the service organisation is ignoring user specified priorities and arbitrarily assigning their own. The concept of internal and external priorities within an internal support environment is flawed as it presumes that the user population is unaware of the needs of the business when they are a part of that very business themselves. In such cases it is always better to be transparent and open regarding ticket prioritisation and to be willing and able to explain how the incident was prioritised if asked.

15.7.3 A Crude Approximation of Incident Priority...

Many systems will not be sufficiently advanced to be able to evaluate all of the varied factors associated with the prioritisation of an incident. In such cases the following approximation may be used to calculate the relative priorities of open incidents within a work queue in order to assist with workload management:

Priority $=$ Severity $\times$ Scope $\times$ Urgency

The following list outlines an example (and it is only an example of how it could be done) of how such a system could manifest itself within a three tier menu selection to determine ticket priority:

		Immediate action required (5)	Resolution required before close of business today (3)	Resolution needed within 3 working days (1)
User unable to work (5)	Single user affected (1)	25	15	5
	Department/Group of users affected (3)	75	45	15
	Entire organisation affected (5)	125	75	25
User productivity impacted (3)	Single user affected (1)	15	9	3
	Department/Group of users affected (3)	45	27	9
	Entire organisation affected (5)	75	45	15
User able to perform normally (1)	Single user affected (1)	5	3	1
	Department/Group of users affected (3)	15	9	3
	Entire organisation affected (5)	25	15	5

You will note that the weightings have been kept the same across the 3×3 matrix of options. In reality, it is likely that the weightings for incidents which do not immediately impact the productivity of a user would be lowered.

15.8 Incident Status Model

Irrespective of the underlying process being used to log, track and resolve incidents there is a need to be able to describe whereabouts within the overall incident lifecycle that an individual case is at any point in time. This is often achieved using the 'state', 'status', 'current stage' or 'next action expected' attributes or fields,

The status attribute of an incident is supposed to fulfil a variety of roles including:

- Informing the requester, and others, where their incident is currently within the incident management process
- Enabling IT management to determine the current workload and progress of the work throughout the system
- Allow persons working on an incident to make others aware that they have completed their work and to possibly progress it to the next stage in the process via automation etc

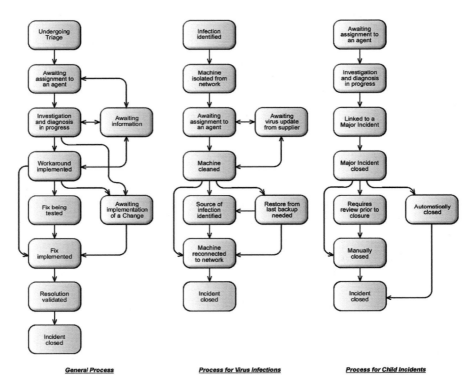

Fig. 15.6. Example status models for various types of incident

15.8.1 Enemy of the State . . .

Unfortunately, the status field is often misused and abused in order to track data that cannot be collected through other means. Such behaviour detracts from the primary purposes of the status attribute and may cause user dissatisfaction if they are forced to repeatedly change the ticket status and save it in order to close out an incident.

15.8.2 One Size Fits All

Unfortunately many commercial incident management solutions apply a standard process flow against all incidents irrespective of the needs of the business or requester. Such a limitation may be worked around by the use of predefined task or activity templates based upon incident type and classification, but this is usually always a sub-optimal approach. Different types of incidents will require different process flows. Incidents regarding security issues (e.g. virus infections etc) may require additional investigative steps to try to ascertain the method of infection and the performance of a comprehensive security assessment etc. Production system related incidents may require approvals from system and process owners to perform intrusive diagnostic tests within the live production environment. Major incidents may have additional notification requirements and steps to broadcast status reports to the business. Solutions for complex incidents may require additional testing and review cycles prior to implementation. In comparison, requests for information, questions regarding entitlements, "How do I?" enquiries etc will have very simplistic process requirements.

15.8.3 State Transition Rules

Typically the business defines a series of rules to restrict when an incident record can have its status changed from one state to another. These rules may be based upon a wide variety of constraints including:

- User profile (e.g. group membership)
- Completion of incident related data (e.g. solution field must be filled before the record can be set to a status of 'resolved')
- Status of related records (e.g. completion of related activity/task records before the incident can be finally 'closed')

15.9 Assignment, Ownership, Responsibility and Accountability

When defining an example of a state model (or process flow) for incidents, ITIL uses a status of "assigned" to designate the status of an incident that has previously been "accepted" or "scheduled", but is not yet "in progress". Now this example may have been jotted down without thinking or it may have been subject to many weeks of editorial review – I do not know. However, it has become ingrained into many of the leading off the shelf commercial ITSM solutions without thought or debate. Assignment is not a status or stage of the incident lifecycle; it is an attribute of the incident at worst and a dynamic relationship with another entity at best. Using "Assigned" as an incident status is meaningless and does nothing to help the requester or wider world understand the current progress of the incident in question.

Today's IT environment is a complex and multi-disciplinary place, to have an incident status of "assigned" implies that an IT problem can readily be resolved in one simple step by a single individual or group. All too often incident resolution requires a multi phased approach utilising various specialist groups through an iterative cycle to identify the underlying cause(s) and implement appropriate remedial action(s).

"Assignment" is better thought of as a series of transient relationships between individuals or groups and incident records i.e. Person A logged incident 1234, Person B worked on incident 1234 between then and yesterday, Person C has been working on incident 1234 since then and Group D will be working on incident 1234 from tomorrow onwards... Such an approach allows multiple groups or individuals to be associated with an incident at the same time and enables them to be involved multiple times throughout the incident lifecycle.

15.9.1 Automatic Assignment vs. Self managed Teams/Self Selection

Automatic assignment is the automated method of allocating incidents to specific individuals and/or functional groups/teams for them to work upon. Automatic assignment is often considered one way in which an Incident Management solution can improve productivity.

Group and Person Level Assignment

There is often a lot of resistance to automatically assigning incidents to specific individuals directly. Management often believe that the administration and configuration overhead associated with person level assignment rules are sufficiently onerous to outweigh any benefit that could be derived. Instead they decide to opt for a high level broad brush approach and automatically assign tickets to the functional group level, allowing individuals to then self select which incidents they work upon from their groups combined work queue. Sometimes this group level assignment is supplemented by a team leader then distributing the group workload to named individuals but this is relatively rare in all but the largest people heavy organisations.

15.9.2 Unfortunately, Self Selection can have its Problems.

"In the long history of humankind (and animal kind, too) those who learned to collaborate and improvise most effectively have prevailed"

Charles Darwin, Naturalist, 1809–1882

If we learn anything else from Darwin it is that it is not always the best or brightest that survive but those that are able to adapt to change the most effectively. As in evolutionary theory, this is also true in the help desk environment. Agent longevity is not always dictated by how well they service user requests and resolve incidents, but instead by how well an individual support agent plays the management's current numbers game. Self selection of work allows unscrupulous agents to cherry pick prime tickets to ensure that their performance and productivity metrics are sufficient to avoid unwanted scrutiny.

The reasons for cherry picking are as varied as those picking the low hanging fruit themselves and include:

- Selecting the simplest, easy to resolve incidents, to improve ones performance and/or productivity metrics
- Monopolisation of a specific niche area in an attempt to make oneself seem indispensable
- Keeping within ones comfort zone avoiding having to stretch oneself, or indeed, think
- Working with specific individuals or avoiding working with specific individuals due to personal preference/conflict
- Selecting high profile cases that will attract kudos and/or recognition

The organisational impact of cherry picking may include:

- Misrepresentation of the value of, and contribution made by, an individual to the organisation
- Creation of silos of knowledge and expertise
- Stagnation of agent skill sets
- Hoarding of 'simple' incidents causing them to miss their SLA
- Skewed user satisfaction metrics

The following list of questions will help determine if an organisation is susceptible to, or is suffering from, cherry picking behaviour:

- Are agents, or teams of agents, measured/rewarded by the number of incidents they resolve?
- Do agents keep an unhealthy watching eye on their group's work queue? i.e. Is the work queue open and constantly updating on their workstation?
- Are incidents being assigned outside of their priority? i.e. are low priority incidents being assigned before all medium and high priority incidents have been allocated?

- Are incident types/classifications unevenly distributed across the members of the support team?
- Are low priority incident Service Level Agreements (SLAs) being missed on a regular basis?

Answering 'Yes' to any or all of the above may be an indicator of sub-optimal performance related to cherry picking behaviour.

15.9.3 Automatic Assignment Methods

Irrespective of whether group or individual assignment is being used, the criteria and mechanisms used for automatic assignment will be similar. Automatic assignment is usually a two stage process, initially there is some form of grouping or filtering to come up with a list of possible candidates and then this list is refined using some form of weighting or ranking criteria. At the end of the process a single individual and/or group is selected to be assigned against the incident.

15.9.4 Short List Selection

There a several methods of selection criteria in common use today. These may be used in isolation or in combination to give a list of contenders from which to pick. Common selection criteria include:

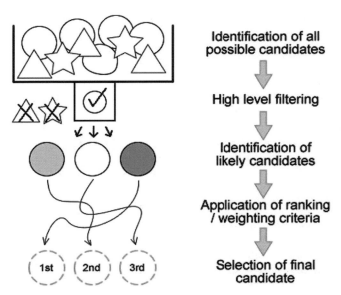

Fig. 15.7. High level automatic assignment process

- Skills based routing
- Experience based routing
- Geographical routing
- Personnel availability

Skills Based Routing

Assignment candidates are selected based upon their known skills and competencies. Typically incident classifications are used to describe skills and as such they may not be too intuitive to users and management. It is better to define meaningful skills and/or roles e.g. network troubleshooting, script debugging, application specialist etc and to relate these skills to individuals or groups. These skills, or combinations or skills, can then be linked with incident classifications to identify what skills are required to work upon a particular type of incident.

Experience Based Routing

Individuals are selected depending upon their historic record of dealing with incidents of the specific type in question. The theory being that if someone has successfully worked extensively on a specific issue type previously then they would be well placed to resolve similar incidents in the future. Such an approach can be used where an organisation hasn't been through a formal skills audit and competency identification process and lacks a documented skills database that it can leverage within the automatic assignment process.

Geographical Routing

Physical proximity to the incident being assigned is used to identify the optimum individual or group to work upon the ticket. Geographical matching is often completed using a basic location based hierarchy e.g. country, state/county, town etc which is related to both the requester and the delivery team. Where more accuracy is required GIS and GPS solutions can be incorporated to identify the closest resource to an incident site in real time.

Personnel Availability

Assignment decisions are based upon which personnel are available at the time of incident allocation. Availability based assignment processes should take account of operational working hours, shift patterns, planned absence (vacation, training etc) and should be capable of handling unplanned absence such as sickness etc.

15.9.5 And the Winner is... Refining the Shortlist

Having created a shortlist of potential assignment candidates the following allocation or distribution criteria can be used to select a specific individual or group:

- Round robin
- Workload balancing
- Relationship continuity
- Previous success rate

Round Robin

Members of the subset of individuals, or groups, that are eligible to be assigned against the incident are allocated in turn for subsequent incidents, thereby ensuring that all eligible parties are utilised evenly. Distribution order is often based upon something meaningless like the alphabetical sort order of the individual's or group's name – such a distribution method is not usually problematic providing there is sufficient incident volume to ensure those at the bottom of the distribution listing are utilised as much as those at the top.

Workload Balancing

Incidents are assigned to the members of the subset of individuals, or groups, that are eligible for assignment with the fewest number of open incidents assigned against them. This methodology is based upon the premise that agents working on particularly difficult, complex or time consuming incidents should not be overloaded beyond their current capacity. This is intended to prevent incident service level agreements being breached before the assigned agent even has an opportunity to begin working on the issue.

Relationship Continuity

Tickets are assigned based upon which support agent has assisted the person affected by and/or reporting the incident in the past. Doing this allows the support agent to develop a personal rapport with the requester and enables them to leverage previous experience of the user (e.g. their equipment setup, role, skill levels etc) in order to be able to deliver a more personalised and effective service. The intention is to enable personal relationships to form between the support organisation and the business, fostering closer links and improving understanding on both sides.

Previous Success Rate

Support agents are selected based upon their previous success, or otherwise, with similar incidents to the ticket being assigned. Such an approach can be used to give weaker agents increased exposure to subject areas which require improvement or additional experience. Alternatively, this method can be used to develop subject matter expertise within the support organisation.

15.9.6 Ownership vs. Assignment

The owner of an incident can be thought of as someone who, whilst not necessarily taking a direct hands-on-role in its resolution, keeps a watching brief to ensure that progress is made, the affected parties are kept informed and momentum is maintained until incident resolution and closure. The incident owner may instigate corrective actions proactively or they may take a more reactive stance and behave as the customers advocate.

15.9.7 Responsibility vs. Accountability

Let's have a quick look in the dictionary first before we see how these two terms apply within an IT context:

- *"Responsible – having control or authority (over)"*
- *"Accountable – answerable to someone or for some action"*

There is much talk of responsibility within the IT service management space... Specific delivery groups are given responsibility for completing specific tasks and actions. And yet, there is often little or no accountability to reinforce these assignments. Unless the management loop is closed and individuals / groups are held to book for their actions then mistakes, errors and omissions will continue to be ingrained within the culture of the IT organisation. All too often management blindly accept IT failures as being part and parcel of working life and do not even question why or how they came about. It is true that many of these events are unexpected and unpredictable but it is also true that many such events are caused by inattentive personnel and sloppy working practices. In such a culture, failure becomes a self fulfilling prophecy which stifles innovation and prevents significant process improvement.

15.9.8 Three Strikes and you're Out!

In cases where a persistent problem recurs numerous times it is often a good idea to get a fresh pair of eyes to look at the situation rather than to continually re-assign the same individual to deal with the immediate symptoms of the incident. Such an approach is sometimes known as "3 strikes and your out" indicating that a support agent is given three opportunities to resolve the underlying issue before being taken off the case. Unless implemented tactfully, this methodology can have a detrimental effect upon agent morale if they are openly taken off a problem in front of their peers. It may be better instead to assign an overlay troubleshooting resource, of a higher technical capability, to assist the originally assigned agent. Such a coaching/mentoring role can be used to develop and enhance the skills of the entire support team and can be a good way of stretching more able support agents and increasing their contribution to the organisation as a whole.

15.10 At your Service . . .

It is common for the suppliers of commercial incident management solutions to suggest that an incident be arbitrarily assigned against a 'service' with little thought as to what that really means to the organisation. Today's highly virtualised and pooled/shared resource based IT environments mean that such a crude allocation may be inappropriate at best and misleading at worst. In order to truly reflect the situation it is necessary to track service to incident relationships against the following criteria:

- Affected service(s) – i.e. the services whose operation has been negatively impacted by the incident (whether that be an outage or 'just' a performance degradation)
- Service under which incident is being reported – The service which defines the terms and conditions that the person reporting the incident may expect to have their issue dealt in accordance with i.e. the service covering the delivery of 'Email' may exclude the support of the service as this may be delivered under the banner of 'Workstation support' etc
- Service(s) under which the resolution is being applied – The services under which the people or groups attempting to resolve the issue are working i.e. This may be a series of internal IT services such as 'Database support', 'Network monitoring' etc which are only visible to the IT function.

15.11 Piff Paff Puff! Magic Happens here!

"Become a fixer, not just a fixture."

Anthony J. D'Angelo, Author, The College Blue Book

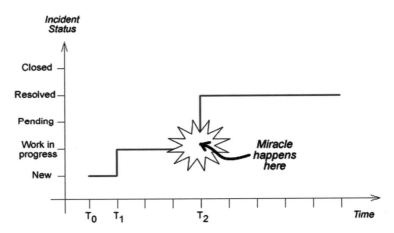

Fig. 15.8. The incident resolution process

The art of actually resolving issues is one which is often overlooked by management who are sometimes more concerned with call volumes and call durations than actually fixing problems (I mean "incidents" ...). They forget that the purpose of the process is to get people or systems up and running again as quickly as possible. There are many methodologies which can be employed for incident investigation, diagnostics and development of remedial action plans. Before we come to how we could or should go about finding out what is wrong (and maybe even how we could go about fixing it), let us first consider some fundamental and unquestionable truths of the incident management process. It is an undeniable fact that:

- Everybody lies
- Nobody listens
- If you don't ask the right questions, you won't get the right answers
- Be careful what you ask, they might just tell you

15.11.1 Everybody Lies

The word 'lies' might be a little harsh but the sentiment is spot on. Knowingly or not, 99.9999 % of users will give misleading or contradictory information during the course of a typical conversation to report an IT incident. It may be that they are trying to cover up their lack of understanding, it may be that they have a little knowledge in the subject and have extrapolated it beyond the realms of all credibility, it may be that they are trying to hide a guilty secret, it may be that they are just repeating an urban myth or inaccuracy that they themselves have been told. Whatever the reasons behind the intentional or unintentional deception, it is important to remember that any information provided by the end user must be treated with healthy scepticism until such time that they can be proven to be a reliable and credible witness.

15.11.2 Nobody Listens

People have a tendency to process oral information erratically, often missing vital pieces of a statement and filling in the blanks themselves, interpreting the inbound message as they believe to be appropriate. This is a problem for both the user reporting the issue, explaining its importance, responding to questioning etc and the frontline agent who is trying to determine what is wrong. The advent of web browsing, instant messaging, multi-tasking and the like have provided considerable distractions for your average front line agent and it is critical that they listen attentively to the caller if they are to glean the information they need from the conversation in order to resolve the incident to the users satisfaction.

To prove this point, if proof is needed, simply conduct the following experiment; The next time someone asks you how you are as you pass them in the corridor reply with something like "awful", "not too good" or "terrible".

Repeat this experiment a few times to gain a reasonable sample upon which to base your results. Count how many times the questioner smiles back and says "that's good" or similar. Bonus points should be awarded to people who respond with "fine thanks" or similar as they have imagined an entire conversation with you. Its not that they are revelling in your reported unhappiness, its just the way in which human beings process aural stimulus...

This phenomenon also manifests itself with written communications, in particular with email messages. Many people scan messages rather than reading them carefully and often miss important details (especially towards the end of longer messages). It is for this reason that email communications work best when a single email is used for a single topic and the text is kept short and focused upon the point in hand. To prove this to yourself why not add some random text to your email signature block and see how many people comment upon it. It is often interesting to see who actually reads your emails and who doesn't...

15.11.3 If You don't Ask the Right Questions, You won't Get the Right Answers

The key to an accurate and efficient diagnosis is the ability to ask the right questions at the right time, interpreting the responses correctly and using them to refine ones hypothesis through additional questioning until one is able home in on the actual problem and/or root cause. It sounds trivial when put like that doesn't it?

Unfortunately the vast majority of users are completely incapable of providing any useful additional information without being prompted. It is also important to remember incident process fact 1 (i.e. everybody lies) and ensure that if they do provide you with unprompted information it should be treated with extreme care!

15.11.4 Be Careful What You Ask, they Might Just Answer You

The only thing worse than not asking the right question is to ask the wrong question. Countless hours are lost every year chasing imaginary causes to equally imaginary problems because someone asked an overly vague question or failed to refine an initial finding appropriately. Requesters will usually provide responses to any and all questions that are asked of them, this does not mean that such responses are either relevant or useful. It is important to remember that in the majority of cases that the person requesting help doesn't know how to resolve the issue themselves (excluding instances where they don't have sufficient access privileges to fix their own problem) and so their opinions upon the root cause of their predicament may or may not be valid.

15.12 Incident Diagnostic Techniques

Naturally there are formalised and proven incident investigation and diagnostic techniques such as Kepner-Tregoe, Universal Troubleshooting Process (UTP), Oslerian analysis and others... However, in addition to these tried and tested 'scientifically proven' methodologies the following list outlines some of the most prevalent real life diagnostic systems in use within the IT space today:

- Have you turned it off and turned it on again?
- We have been placed in a holding pattern at 30,000 ft...
- Snap!
- The Spanish inquisition
- Spot the difference
- Newtonian physics
- Log, Look and Refer

15.12.1 Have You Turned it off and Turned it on Again?

This is the classic IT support opener. Despite the fact that 99% of all users will have already turned their machine off and on again multiple times (as well as angrily banging the poor keyboard in time to their current favourite from the top ten), frontline agents still sometimes insist on being masters of the obvious by suggesting this as course of action. Hey! Why bother trying to diagnose the issue and resolve it when we can go straight to the fix...

15.12.2 We have been Placed in a Holding Pattern at 30,000 ft...

Irrespective of what the requester is reporting, the front line agent gives them a long list of standard pieces of information that they definitely absolutely positively require in order to progress their issue any further. In exceptional cases, the front line agent may send the user an incredibly detailed email explaining how to find the requested log files and configuration settings for submission to the service desk. And all this before the user can ask for a password reset!

15.12.3 Snap!

If it looks like a fish, smells like a fish and is flapping about gasping for air, it might just be a fish... But then again it might not. It is very common for front line agents to play a game of snap with incident symptoms in order to try and match the case in hand with one that they have dealt with before. This is a perfectly reasonable approach providing the frontline agent has extensive experience of all of the possible issues that could befall a hapless user and that they recognise the fact that many symptoms can point to multiple underlying issues and causes. Regrettably, this is not always the case and consequently relying on matching symptoms alone is not a very efficient method of incident investigation.

15.12.4 The Spanish Inquisition

Nobody expects the Spanish inquisition! What did you do? What have you changed? Have you received any suspect emails? Did you open any attachments? Have you installed any software? Have you visited any unauthorised websites? Could anyone else have done something? Have you let anyone else use your PC? Are you incredibly stupid? Exactly how stupid are you? Have you committed an act of gross misconduct? Do you want to get fired?

Under this type of aggressive intense 'light in their eyes' questioning few users will be able to withstand a barrage of pointless accusations before they put their hands up and confess to everything and anything from the kidnap of Shergar to their involvement in the Great train robbery. Unfortunately, the majority of users will either not know what they have done, or not done, to cause an issue so even the most rigorous interrogation will fail to provide any clues to help with the resolution of the incident.

15.12.5 Spot the Difference

Identifying a difference between a machine setup that is functioning correctly and one that is not would appear at first glance to be a good way of approaching an incident in order to identify the underlying cause. Unfortunately, modern IT work stations have literally tens of thousands of configuration settings spread across hundreds of ini files, registry entries, application configuration screens, operating system parameters, bios settings, hardware level dip switches and the like. In reality, there are often dozens of seemingly trivial differences between apparently identical machines that may conspire together to cause the issue that is impacting the issue. Finding the one specific difference, or combination of differences, that is causing the issue is often akin to finding a very small needle in a very very large haystack.

15.12.6 Newtonian Physics

Disciples of Sir Isaac are committed to the notion of cause and effect. Every action will have an equal and opposite re-action. This may be true. But attempting to recreate the dying moments of a server with a low level systemic memory leak is a painful and difficult process. Especially if all you have to go on is an incomplete or corrupt dump file and your intuition.

15.12.7 Log, Look and Refer

Inexperienced or lazy agents (or agents whose bonuses are solely related to the number of incidents that they 'handle') sometimes abdicate all responsibility for the diagnosis of an incident and do nothing more than a cursory search of the corporate knowledge repository before automatically referring it on second line support or a specific delivery team. Obviously this does nothing to improve the incident resolution rate and can create animosity between the frontline and back office teams if left unchecked.

15.12.8 There is a Better Way...

And if I knew what it was I would be bottling it and making a fortune! However, without access to the magic elixir of incident diagnosis, I am left to offer a few words of guidance based upon my observations in the field. As with all things in life, everything in moderation is a good mantra to bear in mind when trying to determine why a particular incident has occurred. All, bar the first and last, of the above methodologies have their place in the frontline agent's arsenal and should be used in combination if a balanced and optimal approach is to be applied.

In addition to these techniques it is sometimes worthwhile applying basic situational analysis concepts to a particularly knotty issue. Such analysis techniques require the person investigating the incident to consider and write down responses (as the act of putting it down on paper will help to clarify and solidify ones thoughts, ideas and concepts within the writers mind) to questions such as:

- What is the current situation?
- How did you become aware of this situation?
- What information do you have to support the definition of the situation?
- Are you sure that the information is fair and accurate?
- How will you know when the situation is resolved?
- How long have you got to resolve the situation?
- Who is involved in the situation?
- Do anybody's perceptions need to be adjusted?
- What are the motivations of the relevant participants?
- What are the internal politics between the involved parties?
- Do you need to gather additional information to support your analysis?
- What do you intend to do to resolve the issue?
- Have you tested your hypothesis using actual data?
- What are the steps needed to resolve the situation to the satisfaction of all concerned?
- Are there any obstacles to implementing these steps?
- Whose mind do you need to change to clear the way for the solution?
- How can you frame the solution as a win-win scenario for all concerned?

You will note that almost half of these questions relate to people rather than things. This is deliberate. Even the most complex technical issues come down to people in the end, consider a poorly performing corporate back office system – the problem may be due to poor application design, insufficient network capacity/performance, inadequate client machine specification, user bad habits, slow back end database performance, delays waiting for data from integrated systems, congestion at the web farm tier etc etc . . . Naturally, the persons responsible for each of these areas will not want to be seen as the root of all evil and as such it will be necessary to apply considerable people skills to come up with a solution that allows everybody to keep their dignity and not to lose face in front of their peers. Who said that technical support was easy?

15.12.9 Perfecting Your Bed Side Manner

A study of medical malpractice attorneys in the US found that the single most important factor when patients were deciding whether or not to sue their doctor was the way in which they were treated. It had little to do with the physician being competent or never making a mistake, it was in fact much simpler. Patients who genuinely liked their doctors rarely felt inclined to sue them. In fact, US attorneys often shake their heads in disbelief after they point out that it was actually their client's doctor who made the mistake only to hear, "I don't care. I'll sue the hospital but I like him and I'm not going to sue him."

What can we, as IT support professionals, learn from this? Simply that as we dispense our own brand of advice and assistance, that our customers will subconsciously notice our ability to show that we believe in them and our empathy and concern for their situation. Treating a requester as a peer, worthy of your respect, has just as much of an impact on the perceived quality of our service delivery as all of the knowledge, workarounds and fixes that we impart. In fact, when a support agent is committed completely to their customer's success, their customer's become their biggest evangelists. It is imperative therefore to never forget to invest time and emotional capital in your customers. If their behaviour needs correcting, it is more helpful in the long run to point out an area of their skill set which needs enhancing or refreshing than simply to ignore it and label them an 'idiot'. No one likes to be told that they are in the wrong, but the skilful communicator can introduce such concepts subtly without having force a confrontation.

Support agents should be prepared to open, honest and frank with customers because they can tell if your heart isn't in it. The hearts and minds of the wider business need to be won on a one to one basis and the support team are ideally placed to take the fight to them and smother them with kindness.

When dealing with callers reporting and incident the following opening questions may be useful to avoid confrontation and help to develop a meaningful two way dialogue:

- What appears to be the problem?/What seems to be the matter?
- What symptoms are you experiencing?/How is the issue manifesting itself?

- How is the problem impacting you at the moment?
- Is there anything we could do to help mitigate the effects of the problem whilst we work on it?
- When did you first notice this/these symptoms?
- Are you aware of anything that happened prior to this that may be related?
- Are the symptoms constant?/Is the problem occurring intermittently?
- Do you know of anyone else with the same symptoms?
- Can you talk me through the steps you complete(d) to find the issue?
- What were you trying to do when you became aware of the issue?

And above all else remember the old mantra of the call centre agent – SMILE! It really does come across in your voice and helps to establish a rapport with the caller far quicker than a dull monotone mumble.

15.13 Notifications – Needing to Know What You Need to Know...

"Bernard, Ministers should never know more than they need to know. Then they can't tell anyone. Like secret agents, they could be captured and tortured."

Sir Humphrey Appleby, Yes Minister, BBC Television

Practically every ITSM system I have implemented over my career has, at one point or another during their lifecycle, had too many automated notifications flying about to be useful. The danger with such in-house spam generation is that important messages become lost in the system generated fog of communication. To add insult to injury, the content quality and usefulness of many system notifications is questionable in the extreme. Fragmented computer generated sentences with obvious variable substitution are annoying on their own. However, such annoyances are often compounded by the level of information contained within the notification itself. Either the message contains so much data regarding the issue in hand to make finding the pertinent point impossible or it contains so little data as to make it worthless.

Some common trigger points used to generated system messages which invariably lead to over notification are as follows:

- Every status change
- Transfer of ownership/re-assignment
- SLA milestones
- Updates to the work log
- Receipt of inbound email
- Changes to priority, severity etc

15.13.1 Less is More

Notifications should be used sparingly if they are to be effective. In an ideal world, the system should be 'intelligent' enough to send context sensitive messages to the right audience which contain the necessary information to be able to enable the reader(s) to make value judgements and take appropriate actions in response to the notification.

15.13.2 Registering an Interest

In addition to proactive notification to the persons directly associated with an issue, it is helpful to enable interested parties e.g. account executives, product managers, process owners, problem managers etc to register their interest in a particular type of issue, product, customer location, system, ticket etc and for them to thereafter receive notifications as the item of interest changes or develops. Advanced systems would also allow the registrant to determine which types of event they are particular interested in and to restrict their notifications accordingly.

15.14 Incident Management Aides

"I am endeavouring to construct a pneumatic memory board out of stone knives and bear skins."

Mr Spock, Science Officer, USS Enterprise

Thankfully, most help desk personnel are more suitably equipped than Mr Spock was when he visited "The City on the Edge of Forever" with Captain Kirk. There are a wide variety of niche tools available to assist with incident diagnosis and resolution currently available in a variety forms from open source solutions to full proprietary products.

15.14.1 Predefined Response Plans/Remedial Action Plans

Predefined response plans are not typically a standalone tool but are instead an inherent function of the incident management solution. These plans can be thought of as an aide memoir, or crib-sheet, for the support agent listing a series of tasks or activities that may be undertaken to assist with the diagnosis and resolution of an incident.

The plans should be related to the type and classification of incident being reported in order to ensure that they are pertinent and relevant to the case in hand. For example a predefined task or action list for a suspected virus infection may include:

- Isolation of the machine from the network
- Check current antivirus level

- Apply antivirus update if required
- Scan and clean machine
- Identify source of infection if possible and notify security team
- Broadcast a warning to the user community if appropriate
- Restore corrupted/lost data from most recent back up
- Reconnect machine to the network
- Perform basic connectivity testing

The key to successfully using response templates is to make them a help rather than a hindrance. Users should decide whether to implement every suggested action for the case in hand and should be able delete or cancel unnecessary actions with a minimum of effort (although an audit trail recording of this decision may be kept for analysis at a later date if required). Systems that force users to update/complete every task, are invariably filled with random garbage text and do nothing more than irritate the service delivery community.

15.14.2 Remote Control

Remote control solutions that enable a help desk agent to assume control of a users PC over the network have been available for many years now and are used in many organisations to good effect. It is often claimed that they dramatically improve incident diagnostics by allowing the support person to see for themselves exactly what is going on. This may be true, as such tools enable the agent to observe everything that occurs on the users screen (admittedly they wouldn't help to identify a user with oversized frilly cuffs that keep catching the 'Alt' key when typing etc, but they do help with diagnosis in some cases) and therefore allows them to correct any user induced errors more readily. However, where the problem is not related to the immediate short term actions of the user reporting the incident, remote control systems do not necessarily provide the agent with any additional information that could not be obtained through careful questioning.

One significant benefit of remote control tools is their ability to help ease the communication void between the user and the front line agent as there is no requirement for the user to know the difference between a scroll bar and a toggle bar or a drop down menu and a list box in order to be able to explain what is happening and what they are doing immediately before it happens.

Perhaps the most useful use of remote control technology is in the application of fixes and/or temporary workarounds to resolve the incident in question. Agents can quickly redirect print jobs to an alternative printer, add entries into a local hosts file for un-resolvable server names, alter network connection settings, connect to a secure file server to download a patch for installation etc. In short, remote control tools are an ideal means of implementing routine simple fixes/workarounds to common issues without having to visit the users' physical desktop in person. The potential productivity gains are obvious, at least according to those trying to market such tools, however the overall cost

in terms of service quality and user perception, due to the lack of personal
face time etc, need to be considered.

15.14.3 Black Box Recorders

The use of software that mimics the role of an aircraft black box recorder is
gradually beginning to be more common in larger complex IT environments.
These solutions can be thought of as legitimate or benign spy ware that is
continuously monitoring the usage and condition of the host machine and
storing the previous X minutes worth of data in a local buffer. In the event
of a system crash the support organisation can replay the events (including
in some cases screen captures and key logging) in the immediate run up to
the problem to see if they can determine what it was that went wrong and
potentially what caused it. These client side recorders may sometimes be
linked to server side equivalents to give help desk agents a complete view of
the system and allow and end to end view to be constructed.

Despite being touted as the next best thing since sliced bread, black box
recorders are little more than a reliable means of capturing data regarding the
moments immediately before an incident occurs without having to interrogate
the user directly. It is fair to say that the breadth and depth of information
available is significantly more detailed than what would be possible to extract
from all but the most technically savvy user. However, the point remains that
the data still needs to be reviewed, analysed and interpreted by someone with
diagnostic skills in order to become useful.

15.14.4 Self-healing Systems

Self healing systems are typically a misnomer. More often than not they are
little more than mechanisms for comparing the current situation (e.g. the files
associated with an application) against a defined standard or packing list.
In the event of a problem being encountered with the application then the
system reviews what is in place locally against what it believes should be
in place and rectifies any anomalies. This is fine when an employee's Siebel
client has stopped working because the copy of Quake that they installed over
the weekend has overwritten a shared DLL file with one that is incompatible
with Siebel, but it is less useful when the problem is due to a legitimate
software installation that needs to be able to run in parallel with the existing
configuration.

15.14.5 Event Management/Intelligent Agents

Systems management monitoring tools are now more sophisticated than ever
and can predict system failures and performance degradation with higher
accuracy than previously. Event management agents monitor system characteristics, attributes and transaction times in real time and in cases where

these parameters exceed predefined thresholds the agent's pass alerts to a centralised management system which consolidates inputs from around the infrastructure and raises incident reports etc if required.

By reviewing the outputs of these systems in the run up to a failure, the incident management function can gain an insight as to the factors that may have combined to cause an issue e.g. a server that routinely has high CPU and memory usage may continue functioning adequately indefinitely, however if disk capacity reduces to a point that the operating system needs to start swapping data to and from the physical disk this may be enough to cause a fatal system lock up... Event management agents would typically track all of these three metrics as a matter course, however the rules engine within the event management console may not have had a combined business rule applied to raise an alert for such a combination of events.

So we've worked out what's wrong, all we need to do now is fix it...

15.15 Workarounds, Fixes and Resolution

ITIL defines a workaround as *a means of avoiding an Incident or Problem, either via a temporary fix or from a method or procedure that means the Customer is not impacted by an element of a service that is known to have a problem.*

The term 'Workaround' doesn't appear in the classical dictionaries but thankfully dictionary.com comes to our aid with the following:

"1. A temporary kluge used to bypass, mask, or otherwise avoid a bug or misfeature in some system. Theoretically, workarounds are always replaced by fixes; in practice, customers often find themselves living with workarounds for long periods of time. "The code died on NULL characters in the input, so I fixed it to interpret them as spaces." "That's not a fix, that's a workaround!" 2. A procedure to be employed by the user in order to do what some currently non-working feature should do. Hypothetical example: "Using META-F7 crashes the 4.43 build of Weemax, but as a workaround you can type CTRL-R, then SHIFT-F5, and delete the remaining cruft by hand."

I think that in this instance dictionary.com's definition wins hands down! Workarounds are the short term disposable sticky plasters to get people up and running quickly. Their purpose should be to prevent the wound becoming infected and to stem the flow of blood – that is all. They should never be left if place for any longer than is absolutely necessary as they may jeopardise the integrity of the wider IT ecosystem. After all, how often do workarounds undergo formal compatibility testing within the real world environment. Just because the workaround has alleviated the symptoms of one particular issue, does not mean that it won't conspire to cause potentially greater problems in the future if left in place.

15.15.1 When does a Workaround become a Fix?

In an ideal world, a workaround would never become a fix. In the, far from ideal, real world workarounds are all too often left in place to permanently resolve an incident. But what if there is no alternative but to leave a workaround in place e.g. the equipment manufacturer/application developer is no longer in business? In such cases, the workaround should be subjected to the same kind of design review and testing standards that would be undertaken if it were a planned change to the environment. If after following due process, the workaround is found to be sufficiently benign to not adversely affect the rest of the infrastructure then it may be reclassified as a permanent fix.

15.15.2 Is an Incident that is 'Resolved' by a Workaround Really Resolved?

Yes and no. In so far as the user being able to continue with their work then "yes", the incident can be considered 'dealt with'. But being 'dealt with' is not the same as being 'resolved'. Metrics regarding the time taken to restore service can be calculated at this point but the time to resolution is as yet unknown. More often than not, helpdesk's consider incidents where a workaround has been successfully applied as resolved and attempt to close them out as quickly as possible thereby improving their performance statistics. This may not necessarily be the best course of action for the business but conflicting departmental objectives may mean that this is the course of action pursued nevertheless.

15.15.3 Closing the Workaround Loophole

All too often workarounds are left in place permanently. This is due to one of two factors; ignorance and ignorance.

- Ignorance of the fact that a workaround should not be treated as a formal fix.
- And ignorance of the number and identity of those incidents that have been dealt with using a workaround.

It is important to try and identify which incidents need to be revisited to remove the applied workaround and implement a permanent fix (where possible) when it is convenient to the user. Such attention to detail resonates well with users, as well as helping to maintain the overall systems integrity of the IT environment. People sometimes get hung up regarding the vehicle to use to facilitate these follow up actions. It doesn't really matter (well it might after you read the section following this one) if the originating incident is 're-opened' or if a related incident or problem/change record is created to track this activity. The important thing is to ensure that temporary workarounds are replaced with permanent fixes wherever practical.

15.15.4 When can a Resolved Incident be Closed?

Closure of an incident typically results in the incident being locked for all time and it ultimately being archived. Some organisations take the view that they want to wait a specified period until closing the incident automatically whereas others prefer to wait for the requester to acknowledge that the issue has really been resolved before putting the incident to bed. Where user feedback is solicited it is necessary to define a time out period after which incidents are closed automatically as not every requester will respond to requests to confirm all is well ... The reasons for such delaying tactics are to enable additional work to be completed against the incident record in the event that the original fix was inadequate. Such a policy prevents the easy analysis of incomplete fixes and may even be used by unscrupulous managers as a means of cheating the system by arbitrarily 'resolving' open incidents in an attempt to improve their SLA performance, safe in the knowledge that they can then continue working on the issue long after the clock has stopped ticking without fear of escalation processes being initiated.

15.15.5 Closure Codes

Closure codes (sometimes known as disposition codes) are used to describe the way in which incident has been resolved. An excellent use of such a data point is to use it to identify cases which were dealt with a workaround and need revisiting with a formal fix in due course.

But what if it's really really broken? What then?

15.16 Follow up Actions – Closing the Stable Door ...

15.16.1 Do Nothing – Part 1

On occasions, incidents will be reported that cannot be replicated no matter how hard you try. Such random blips may or may not be the figment of the imagination of the person(s) reporting them. However, where all diagnostic tests and investigations turn up absolutely nothing it is wise to keep the old adage, "If it ain't broke don't fix it" in mind. Better to await a recurrence of the anomaly than to jump in feet first and risk making the situation worse. Such cases should be closed with a classification of "Unable to reproduce the problem", in the event of a recurrence then the previous ticket can be related to the new report and the hunt can continue where it left off ...

15.16.2 Escalate it to a Higher Level

Where an incident cannot be resolved by the person working on it (due to insufficient knowledge, technical skills or lack of access to specialist diagnostic tools or source code) it may be necessary to escalate the incident to another individual or group. Many IT organisations are divided into tiered functional hierarchies with 1st, 2nd and 3rd line support teams dealing with progressively more complex and tricky issues. An escalation in this context is nothing more than a reassignment of the case to someone else to work upon it.

15.16.3 Do Nothing – Part 2

Sometimes, despite the best efforts of every level of support (including vendor support were appropriate), it may not be possible to resolve an incident to the satisfaction of the business. These cases are rare – but they do happen. If the incident impacts the operation of the business significantly then it may be necessary to re-design the business process to avoid the problem. In such cases IT and business management must make the judgement call as to when to stop burning resources searching for a cure that may never be found.

15.16.4 Raise a Change Request

Many incidents will require changes to the IT infrastructure to be implemented in order to resolve them. In such cases it is important to follow due process and raise an appropriate change request and have it formally approved before rushing to the spares cupboard and starting the repair/replacement etc. Change management processes act as the conscience of the IT organisation, ensuring that the relevant due diligence is completed and that all potential impacts and side effects of a course of action are considered before diving in with screwdriver in hand.

15.16.5 Request a Problem Investigation

It may be appropriate for support personnel to request a formal problem investigation for issues which cannot be resolved fully, or for issues that are overly common. Such an investigation, if undertaken, should evaluate all of the potential causes for the incident and identify which factor, or factors, contributed to be the root cause of the problem.

15.16.6 Identify it as a 'Known Error'

This can be thought of as the IT equivalent of annotating a nautical chart with a picture of a large ferocious reptile and inscribing the legend "Here be dragons!" ... The warning is intended to make other system users aware of the potential issue and allow them to take appropriate action to avoid the incident if possible, or if it is unavoidable it should give them pointers as the best course of remedial action to take. Known errors are typically recorded within the knowledge management system repository and would include details of symptoms and any known workaround or fix.

15.17 Parent Incidents and their Children

Practically every RFI/RFP/ITT I have seen over the past ten years has made reference to the need to be able to link similar incidents together underneath a master or parent incident record. The theory being that in cases where there is a major outage etc that all of the people affected would raise an incident report and the fix applied to the centralised system would resolve everyone's issue in one fell swoop. This is a nice idea. Unfortunately, it is based upon the assumption that every incident will be categorised correctly and that the frontline support team will ensure that 100% of incidents related to a parent ticket are indeed related to the major incident in question. More often than not, during a major system outage/service disruption anyone calling in regarding the system in question is told that there is an ongoing problem and that their issue will be resolved when the system is restored. But not every call will be due to the outage. Some calls will inevitably be mistakenly attributed to the parent incident when in fact they require their own investigation and diagnosis.

15.17.1 Automatic Closure of Child Tickets upon Resolution of the Parent

Be careful. You may not be resolving the customer's issue. And no-one likes to be told something is fixed when it isn't.

15.18 "Near Miss" Management?

No, not a commentary upon the state of IT middle management, but instead the tracking, diagnosis of potential incidents before they manifest themselves into service impacting events. Examples of such 'near miss' incidents would include excessively noisy disk drives, random failures of batch transfers/backup jobs, sticky cooling fans, unusual noises/levels of vibration/odours emanating from hardware (or indeed personnel) etc.

15.19 Major Incident Planning

Large and small IT functions should have plans in place to handle major events that impact IT service provision. A detailed discussion on the various approaches to business continuity planning is out of the scope of this book but the following notes may help the uninitiated on their way. Examples of major incidents that would typically have a business continuity response plan:

- Core service failure
- Significant network outage
- Virus infection

- Publication of a known security risk
- Denial of service attack
- Detected intrusion/security breach

Response plans should define:

- Who is to be notified?
- Communication plans
- What actions are to be taken immediately?
- Service restoration/cut over plans

15.20 Is a Help Desk Really a Commodity Item?

Unfortunately, the market believes "Yes" – But as can hopefully be seen from this chapter, the Help Desk market has stagnated over the past decade or so and, in general, only delivers solutions that partially satisfy the needs of the IT function. I believe that there is still a significant opportunity for a Help Desk solution that turns it back on conventional wisdom and addresses incident management requirements from first principles.

Knowledge Management

Also known as knowledge base, solutions database, FAQs etc

Knowledge management is much more than a tool or database. It is the systematic identification, capture, dissemination and use of information for the good of an organisation and its customers. All too often, knowledge management initiatives fail to address the people, cultural and procedural elements of the process, insteadrelying upon the capabilities of a software tool. Such an approach will always fail in the long term, despite some possible short term wins.

"Knowledge is power"

Sir Francis Bacon, Philosopher, 1597

"With great power, comes great responsibility"

Ben Parker, Spider-Man, 2002

The key to successful knowledge management is to instil a continuous learning and improvement culture within the organisation. Using and contributing to the knowledge repository should be considered part of the day to day routine for everyone handling incidents and researching and resolving problems.

16.1 Process Objectives

The knowledge management process should be focused upon the following core objectives:

- To provide quick and easy access to pertinent information to assist with the resolution or mitigation of incidents
- To prevent corporate knowledge loss when personnel leave the business
- Reduce the time taken, and number of interactions required, to diagnose and resolve incidents

16.1.1 Quick and Easy Access to Pertinent Information

The primary goal of users of any knowledge management system is to get the information they need when they need it. Search capabilities are a crucial element of such a system as they allow users to find information relating to their current need. But search on its own is not enough, it must be combined with suitable, relevant and useful content to become a truly useful resource for the business as a whole.

16.1.2 To Prevent Corporate Knowledge Loss when Personnel Leave the Business

Organisations which allow valuable corporate knowledge and experience to be retained solely in the heads of key members of staff are exposing themselves to significant business risk. Employee turnover is a fact of business life and it is critical that provision be made to capture all information that can potentially help the business achieve its objectives better.

16.1.3 Reduce the Time Taken, and Number of Interactions Required, to Diagnose and Resolve Incidents

By leveraging the collective knowledge and experience of the entire organisation front line agents should be capable of improving their first time fix rate and diagnostic accuracy. Existing workarounds for known errors, canned responses for frequently asked questions and step by step resolution instructions prevent service desk personnel reinventing the wheel at every interaction and improve the consistency and quality of service delivered irrespective of the skill and experience of the individual servicing the request.

16.2 Common Issues

Common issues associated with Knowledge Management include:

- Reluctance of employees to contribute knowledge
- Quality of information stored within the knowledge repository
- Information getting out of date/becoming irrelevant
- Difficulty accessing the relevant content when it is required
- Inaccuracies and/or omissions within the knowledge base
- Level of information inappropriate for the audience
- Lack of trust in the usefulness of the information held
- Inadequate approval and proofing cycles before publication
- Duplication of solutions
- Insufficient time and resources allocated to maintain knowledge repository
- Business benefit and usage information is difficult to demonstrate
- Knowledge repository not being leveraged as much as it could be
- Local silos of information not included within the central repository
- Poorly written content containing confusing technical jargon and/or grammatical and typographical errors

16.3 Key Players

Person searching for a solution/information – Typically any user within an organisation is able to search for information within the knowledge management solution. However, it is common for knowledge entries to be published to subsets of the user community to prevent general users accessing internal material or information which could be hazardous i.e. a little knowledge can be a dangerous thing...

Service/Support Agents – Often the primary users of the knowledge management system. Focused upon quickly identifying the relevant entry and using it to address a specific incident and/or request.

Implementation Group(s) – Often used as contributors/reviewers for content submissions to check for validity, accuracy and practicality of the recommended approach. May also generate content as a by-product of their day to day activities.

Technical Specialists – Functional specialists which may approve content for publication and provide high level direction to those tasked with creating KB entries.

Knowledge Worker/Engineer – Dedicated resource responsible for researching known issues and creating content in accordance with organisational policy.

Knowledge Manager – Dedicated management resource to oversee the knowledge management process and to oversee approval, publication processes, reporting system usage to the business.

16.4 Process Metrics

Key Metrics include:

- Number of new knowledge base entries submitted for review within specified period
- Number of knowledge base updates/modifications submitted for review within specified period
- Number of new knowledge base entries published within specified period
- Number of knowledge base entries updated within specified period
- Number of incidents that used knowledge base solutions within specified period
- Time saved by using knowledge base (calculated by comparing average time to resolution of incidents that were closed using the knowledge base against those that didn't)
- Number of self-help requests that stated that the knowledge base entry helped them with their issue within a specified period

16.5 Elements of a Knowledge Management Solution

16.5.1 Content

Central to the success of a knowledge management solution is the content that is available to its users. The content should be clear, precise, well written, technically accurate and focused upon specific issues. All text should be reviewed for clarity and ease of understanding as well as for its technical merit prior to publishing. Elements of a knowledgebase entry may include:

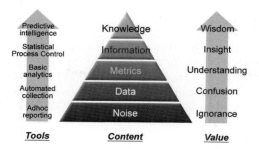

Fig. 16.1. Traditional knowledge hierarchy

- Type of entry (e.g. FAQ, Known Error, Common Issue etc)
- Search enablers (e.g. keywords, links to classifications/products/services, synonyms etc)
- Symptoms description (i.e. a list of all of the ways in which the issue is likely to manifest itself)
- Diagnostic script (i.e. a list of steps needed to reproduce the incident and/or confirm the nature of the issue)
- Workaround (i.e. the temporary action(s) necessary to get the user/service back up and running as soon as possible)

16.5.2 Search

The best quality content in the world is pointless unless those users that need it are able to find it when they need it. Search technology has come a long long way in recent years and it can significantly improve the usability of knowledge repositories when leveraged to good effect. Searching can be considered as the combination of three separate technical elements:

- Indexing – the crawling of the knowledge repository, and associated attachments, to determine index structure and grouping, categorisation of entries etc
- Subset identification – the actual search itself i.e. the selection of a group of records that match the user entered search criteria
- Ranking/Weighting – the relative ranking of the search results in order of usefulness, applicability etc

The advent of reliable and affordable Natural Language Processing (NLP) technology has significantly improved the ease with which complex searches can be completed using free format text input. The application of a self learning engine, based upon linguistic science, to apply fuzzy logic to user entered text in order to determine not only the subject, but the context and intent behind the phrase or paragraph means that systems are able to provide automated or semi-automated responses with a higher degree of confidence and accuracy than ever before.

16.5.3 Approval Process

The process by which entries are submitted for potential inclusion within the formal knowledgebase will vary from business to business. The key for any such process to be successful is transparency. If the process is to remain credible then the people submitting content must be able to see who is conducting the review and the criteria they are using to evaluate their submissions.

16.5.4 Ongoing Maintenance

Few things are worse than obviously out dated material. Every entry within the knowledgebase must be reviewed periodically to determine if its content remains valid and useful. Obsolete content should be archived/removed from the repository as required in order to prevent it obscuring useful information.

Where possible content should be reviewed and revised by someone other than the original author, this ensures that a fresh perspective is used and helps to prevent unintentional bias and complacency. Irrespective of who updates a knowledgebase entry it is imperative that the revised version undergoes the formal review and approval process used for new content submissions.

16.5.5 Solution Usage Tracking

By monitoring how often specific knowledgebase entries are accessed and/or used, the IT organisation can proactively identify incident trends earlier than relying upon after the fact incident reports alone. Usage tracking can also be used to help identify content that is obsolete, irrelevant or hidden (i.e. it cannot be found by the people that it is supposed to help).

To be truly useful, usage tracking will identify not only when a knowledgebase entry has been used against a specific incident but also how often it is accessed and how long users spend reviewing the content (i.e. large numbers of very short duration uses could possibly indicate a poorly indexed or classified entry that is being returned incorrectly by the search engine).

16.5.6 Feedback Loop

Effective knowledge management solutions include provision to allow users to pass feedback upon content quality and search applicability back to the system administrator. Such a closed loop feedback system is essential to ensure that the repository remains effective. Feedback collection need not be an overly onerous task if implemented carefully, many systems simply ask the user "Did this help?" when they review a knowledge base entry.

16.6 Approaches to Content Creation

16.6.1 Dedicated Teams

Some organisations take their best individual contributors out of their normal day to day roles and ask them to perform a brain dump of everything they know into the repository. Providing the contributor is widely accepted within the business as a subject matter expert then content adoption and 'not invented here' issues may be avoided. However, it may be more difficult to convince the contributors themselves of the benefits to them of imparting all of their hard earned knowledge and experience in an act of selfless charity. Their knowledge gives them kudos and a position of power/respect within the business – by giving this information away they may feel that their position is undermined and that they are no longer 'indispensable'.

16.6.2 Bonus Incentives i.e. Pay per Clue

Employees are compensated based upon the number of knowledge base entries they have approved for publication within the knowledge repository. The danger is that multiple entries for a given topic will be submitted and the organisation will be faced with having to reject perfectly good content because someone has got there first. Generally such approaches are not recommended as they can lead to conflict between the reviewing panel and those submitting entries.

16.6.3 Peer Review and Community Credibility

Many online knowledge repositories and technical forums use the concept of peer review and virtual payments for knowledge usage to ensure content is kept up to date and that content quality is maintained to a high standard. Knowledge users have to 'pay' for the right to access information, they themselves determine the amount that they wish to 'pay' based upon how useful they found the entry. Knowledge contributors are then 'credited' based upon the volume of usage and usefulness of their contributions. Credit may be allocated via virtual payments and/or the assignment of medals of honour i.e. Contributors are often ranked on a sliding scale from newbie through to harmless, competent, useful, expert, guru etc to let other system users know of their relative position within the community. Alternatively the community may regularly award titles such as 'Most Valuable Poster' (MVP) to individuals that have earned particular respect and kudos. Such a system creates a marketplace of sorts whereby users of the system continually contribute information on the understanding that they will be able to find, or request and receive, help when they need it in future.

Problem Management

Also known as Preventive Action, Continuous Improvement, Incident/Outage avoidance program, Service improvement program etc.

ITIL definition of a problem:

A Problem is a condition often identified as a result of multiple Incidents that exhibit common symptoms. Problems can also be identified from a single significant Incident, indicative of a single error, for which the cause is unknown, but for which the impact is significant.

The above definition is overly reactive in nature. ITIL doesn't consider it practical to prevent issues before they occur and yet it is at the service design stage where the most effective prevention activity can be implemented. Problem management should be thought of as the proactive analysis of current and historic situations, risk assessment findings and service design review outputs aimed at initiating actions to improve existing system performance and/or eliminate the factors that contribute to system / process failures.

Problem management processes are primarily aimed at incident/outage avoidance in order to improve service reliability and performance to the levels required by the business. The prevention of incident recurrence and the identification of known errors is not an easy task and this level of complexity and difficulty often leads organizations to neglect this particular ITIL discipline. Instead, Problem management is used as a mechanism for attributing blame and performing witch hunts following catastrophic service failures. Such an approach has a counterproductive effect and causes employees to conceal errors and mistakes to prevent retribution. Traditional solution vendors have done little to improve this situation and existing management systems tend to act as little more than a searchable repository for the minutes of trials and executions.

17.1 Process Objectives

The problem management process should be focused upon the following core objectives:

- Incident/outage avoidance
- Improve service reliability and performance to levels required by the business
- Prevent recurrence of issues
- Identification of known errors/probable causes
- Process improvement

17.1.1 Incident/Outage Avoidance

It is always far better to avoid an incident completely than to merely recover from its effects quickly. By preventing an incidence of service disruption, the business avoids incurring the costs associated with failure including opportunity costs, loss of productivity, investigation and recovery costs etc. Prevention is the only goal worth aiming for within the service management space. Such an approach is commonplace when considering business critical issues such as health and safety and environmental impact where the potential costs of failure are so much greater. It is time for service management to join these ranks and play its role on the wider business stage. How long will it be before service functions follow the lead of their counter parts within the safety and environmental arenas and begin posting details such as "X days since last service impacting event" on their intranet sites?

17.1.2 Improve Service Reliability and Performance to Levels Required by the Business

Carefully focused analysis of historic outage and incident trends coupled with prevention based remedial actions enable the business to begin accurately predicting when systems are likely to fail or suffer from significant performance degradation in the future. When combined with a fact based preventive maintenance and preventive replacement program, this enables the IT organisation to begin to feel confident in its own capabilities and start assuring the rest of the business of continued service availability and performance.

17.1.3 Prevent Recurrence of Issues

Few things are as soul destroying as continually fighting the same fires again and again. Careful analysis of root causes and contributory factors allow the IT function to plan and implement suitable controls and precautions to prevent common issues from reappearing and causing service interruptions. The effectiveness of preventive actions demonstrates the overall effectiveness of the problem management process.

17.1.4 Identification of Known Errors/Probable Causes

The identification, classification and documentation of known errors allow frontline service agents to quickly diagnose incoming incident reports and apply tried and tested workarounds where available. This can significantly improve the first time closure rate for incidents and prevent effort being wasted re-inventing solutions to problems that have already been solved. Known errors form part of the organisations knowledgebase and can often be leveraged from self service interfaces as well as via the help desk.

17.1.5 Process Improvement

If you're not moving forwards, then you're going backwards. Technology and business practice evolve at an alarming rate these days. What was considered best practice yesterday could be seen as quaint and antiquated tomorrow... Unless every department of every function continually strives to improve the way in which it operates, then the business will begin to lose ground against the market and its peers. Prevention based approached to process design often help improve efficiency by eliminating rework and the costs associated with process failure etc.

17.2 Common Issues

Common issues with Problem Management include:

- Insufficient focus and/or time and resources given to preventive action
- Lack of sufficient data for meaningful analysis
- Difficulty collecting the data necessary to facilitate analysis
- Poorly defined relationships between configuration items
- Relationship structure does not allow indirect cross object analysis
- Inappropriate resource allocation to preventive action efforts
- Limited involvement of appropriate technical specialists
- Unrealistic expectations that issues can be prevented easily
- Seemingly random events/Undefined and/or unknown causal links prevent true causes being identified
- Control measures fail to prevent recurrence of incidents
- Problem management used as a means of determining/attributing blame for
- outages and/or incidents
- Reluctance on the part of employees to participate within the process

17.3 Process Flow

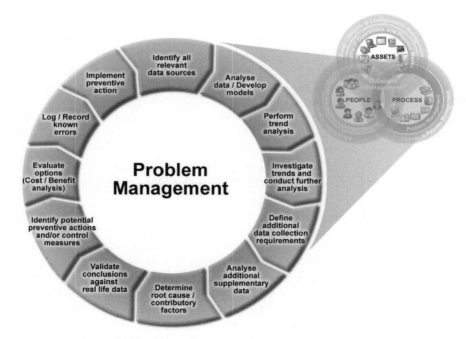

Fig. 17.1. High level process overview for problem management

17.4 Key Players

Person requesting/suggesting problem investigation – Suggestions for potential problems that should be investigated can come from all parts of the business. It is important to respond to all such suggestions and to ensure that the person suggesting the investigation topic be kept up to date with developments etc.

Service/Support Agents – Service personnel will often be required to capture additional data for subsets of inbound issues at the request of the problem management function in order to enable targeted analysis to be completed.

Implementation Group(s) – Workarounds and problem solutions are often devised, developed and ratified by the people that work with particular technologies day in and day out.

Technical Specialists – It may be necessary to enlist the assistance of highly skilled and experienced technical resources to troubleshoot a particular issue and to identify potential ways in which a problem could be eliminated or its effects mitigated.

Problem Investigator – Person charged with overseeing a specific problem investigation. The investigator may include additional resources to assist them with any identified data collection activity and then use this within their analysis to identify the factors which may be contributing to the problem.

Problem Manager – Individual responsible for overseeing the end to end problem management process, reporting activity and performance to senior management and acting as a mediator between internal functional groups to ensure that problem investigations remain objective and avoid becoming 'personal'.

17.5 Process Metrics

- Number of preventive action programs currently running
- Number of incidents attributed to the cause(s) being addressed by each preventive action program within specified period
- Business cost of incidents attributed to the cause(s) being addressed by each preventive action program within a specified period

17.6 The Problem with Problem Management...

17.6.1 Witch Hunt vs. Prevention

When done well, problem management can be a powerful tool to help improve overall service quality and IT value. Unfortunately, it is very rarely done well. All too often the problem management process is bastardised into nothing more than a tool to attribute blame to the guilty and hapless. By focusing upon finding the root cause, and eliminating it, the standard ITIL problem management process lends itself well to anyone wishing to instil a culture of blame and retribution. Consequently, many people resist attempts to be included within the process and unfortunately the process suffers for it.

17.6.2 What's in a Name? A Rose by any other Name would Smell as Sweet

It is a sad fact of business life that the majority of people employed in an organisation spend their much of time protecting their flanks and rear. People are inherently insecure and are often desperate to hold on to their positions, benefits and hard earned reputations irrespective of the cost to the organisation. Such behaviour can sometimes be counter productive and diametrically opposed to the wider needs of the business. In order to maintain ones position and status, people may hide mistakes, cover up errors/omissions and tend to avoid becoming embroiled in conflict, trouble and situations which require them to stand out from the crowd. If we add a healthy dose of paranoia to the mix you will begin to see why so many people shy away from participating within the problem management process.

The name "Problem Management" conjures images of pain, inefficiency, waste and risk in the minds of many. Such negative overtones and language may hide or obscure the true purpose of the process but these virtual barriers may be sufficient to prevent the process from functioning. How many times have you heard a manager say "Don't bring me problems, bring me solutions!"? This exasperated plea often comes from having to continually think on behalf of their entire team, but it must be remembered that the reason such a manager is overwhelmed with minutia and trivial decisions is likely to be because they don't promote and encourage an open environment where employees work together and resolve issues locally.

17.6.3 Cultural Shift

In order to get real benefits from a prevention based approach to problem solving it is essential that all levels of the organisation contribute to the effort. The cultural change needed to effect such a change requires the hearts and minds of the business to be convinced that everyone is on board and that the process has the total and complete support of the most senior management within the company.

17.6.4 Changing Perception is one of the Most Difficult Changes of All!

"I haven't time to prevent issues, I'm too busy fire fighting..." How many times have you heard this within a business environment? Dozens, if not hundreds maybe. This is the rallying cry of the line manager who doesn't know how to prevent minor issues from escalating into bona fide major incidents. If prevention is to become common place, such perceptions must be challenged at every opportunity.

17.6.5 The Lack of Tools

"For the want of a nail, the shoe was lost; for the want of a shoe the horse was lost; and for the want of a horse the rider was lost, being overtaken and slain by the enemy, all for the want of care about a horseshoe nail."

Benjamin Franklin

Commercially available problem management tools are predominantly little more than filing cabinets within which to store details of problem management activity. The lack of useful, usable tools is one of many the reasons that the discipline is as it is. Until such time that the software vendors invest time and resources in developing aides to the problem management effort, the process will remain highly dependent upon the skills and experience of those charged with performing prevention based analysis . . .

17.7 Problem Selection

"If one person tells you you're sick; don't worry. If ten people tell you; lie down!"

Proverb

There are several ways in which issues deserving of formal problem investigation can be identified including:

- Statistical analysis
  - Common/Recurring issues
  - Most costly issues
- Automated potential problem suggestion
- Biggest problem lists from departmental heads
- User requests/improvement suggestions
- Management sponsorship
- Major incidents
- Risk assessment

17.7.1 Statistical Analysis

The most common way of determining which issues to focus upon is by slicing and dicing historic incident statistics to identify the most common or costly issues affecting the business. Care should be taken to ensure that the output of such analysis is not taken as gospel without validating it against the business – it is not unusual for common trivial incidents and minor annoyances to be identified in this manner whilst real issues that the business is concerned about go unnoticed.

17.7.2 Automated Potential Problem Suggestion

Incident management systems are sometimes configured to automatically suggest potential problems based upon the frequency that incidents with specific categorisations are raised. Such a system may look for X incidents of category Y within the past Z hours and raise a potential problem record for further analysis. The usefulness, or otherwise of such a system will be dependent upon the accuracy of classification employed by those logging incidents and the granularity of the classification structure being used.

17.7.3 Biggest Problem Lists from Departmental Heads

As part of ongoing dialogues with business owners, the IT function should routinely ask for top ten lists of the business's biggest IT related concerns. The creation of these lists will force the business to evaluate the level of service they are receiving and will allow the IT function to collate issues and concerns from around the organisation to help identify which areas need work.

17.7.4 User Requests/Improvement Suggestions

The average IT manager can count the number of unsolicited improvement suggestions they receive per month using a single binary digit (and I don't mean a 'one'). However, this is not to say that pearls of wisdom are not out there to be uncovered . . . It is therefore useful to proactively solicit improvement suggestions from the field and the user base. These suggestions can be submitted anonymously or entered into a monthly draw for a prize etc. Not every suggestion will be implemented, but the important thing to remember is to acknowledge every suggestion and to review it and respond with feedback (positive or negative) as soon as is practicable.

17.7.5 Management Sponsorship

It is often said that "He who pays the piper, calls the tune". Nowhere is this more true than in the world of work. Every employee, be they a frontline support agent or a CIO, has someone to whom they are accountable. Management sometimes identify problem issues in a variety of ways (such as water cooler chats, informal corridor conversations, casual remarks during a round of golf and other such reliable sources), irrespective of how the information is imparted, once logged it is common for managers to doggedly pursue such issues until they are satisfied they have a response ready for their next encounter with the originator of the (bad) news. Not all issues identified in this manner will be ill researched, poorly defined and biased. It is important therefore to take time to understand how such issues have come to the fore and to take appropriate actions to ensure that ones management are better prepared to handle such approaches in future.

17.7.6 Major Incidents

It is important to avoid the temptation for knee jerk reactions to major outages/incidents, normal incident management procedures should be allowed to be followed to their conclusion before instigating the problem management process if deemed necessary. Political pressure and the need to be seen to so something proactive sometimes mean that IT functions immediately launch into a full problem investigation without first evaluating the true nature of the incident and its potential cause.

17.7.7 Risk Assessment

Risk assessment activity will highlight numerous areas which could be improved in order to improve the stability, reliability and performance of the IT environment.

17.7.8 Qualative vs. Quantative Evidence

Unfortunately the scope of every problem will not be demonstrable using statistical analysis. Issues affecting potential risk, service quality and user satisfaction, particularly perceived user expectation related issues, are often difficult or impossible to express in numeric terms. It is therefore important to make value based judgements on the potential tangible benefits that could be realised by removing the root cause of a particular issue.

17.8 Problem Analysis

When analysing an identified problem area the following actions will need to be addressed in order to come up with concrete preventive action plans:

- Clearly define problem scope/boundaries
- Review historic data and trends
- Identify common symptoms
- Analyse underlying processes, tools and environmental factors
- Identify potential root causes
- Develop a hypothesis
- Gather and additional data points as necessary
- Test the hypothesis
- Refine hypothesis
- Accept or reject hypothesis

17.8.1 Root Cause Analysis

Today's IT environment is a complex and contradictory place, the chances of finding the proverbial smoking gun for every problem is slim to say the least. Realists understand the nature of the ecosystem within which they operate and take account of the fact that chaos theory has as much of a role to play in the prevention of problems as does traditional deductive reasoning based detective work. The absence of a definitive and proven root cause does not mean a problem is not preventable. It is just that multiple actions may be necessary that combine to mitigate the risk of reoccurrence.

17.8.2 Known Knowns, Known Unknowns and Unknown Unknowns

"As we know, there are known knowns.
There are things we know we know.
We also know there are known unknowns.
That is to say, we know there are some things we do not know.
But there are also unknown unknowns,
The ones we don't know we don't know."

US Secretary of Defense, Donald Rumsfeld - 2002

As Mr Rumsfeld so eloquently explained sometimes we just don't know why something happened. In such instances we have a variety of courses of action open to us:

- Do nothing at all
- Look for indirect links between similar events
- Attempt to gather additional data points
- Develop a hypothesis and test it
- Perform a failure assurance assessment

Obviously bad things do just happen sometimes but not usually within an IT environment. For this reason it is always better to try and understand why a particular event, or series of events, occurred rather than simply burying ones head in the sand and awaiting a repeat performance.

17.8.3 Guilty by Association...

Sometimes it is difficult to identify a direct statistical correlation between cause and effect. In such cases, it may be possible to draw conclusions by comparing parallel information e.g. show me all incidents related to servers that are related to change requests that were related to service X in the past Y months. Comparing specific attributes of such a dataset (using techniques such as scatter plots etc) may well reveal a linear correlation or relationship between two seemingly unrelated variables.

Indirect relationships are by their very nature difficult to analyse simply. As such analysis typically requires an iterative approach across multi-dimensional datasets it is something best left to automated analytical toolsets. Providing circular references are avoided and sufficient relevant data exists then such approaches may sometimes be used to identify potential hypotheses for further detailed analysis and testing.

17.8.4 Trying to Know the Known Unknowns ... Data Collection

The nub of the problem may very well be related to specific data that you are not currently aware of i.e. known unknowns. If only there were a way to capture additional data points for specific types of incident over the short term in order to be able to test your hypothesis and definitively identify the cause or causes of the problem.

Unfortunately few, if any, commercial ITSM solutions currently offer such a feature at present. The next best option is to try and piggy back upon existing agent scripting tools and/or pop up notes/alerts functionality that has been associated with inbound incident classifications in order remind the frontline support personnel to capture the required information and record it within the ticket details section. Inevitably the problem investigator will have to develop strong links with the frontline support organisation and use their powers of persuasion to get them to capture the additional information they need to test out their theories. Such supplementary data will often be collected via tally sheets or spreadsheets and will need a considerable amount of effort to be entered into a computer system and cleaned sufficiently to enable meaningful analysis to be completed.

17.8.5 You can Feel it in your Water ...

Sometimes gut instinct can be the most accurate and effective tool in a problem managers arsenal. In the absence of any plausible alternatives, going with your gut is as good an option as any – it may even be right!

17.8.6 Failure Assurance

Failure assurance is the art of making sure the problem re-occurs on demand. Put simply, this is achieved by listing every possible way in which the problem in question could be made to happen. This produces a list of possible causes. Reviewing the effectiveness of the current controls for each mode of failure on the list ensures that every conceivable angle is covered and may highlight vulnerable areas that are contributing to the problem.

17.9 Trend Analysis

"The price of freedom is eternal vigilance."

Thomas Jefferson

17.9.1 You may Know More than you Think you do . . .

Somewhere, buried deep within your organisation are the answers to most, if not all, of your IT related problems. The trick is knowing where to look for them, and to know what you're looking for so that you recognise them when you find them. Analysis needs to become a routine part of the operation if prevention is to become the normal modus operandi. To paraphrase Thomas Jefferson, ongoing analysis is the price to be paid for service assurance and incident avoidance.

17.9.2 Standard Tests

Everyone who has watched a TV medical drama is aware of the vast array of standard tests that patients are subjected to when the heroic (yet tragically flawed) doctor is attempting to diagnose what ails them. The following basic tests can be considered as the routine toxicity screens and blood work of the IT world, whilst they may not produce conclusive results they may give pointers to the true problem and pay early dividends:

- Analysis of related incidents by time
  - Day of the week
  - Day of the month
  - Day of the quarter
  - Time of day
- Analysis of related incidents by user
  - Role/Job title
  - Business unit/Department
  - Geographical location
  - Machine specification

17.10 Statistics and IT

"Not everything that counts can be counted, and not everything that can be counted counts."

Albert Einstein

Considering the volume of data generated by the function, the level of statistical analysis used within many IT shops is pitiful. So called analysis is often limited to a series of pie charts and bar charts depicting the distribution of issues discovered in the preceding month. If IT is to be taken seriously within the business community it must develop the analytical skills necessary to meaningfully interact with its peers. The concepts of business statistics (i.e. statistical analysis governing forecasting, trend analysis and the identification of correlations between multiple factors) are beyond the scope of this book, however I heartily recommend that every IT manager take some time to read up on the subject so that they are fully conversant with the basic principles of probability, variance, standard deviation and distribution models. These skills will prove themselves invaluable in the analysis of IT related performance data and the identification of root causes and potential issues.

17.10.1 Statistical Process Control (SPC)

SPC is a quality management methodology, which is commonly used within manufacturing processes, to proactively monitor and improve the performance of a process which has characteristics that vary slightly from their defined values when the process is running normally. These variances can be analyzed statistically to identify underlying changes to the system and can be used to proactively control the process. For example, a submit transaction for an order management system may be designed to complete each record insert in 0.2 seconds, but some transactions will take slightly longer, and some will complete slightly quicker, producing a distribution of net transaction times. If the submission process itself changes (for example, if the underlying data table grows exponentially due to the lack of a suitable archiving policy etc) then this distribution can change, either shifting its average or spreading out or contracting. For example, as the burden associated with updating an index entry for each record increases, the order management system may take longer to complete a transaction than it was designed to. If this change in behaviour is allowed to continue unchecked, the average transaction time may shift to a value that falls outside of the tolerances defined by the original system architect, and could potentially lead to a SLA breach and/or user dissatisfaction. More importantly, these incremental shifts in performance may be the early warning signs of a potentially catastrophic event and should be carefully addressed to prevent unplanned outages and service impacting failures.

By using statistical tools, the IT function can discover that a significant change has been made to the process and/or the environment, although at this point they may not know what factors are influencing this change, and take proactive steps to investigate and correct the problem before application performance degrade significantly or the underlying issue leads to a service impacting incident.

SPC does not have to be restricted to the analysis of performance data. The example cited above is just that – an example. SPC is equally valid for the analysis of incident data across an organisation (for example tracking the number of incidents of a specific category raised over time) to identify areas which are either performing better or worse than the usual background noise of infinite variation.

17.10.2 Control Charts

A control chart is nothing more complicated than a basic run chart of a series of quantitative data with five horizontal lines drawn on the chart. The exact nature and definition of these lines may vary depending upon the sampling and statistical models being used but generally the lines will represent:

- A centre line, drawn at the process mean
- An upper warning limit drawn two standard deviations above the centre line
- An upper control-limit (also called an upper natural process-limit drawn three standard deviations above the centre line
- A lower warning limit drawn two standard deviations below the centre line
- A lower control-limit (also called a lower natural process-limit drawn three standard deviations below the centre line

A series of rules have been developed to determine conditions when a process can be considered to be going out of control and these conditions can act as triggers for investigation and preventive works. The rules (either the General Electric, Donald J Wheeler or Nelson rules) define circumstances which indicate that the process being monitored is not performing as expected.

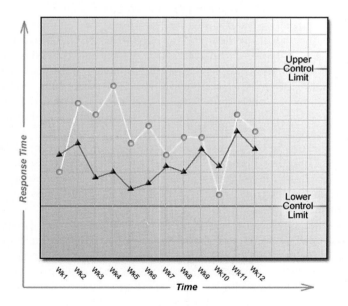

Fig. 17.2. An example of a control chart

The General Electric rules are as follows:

- Rule 1: Any single data point falls beyond 3 standard deviations from the centerline (i.e. any points fall outside of the upper or lower control limits)
- Rule 2: Two out of three consecutive points fall beyond 2 standard deviations from the centerline, on the same side of the centerline
- Rule 3: Four out of five consecutive points fall beyond 1 standard deviation, on the same side of the centerline
- Rule 4: Eight consecutive points fall on the same side of the centerline
- Rule 5: Fifteen consecutive points fall within one standard deviation of the centerline

The use of control charts and other SPC tools allows the IT function to focus upon real process issues rather than being diverted by singular events that are part and parcel of the normal operation of any fluctuating process. By avoiding knee jerk reactions, the problem management function can target its limited resources at significant issues that will deliver real process improvement rather than wasting effort addressing today's current political hot potato.

17.11 The Usual Suspects

In the absence of any hot analytical leads regarding the root cause, or causes, of an issue the following hit list of common contributory factors may be useful as a starting point:

- People
  - Training issue
    - Suitable training unavailable
    - Training received not relevant
    - Insufficient training
    - Refresher training required
  - Unrealistic workload
  - Lack of attention
  - Insufficient communication
- Process
  - Not enough time allowed
  - Process Requirements
    - Lack of defined requirements
    - Conflicting requirements
    - Requirements not agreed
    - Not published
    - Poorly designed requirements
  - Process Resources
    - Insufficient resources
    - Lack of appropriately skilled resources

- ○ Process Controls
  - ■ Process Controls are not effective
  - ■ Process Controls not implemented
- ○ Process Inputs
  - ■ Did not meet specifications
- • Materials/Equipment
  - ○ Contained flaws/imperfections
  - ○ Incorrect materials/equipment used
  - ○ Failed under load
    - ■ Preventive maintenance not completed
    - ■ Proactive replacement missed
    - ■ Usage profile exceeded design parameters
- • Design
  - ○ Errors in calculations
  - ○ Did not account for actual use
  - ○ Corner case not accounted for
- • Information
  - ○ Not generally available
  - ○ Not up to date
  - ○ Not useful/understandable
  - ○ Information is erroneous
  - ○ Documentation
    - • Contains errors
    - • Incorrect version used
    - • Difficult to understand
- • Change
  - ○ Unauthorised changes
  - ○ Change side effect
    - • Scope of works not wide enough
    - • Conflicting requirements
    - • Configuration not tested fully
    - • Unexpected results
  - ○ Change Implementation
    - • Incorrect application of change
    - • Applied change to wrong CI
    - • Change not fully implemented
      - • All tasks not completed
      - • All tasks not applied to all CIs
  - ○ Change Incomplete/Ineffective back out

17.12 Testing Your Hypothesis

A hypothesis is nothing more than a question without an answer. By asking the right question, problem investigators can unlock the way to a permanent solution for troublesome issues. When testing a hypothesis the objective is to "prove" ones theory (or at least not to be able to disprove it), thereby clearing the way to implement a permanent fix. It is common for various levels of "proof" to be used as described below:

- Recreate the problem on demand using a defined series of repeatable steps
- Predict with sufficient accuracy when the next incident related to the problem will occur
- Logically demonstrate a correlation between suspected causes and incidents
- Identify scenarios which are statistically likely to give rise to incidents

Irrespective what type of proof is used, the intention is to gain support and approval to apply a series of preventive actions in order to mitigate the problem.

17.13 Removing the Root

Anyone who has tried to dig up an unwanted mature apple tree will know that the complete removal of such a root system is nigh on impossible without the use of an mechanical excavator and the digging of a hole the size of house. The key to success in such a situation is not to even try to get all of the roots and instead to just remove sufficient elements of the root system to make the tree unviable. After removal, the trick is then to remain vigilant in order to deal with the numerous suckers (shoots) that are thrown up from the remaining root system before it finally gives up the ghost and rots away.

It will not always be practical, or possible, to completely remove the root cause of a problem. Instead it may be necessary to mitigate its effects and/or devise methods of working in order to isolate and/or avoid the root cause as far as possible. When selecting actions to mitigate a root cause, it is essential to:

- Determine how the root cause manifests itself i.e. how the root cause came to be in place and how it appears to the outside world
- Determine the level of exposure to the root cause i.e. who may come into contact with the issue and when that exposure is likely
- Identify alternative means of achieving the same end goal which do not have the same susceptibility to the root cause

17.14 Preventing the Preventable

17.14.1 Just Because you Could, doesn't Mean you should or would . . .

There are countless examples in history of instances where the 'best' man did not win and/or the 'best' technology failed to gain market support (e.g. Betamax vs. VHS). The reasons for these failures are as diverse as the examples of them, but it must be remembered that not all preventive action proposals will be greeted with open arms. The following list outlines some of the most common internal barriers to implementing preventive actions, by paying attention to them and shaping ones proposals accordingly, you may help avoid having your suggestions sidelined or rejected.

Reasons for not implementing a proven preventive measure include:

- Cost/Benefit analysis shows the action is uneconomical
- Payback is not expected until too far in the future
- Scale of the change needed is too big to be attempted at this time
- Existing change plans will remove the need for the action in due course
- Personnel involved are resistant to the idea and there is insufficient management support for the proposal to force the issue
- Lack of appropriate skills and/or technical resources to implement
- Insufficient budget to implement the action
- Ongoing change freeze is in process
- Problem isn't seen as a priority by the business

17.15 Preventive Action Plans – Putting the Theory into Practice . . .

Preventive action plans may include a variety of actions and changes that are intended to combine to address the various symptoms and underlying contributory factors of the problem.

17.15.1 Defining Success Criteria

It is imperative that success criteria be defined in order to be able to validate the effectiveness of the preventive action. Examples of success criteria may include:

- Reduction in the number of incidents of a specific classification
- Increase in the availability of a particular asset, system or service

17.15.2 Raise a Change Request

Problems will often need formal changes to the IT environment to be implemented if they are to be prevented with any degree of certainty. All such changes should be planned and implemented in accordance with the organisation's defined change management processes.

17.15.3 Document a 'Known Error'

Ongoing problems, without preventive action plans, should be classified as "known errors" and may include details of symptoms, workarounds, diagnostic tests necessary to confirm that the incident is related to the error etc. These should be logged within the knowledge management repository and are subject to periodic review to ensure that they remain pertinent and accurate. In an ideal ITIL world all known errors would be tracked, and systematically resolved through the implementation of planned changes. In the real world, known errors may be left in place indefinitely with no intention of ever being formally addressed.

17.15.4 Change the Focus of Event Management/Systems Monitoring

Event management and systems management tools allow the monitoring of an almost unlimited number of machine and application parameters and characteristics in real time. Problem analysis may highlight areas that need to have their monitoring policies reviewed and amended in the following ways:

- Initiate monitoring of configuration items not currently within the scope of event management
- Start monitoring new and/or additional characteristics
- Modify event monitoring consolidation rules and/or amend defined escalation thresholds
- Adjust the frequency of polling/data collection

It is common within medium to large organisations to use event management systems extensively. It is even relatively common to have such toolsets integrated with the IT service management system. However, this integration is often limited to the raising of incident reports in response to monitoring events being detected. To get the best out of any event management solution it is important to see it as a proactive tool within the problem management armoury and to review its use and usefulness on a regular basis. The following questions will help you to evaluate your use of systems management technologies and their effectiveness within incident prevention:

- Is event management seen purely as a reactive discipline?
- Do problem management processes leverage event management tools to capture additional data points when necessary to analyse an ongoing problem?
- What characteristics and attributes are being monitored by your event management system?
- Are you monitoring the correct characteristics and attributes?
- How do you know that the current event correlation and associated business rules are useful?
- How often are these rules reviewed and/or altered?
- What drives changes to the event management business rules?
- What process is used to manage changes to the event management business rules?

17.15.5 Refine Control Chart Thresholds, Sampling Methods and Analytical Models

The ongoing statistical analysis of process performance and activity is a powerful tool to help identify issues before they manifest themselves into significant incidents. One of the outputs of the problem management process may be a recommendation to amend the manner in which process data is collected, the type of control chart model selected and the thresholds used to identify where normal system generated variation departs from a statistical random fluctuation and becomes indicative of a more concerning underlying cause. By implementing such changes the problem management function may be able to more accurately predict issues and to take preventive measures before services are impacted.

17.15.6 User Based Initiatives – Education, Awareness etc

People are often at the heart of a particular problem. Even when not at the nub of the issue, people's behaviours and actions, or lack thereof, often contribute to making a bad situation worse. Real business benefits can be achieved if the delicate issue of people issues are tackled head on in a positive manner. Addressing the non-technical issues surround a problem is often overlooked/ignored by problem management processes. This may be because the personnel involved do not believe that such actions are within their remit, or it may be because they do not feel confident dealing with the sometimes sensitive subject of skill sets and competency gaps. Whatever the reason for the omission, it should be addressed if maximum value is to be gained from the problem management process. The IT function should work closely with the HR team to develop user skills profiles and corresponding action plans for inclusion within the standard review and appraisal systems. Examples of IT awareness and education activities include:

- General IT literacy training initiatives i.e. formal training courses
- Focused user training – short courses targeted at common user issues
- Embedding IT training within other courses – Skills training by stealth
- Pre-requisite training before system access is granted – forced attendance in an attempt to ensure a minimum level of competence
- Hints and tips – Communication programme to propagate good practice
- User generated FAQs – Peer to peer support by users for users
- Regular refresher training – to correct bad habits and remind users of features and functionality they may have forgotten

17.16 Measuring the Effectiveness of Preventive Actions

In an ideal world, preventive action would be 100 % effective and following its implementation no further occurrences related to the problem would be experienced. However, in the real world we must often be content with the analysis of post preventive action performance data in order to determine the following indicators of success:

- Reductions in the amount of variance in process performance data i.e. the process is more predictable than it was previously
- Increases in the mean time between service impacting events i.e. there is more uninterrupted service availability
- Reduction in the number of related service impacting incidents within a given period

17.17 But What Happens if a Root Cause cannot be Found?

It may be possible to identify the section of the user population or IT estate that is particularly susceptible to the issue. Notifying these users of the potential problem may allow them to change their working practices to mitigate the impact of any failure i.e. by ensuring they regularly save and back up documents, submitting records to a corporate system at various points of the transaction rather waiting to the end etc.

Change Management

> *"God, give us grace to accept with serenity*
> *the things that cannot be changed, courage*
> *to change the things which should be changed,*
> *and the wisdom to distinguish the one from the other."*

Karl Paul Reinhold Niebuhr, American Theologian, (1892–1971)

Change Management can be defined as the systematic planning and implementation of finite work packages (i.e. a defined series of interdependent tasks) to reach a predefined desired outcome or state. Or as ITIL would say more succinctly;

"Change is the process of moving from one defined state to another."

Change Management is intended to enable organisations to implement an effective and efficient process to identify, plan and manage changes to their infrastructure. It should provide users with functionality to identify and mitigate risk associated with changes so that they can be implemented with confidence. Job planning capabilities enable changes to be planned in precise detail reducing the likelihood of mistakes and unexpected knock on effects and ensures that all interested parties are informed and that the relevant approval processes are completed before the change is implemented. Changes may be scheduled using a graphical planning interface which allows change managers to see how an individual change fits into the overall change calendar, where multiple changes affect common areas of the infrastructure they can be combined to reduce the overall down time, thereby improving service availability and resource utilization.

Task level management and tracking allows organizations to monitor the progress of changes and identify deviations from plan at an early stage, enabling appropriate remedial actions and rescheduling to be completed if necessary to ensure the overall change remains on track.

18.1 Process Objectives

The change management process should be focused upon the following core objectives:

- Efficient and error free implementation of changes to assets and processes
- Minimising the level of service disruption

18.1.1 Efficient and Error Free Implementation of Changes to Assets and Processes

The primary purpose of the change management process is to predictably transform the known current situation into the desired situation via a series of predefined steps and/or actions. The success of a change can be measured in verifiable terms by comparing the defined objectives of the change request against the actual status and attributes/characteristics of the related configuration items etc. involved in the change after it has been implemented.

18.1.2 Minimising the Level of Service Disruption

The change management process wherever possible should follow the guiding principle of the Hippocratic Oath i.e. "...never do harm...". Minimising the level of service disruption during the planning and implementation of the change, as well as attempting to ensure that there are no related incidents caused by the change itself helps to ensure that the business is not negatively impacted by change activity.

18.2 Common Issues

Common issues associated with Change Management:

- Unexpected side effects from changes
- Failed/Aborted changes
- Failures implementing back-out plans
- Insufficient understanding of the risk associated with change
- Uncontrolled/Unplanned changes
- Sub-optimised change scheduling
- Extended change/maintenance windows
- Insufficient consultation during the planning phase
- Poor communication of change and its impact
- Lack of a closed loop process i.e. no closure
- Conflicting resourcing requirements
- Repetition of mistakes time and again
- Lack of a holistic view of all pending change requests and the effects of multiple potential approvals (i.e. 'what if' scenario planning)
- Conflicts between requested/planned/scheduled changes
- One line change plans/Overly detailed change plans

18.3 Process Flow

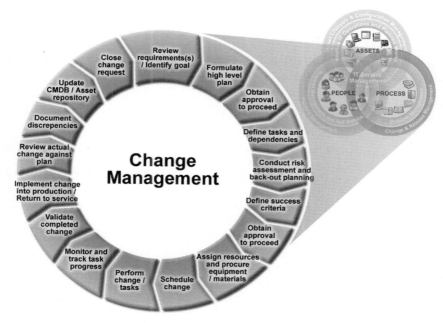

Fig. 18.1. High level overview of the change management process

18.4 Key Players

Requester/Person proposing change – The individual or group that is formally raising the change request in accordance with the change management process.

Request sponsor – The person on whose behalf the change request is being raised. E.g. The helpdesk may raise a change request upon behalf of a senior manager who is out of town and cannot access the system directly.

Recipient(s)/Beneficiaries – The people who are directly impacted by the change and are intended to receive benefit from it.

Approver(s) – Nominated individuals who have sufficient authority to approve or reject change requests on the basis of business, financial or technical judgements.

CAB (Change Approval Board/Change Advisory Board) – A group of individuals that meet on a regular basis to review, discuss and approve or reject requests in light of company policy, ongoing activity, business priorities etc.

Implementation Group(s) – The groups or individuals tasked with performing specific actions/tasks as described within the change implementation plan.

Change Manager – The individual with overall responsibility for a specific set of changes who prepares and validates the implementation plan, schedules resources and monitors the progress of the implementation.

Change Process Owner – The person with responsibility for defining the change management process and evaluating its effectiveness at meeting business requirements with the minimum of change related issues.

Interested Parties – Persons who have some interest in the systems, services or hardware associated with a specific change that have requested to be kept in the loop regarding progress etc.

Affected Users – A subset of the user population that may be directly or indirectly impacted by the change.

18.5 Process Metrics

- Number of changes completed within a specified period broken down by type etc
- Percentage of changes completed on schedule
- Percentage of changes completed within budget
- Number of aborted changes within a specified period
- Average change duration broken down by type etc
- Number of incidents attributed to changes completed within a specified period

18.6 What is the Change Trying to Achieve?

As George Michael put it in Freedom 90; "There ain't no point in moving on, 'til you got somewhere to go". It is essential that the objective of the change is clearly defined in unambiguous terms that can be easily verified and tested. Unless the purpose of the change is understood by all involved with its implementation then there is a danger that they may not all work towards the same end goal. When defining change objectives the following questions may be helpful to ensure that they are clear, concise and useful:

- How will the business evaluate the success or failure of the change?
- What are the business's priorities when implementing the change?
  - Minimising service downtime?
  - Preventing side effects and associated incidents?
  - Keeping implementation costs as low as possible?
  - Getting the change implemented as quickly as possible?
  - Implementing the change without errors?
  - Keeping within agreed budgets and timelines?
  - Minimising business risk?
  - All of the above...
- Do different groups within the business have different success criteria?
- How are the change objectives going to be communicated to the individual's implementing the change?
- Are the objectives documented clearly in easy to understand language avoiding overly technical terminology and jargon?

There is a saying in industry:

"You can have it fast. You can have it cheap. You can have it good. Pick 2!"

18.7 Conflicting Requirements of Various Change Types

Change management processes often struggle with the diversity of changes that they are expected to manage. It is often assumed that the same process that oversees the implementation of a new complex corporate system cannot be used to efficiently implement a simple PC upgrade. And yet each scenario goes through exactly the same logical flow... A requirement is defined, approval to proceed is sort, a plan is crafted, risk is assessed, the plan is reviewed and approved, the pre-requisite resources are assembled, tasks are allocated and implemented in the defined sequence, intermediate checkpoints are monitored and the overall success of the change is measured. Naturally, different elements of this general flow will have different levels of emphasis for the two examples but the overall flow direction should remain valid.

The following list outlines the top ten generic types of changes handled by a typical change management process:

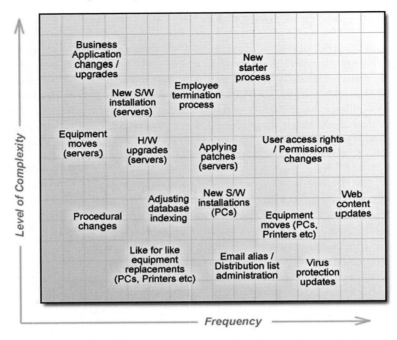

Fig. 18.2. Complexity vs. Frequency for common types of change

- Like for like replacement
- Comparable replacement
- Upgrade component (i.e. Removal and Addition)
- Downgrade component (i.e. Removal and Addition)
- Addition
- Removal
- Modification
  - Meta data
  - Configuration change
- New Installation
- Move

18.7.1 Like for Like Replacement

The replacement of one configuration item for another of exactly the same make, model and version. This type of change is relatively rare due to the rapid rate at which hardware is released by manufacturers. Unless identical spares are purchased at the time of the original equipment purchase it is highly likely that like for like replacements will not be available when required.

18.7.2 Comparable Replacement

Replacing a configuration item with another of equivalent quality, specification and operational performance characteristics. The wide adoption of open technical standards for hardware specifications have meant that such a replacement option is likely to include equipment from manufacturers of the item being replaced. Such substitutions are usually successful with hardware but may be somewhat less robust and reliable for comparable software replacements where adherence to published software standards tend to be more observed to the spirit of the standard as opposed to the letter.

18.7.3 Upgrade Component (i.e. Removal and Addition)

The substitution of one configuration item for another, where the replacement item has increased performance characteristics, enhanced capacity or additional capabilities in comparison to the item being removed.

18.7.4 Downgrade Component (i.e. Removal and Addition)

As upgrade above, but in reverse. Typically used to redistribute and re-use valuable high capacity components that are being under utilised for use within a more demanding function.

18.7.5 Addition

The introduction of a completely new configuration item, data element or component to become an integral part of the existing IT environment and infrastructure. Although sharing many similarities with the 'new installation' change type, additions are incremental extensions to the current setup and as such are likely to involve more risk as the possibilities of unknown side effects affecting existing elements of the environment are greater. Examples of additions would include: Adding new servers to a web farm, fitting additional RAM in a server, installing a new software application onto a production machine etc.

18.7.6 Removal

The removal, or permanent deletion, of a configuration item (or data element) from the environment.

18.7.7 Modification - Meta Data

The change to a piece of meta-data (either amendment or deletion (as deleted data points are really best described as entries with null values)). Meta data can be defined as any attribute or parameter involved with the operation of an application or business system. Such meta data can govern system behaviour in a wide variety of ways and when incorrectly configured may render the application inoperable, cause spurious errors or generate inaccurate output. Meta-data is stored in a wide variety of formats and locations including data dictionary tables, ini file entries, XML configuration records, registry keys, header files, BIOS settings etc. Consider the impact of an inadvertent erroneous change to a payroll system's meta-data regarding tax rates, such a change would affect every person within an organisation and could have long term repercussions if not addressed.

18.7.8 Modification - Configuration Change

A change to the orientation, configuration or hardware settings of a physical piece of equipment. Equipment modifications can include the setting of dip switches, changes to port allocations/mappings, re-positioning cards etc.

18.7.9 New Installation

New installations are the introduction of standalone equipment with minimal dependency upon the existing IT infrastructure. Such equipment may be connected to the corporate network and may access corporate systems but do not themselves play any role in the provision of such services to others.

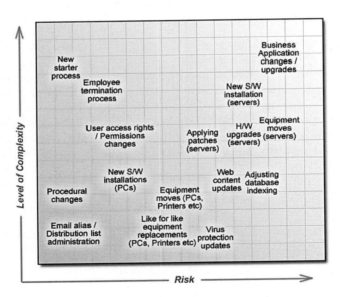

Fig. 18.3. Complexity vs. Risk for common change types

18.7.10 Move

Moves can be defined as a removal and an addition with some transportation in between. Moves are typically thought of as changes in the physical location of a configuration item although they can also be used to describe the movement of data and/or an application instance from one host to another. Large IT equipment moves also bring many logistical challenges as well as technology related issues.

In addition to these ten change types it is common to bundle, or group, multiple change items into a package in order to aid user selection and to streamline and simplify approval processes and task administration.

18.8 Arbitrary Change Classifications/Descriptions can be Dangerous

On 28th January 1986 the American space shuttle, Challenger, exploded during take off killing all seven astronauts on board. The five men and two women were just over a minute into their flight from Cape Canaveral in Florida when the Challenger blew up.

The Rogers commission's subsequent report into the disaster cited the cause as the failure of an "O-ring" seal in the solid-fuel rocket on Challenger's right side. The faulty design of the seal coupled with the unusually cold weather, let hot gases to leak through the joint. Booster rocket flames were able to pass through the failed seal enlarging the small hole. These flames then burned through the Shuttle's external fuel tank and through one of the supports that attached the booster to the side of the tank. That booster broke loose and collided with the tank, piercing the tank's side. Liquid hydrogen and liquid oxygen fuels from the tank and booster mixed and ignited, causing the Space Shuttle to explode.

Even the most seemingly trivial things (such as a ring of rubber) can have a monumental impact upon a system.

The trivial is governed by perception. If people believe something is trivial they will treat is as such. By artificially labelling change requests, ITIL's change management process is fundamentally flawed. According to ITIL, change requests are one of four flavours:

- Standard
- Minor
- Major
- Significant

It is the role of the Change Manager to determine which. Unfortunately, the average Change Manager is not an omni-present entity with the ability to see beyond the here and now and therefore is often ill equipped to make such a value judgement.

18.8.1 Standard Changes

ITIL defines a standard change as *"a change to the infrastructure that follows an established path, is relatively common, and is the accepted solution to a specific requirement or set of requirements."* Now this definition is fine providing that the risk assessments associated with the change are not standardised too. The use of standard methodologies or implementation approaches is to be commended. A predefined list of tasks with the relevant dependency chains and delivery group assignments already configured is an excellent idea and will significantly reduce the administration overhead associated with operating the change management process. However, where ITIL gets it wrong is to assume that just because something is commonplace that it is risk free. It is essential if the integrity of the IT environment is to be maintained that every change be reviewed for its potential impact upon the wider system.

18.8.2 Minor, Major and Significant Changes

Just as the example status model for incident management has shaped an entire generation of commercial ITSM solutions, so has the change process flow diagram within the ITIL documentation. Every major out of the box ITIL compliant solution has blindly used the terms 'Minor', 'Major' and 'Significant' as a means of classifying change requests. Regrettably none of the vendors of these solutions have asked themselves the question "Why?", and consequently such arbitrary segregation of change requests has done nothing but confuse. ITIL doesn't define the differences between 'Minor', 'Major' and 'Significant' changes, it states that each organisation must determine its own change classification structures (and associated definitions) and ensure that they have specific processes and procedures for each depending upon their business needs. How's about that for passing the buck?

18.8.3 Determining the Classification of a Change Request

Don't. By all means, categorise or classify a change based upon the nature of the works to be undertaken or the systems affected etc. Such a classification can then of course be used within management reporting, automatic assignment and the definition of business rules etc. But please refrain from giving changes meaningless labels which can do more harm than good by lulling the unwary into a false sense of security... The important thing to remember when considering change requests is the risk associated with their implementation and the balance of this risk against the opportunity cost of not completing the change. Risk assessment and its uses within the change management process are covered later within this section.

For details regarding categorisation concepts and potential pitfalls etc please refer to the Incident Management section of this book where the advantages and disadvantages of various approaches to ticket categorisation are discussed in depth. The concepts outlined there are equally applicable to change requests as they are to incident reports (well mostly anyhow).

18.8.4 Automation Just Compounds the Problem

Automatic approval of change requests should be avoided for all but the most routine and trivial of requests . . . But you said, no change was trivial - I hear you cry! I know, but obviously some things really cannot have an adverse impact on anything else. Can they? Well yes, there are instances such as the provision of replacement mice and keyboards etc which are incredibly unlikely to have serious knock on effects. If you decide to use the change types outlined earlier then is would be wise to limit automatic approvals to requests for 'like for like replacements' and 'new installations'. Even then I'd like to caveat this section with the fact that the automatic approvals should only cover financial and logical approval cycles and that technical approvals should be sought for pretty much everything. Now there are some of you out there now shaking your head in disbelief, thinking of the paperwork burden of such a system. There is no reason why all approval reviews must be undertaken by the same old group of people, lower risk change types can be delegated to less senior members of staff to reduce the load and increase the general level of accountability within the organisation.

18.8.5 Standard Change Models/Task Templates

Standard change models should rarely be used in their off the shelf state for anything but the simplest of changes. They should be viewed as nothing more than a productivity aide for the Change Manager and resource planning functions to enable them to quickly develop case specific plans to meet the needs of the business. It is essential that the plan be created and reviewed in the context of the current environment and current operational capabilities of the IT function if it is to be valid.

The standard change model should define the following:

- The primary objective of the change i.e. a description of what the change is trying to achieve
- The tasks needed to be completed – including suitable work package descriptions and/or instructions of sufficient detail to enable the target assignee(s) to easily understand exactly what is required of them.
  - Preparatory/Precautionary tasks e.g. back ups, start up procedures for temporary interim solutions, isolation of the system and/or equipment to be worked upon, compatibility testing etc
  - Change tasks i.e. the actual work associated with completing the change itself
  - Back-out/Contingency tasks – placeholders for tasks to be completed in the event of the change being aborted whilst in progress.

- o Post implementation tasks e.g. data synchronisation, performance monitoring/observation, permitting access to the updated system, user base notification etc.
- The sequential order of the tasks and any dependencies between tasks
  - o Linear task chains
  - o Parallel task paths that combine
  - o Optional branching nodes – i.e. points during the change plan where different task plans may be needed in response to actual results in the field e.g. It may not be impossible to determine prior to the change beginning how long a full back up may take and there may be additional tasks needed in cases where this time is excessive in order to improve the resilience of the temporary solution in place.
- Anticipated duration of the task – used to help plan the overall change delivery timeline and to allocate resources against tasks taking into account availability etc.
- Task level contingency – a measure of the likely accuracy of the defined duration of the task.
- The approval cycles to be initiated (as well as identifying when) and the approval processes to be followed in each case.
- Key milestones and/or Check points
- Permitted break points – i.e. points within the change plan at which works may be halted without impacting the change to enable a change to be split across multiple out of hours periods etc.
- The specialist skills and/or tools required to complete the tasks (if appropriate)
- The persons or groups to be assigned against each task (if known) – including the number of resources required for tasks requiring more than one person.
- Any required waiting time between tasks e.g. it may be necessary to wait 24 hours after a new network account has been created for it to fully replicate throughout the organisations identify management infrastructure
- Emergency Contingency – the time needed to implement any back out plan cleanly before the final point of no return has been passed.

18.9 All Changes are Created Equal...

Orwell had a point. To paraphrase - All changes are created equal, but some changes are created more equal than others.

Size, complexity, duration, budget, scope, political support and technical/business risk will all have a role in determining the relative priorities of changes within an organisation.

18.10 If you don't Ask, you don't Get – Approval Processes

"You can't always get what you want
But if you try sometimes you might find
You get what you need"

You can't always get what you want, Rolling Stones

By evaluating change requests against the needs of the business, an organisation can ensure that it focuses it valuable resources on changes that are intended to deliver real business value and minimise the risk and unnecessary costs associated with frivolous or non-strategic change requests.

Fundamental to the effectiveness of the change management process is the verification and validation of change plans prior to implementation. This due diligence helps ensure that untried and unproven changes are not introduced without proper review being undertaken and the appropriate sign off from the relevant business owners that could be adversely impacted by the change.

Various types of approval are used at different stages throughout the change management lifecycle, these include:

- Financial Approval i.e. Can we afford it? Is there a cheaper alternative?
- Technical Approval i.e. Is it likely to work? Is there a better way to do it?
- Logical Approval i.e. Does it make sense to do it at all?
- Implementation Approval i.e. Is the plan plausible and valid?
- Conditional Approval ("yeah but no, but yeah!") – an approval based upon a set of defined criteria that must be met in order to proceed
- Management Checkpoint – an approval cycle intended to ensure that management are fully aware of the current status of a change
- Point of no return validation i.e. Sanity checking that everything that was planned to be done has been completed prior to setting an unstoppable train of events into motion
- Go/No Go decision points – Opt out points within the change lifecycle where the change can be abandoned or delayed with minimal impact to the IT environment
- Approval to place the change into production – i.e. gaining agreement to flip the final switch . . .

Traditional ITSM solution tools tend to have a single approval process initiated once, and once only, throughout the change lifecycle. Such a limitation is contrary to the needs of the organisation as it is often better to have multiple approval points spread across the change lifecycle rather than to load everything up at the initial phase when all of the information needed to make a value judgement may not be known. Consider a large complex change request (e.g. such as the consolidation of a series of distributed database data repositories into a single centralised storage array) that needs thorough investigation, research and detailed design before it can be implemented. It may be appropriate in such cases to have an initial approval cycle to determine whether or not it is right to dedicate the resources needed to conduct the necessary due diligence work before resubmitting the change request for a further approval to proceed.

18.10.1 Types of Approval Process Flows

It is common to have a variety of approval processes defined for changes of varying degrees of risk. It should also be possible to add additional approvers to the process on an ad hoc basis if deemed appropriate by the change manager. Common approval processes include the following elements which combine to form the complete approval cycle:

- Linear/Sequential approval chains
- Parallel approvers
- Group voting
  - Complete consensus needed/Right of veto – Any member can block the request
  - Majority verdict required
  - Any member agrees

18.10.2 Types of Approval Response

Approval requests should be reviewed in light of the current situation and decisions based upon the information provided. However, it will not always be possible for an approver to come to a final conclusion based upon the facts to hand. Approval responses may include the following options:

- Approve
- Reject
- Abstain
- Request additional information
- Require amendments to plan before resubmission
- Delegate decision to someone else (typically a technical expert)
- Conditional approval – i.e. Approved subject to some stated terms being met to the satisfaction of the approver
  - It may be appropriate to require the Change Manager to acknowledge and formally agree to these secondary conditions to ensure that such terms are not overlooked by mistake...

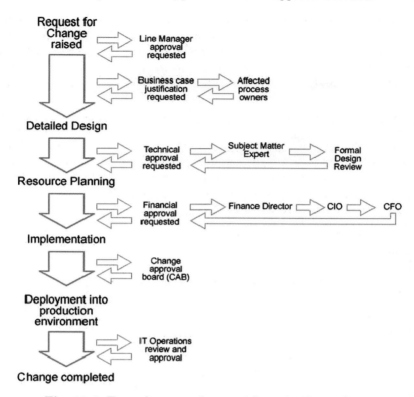

Fig. 18.4. Example approval process for a significant change

18.10.3 Time Limited Approval Cycles – Rescinding the Infinite Right of Appeal

It is sometimes necessary to set a time limit on approval cycles in cases where deliberation and navel gazing are an issue. Where this is necessary, approvers must be informed of these time constraints up front and the process to be followed in the event of them failing to supply a timely response i.e. automatic approval, automatic rejection, majority verdict from those responding within the time limit etc. It should be clear that the responsibility for meeting the approval deadline lies with the approver and that failure to do so removes any right to question the change in the future. Some may consider such an approach as excessive and harsh but it may be necessary within organisations where accountability is poorly defined.

18.10.4 Information Pack for Approvers

In the past decade I have seen hundreds of change management systems in action, and with the exception of maybe a handful, all have left the bulk of the content of a change request up to the discretion of the person raising the change. More often than not, approvals have little to do with evaluating the available information and making a value judgement as to whether or not the change should be allowed to proceed, instead the approval process is used to absolve the delivery teams of their responsibility and/or act as a bottleneck for management to demonstrate their importance. Now some would argue that even if they were furnished with all of the appropriate information that some approvers wouldn't be capable of making a value judgement, this is a different problem which we will come to later. Assuming the right people will be available to review a change approval request, the following list outlines the types of information that should be provided:

- Business justification for the change
  - Why are we doing this?
- Effect/Impact of not completing the change
  - What's the opportunity cost?
- Cost Benefit analysis
  - How much bang do we get for our buck?
- Technical description of change
  - What is that we are planning to do exactly?
- List of dependent systems and services
  - What could we be about to mess up here?
- Worse case impact scenarios
  - How bad could it really get?
- Level of adherence with corporate strategy
  - How does this fit in with our overall direction?
- Risk assessment
  - Have we covered all of the bases?
- Defined success criteria
  - How will we know if we did it right?
- High level implementation plan
  - How do we think we should do it?
- Resource requirements plan
  - Who do we think we need to do it?

18.10.5 Who Should Approve?

Typically, management seniority and an individual's relative position within the organisational hierarchy are used to determine who should review change requests. This may work adequately for financial and business reviews but may be inappropriate for technical and logical assessments. Irrespective of who completes the change review the following points should be kept in mind to ensure that the organisation gets the quality of decisions it expects and requires:

- Is there sufficient business representation from the affected areas?
- Do the technical approvers have the pre-requisite knowledge to be able to validate and review the technical case adequately?
- Are the reviewers sufficiently impartial to make balanced decisions based upon the known facts?
- Are timeline/availability constraints forcing the selection of approvers that would not normally be utilised in an ideal world?

18.10.6 Peer Review

The harshest critics are usually those that are closest to you. Familiarisation is often said to breed contempt, but it also gives an excellent perspective from which to view and evaluate proposals for change. Having change plans reviewed by ones colleagues and peers helps ensure that the person drafting the plan raises their game and includes the details needed to convince even the most sceptical of critics.

18.10.7 The Change Approval Board (CAB)

The Change Approval Board, or sometimes known as the Change Advisory Board, is a group of named individuals tasked with acting as the corporate conscience and defenders of the corporate infrastructure. Such a group meets periodically to review change requests and to determine whether or not they should be permitted to proceed. When assembling the CAB the following principles should be kept in mind:

- Are the members of the CAB credible in the eyes of the technical community? Do they carry sufficient weight with the business?
- Does the CAB have the full support of senior management?
- Is the CAB allowed to operate independently without interference from management?
- Are CAB members allocated dedicated time slots to participate within change reviews or do they fit it in around their other duties?

The change approval process should be defined clearly and published so that everyone who submits a request for change is aware of the procedure that will be followed, who will review their request, the acceptance criteria that the submission will be reviewed against and the timeline for the process to complete.

18.10.8 Automatic Approvals

Don't. See above...

18.11 "Measure Twice, Cut Once" – Or Planning is your Friend . . .

The success of a change is largely dependant upon the level of planning undertaken prior to implementation. Nothing is more critical than the development of a robust change plan which has been validated by all involved as the optimum method of implantation given the business constraints under which the change is to be introduced.

18.11.1 Planning – a Task by Itself

It is important to ensure that sufficient time is allocated to prepare the implementation plan fully. For complex changes, this timeline should include provision for the plan to be reviewed by the appropriate technical experts and allow for a couple of iterative cycles before the final plan is defined and published.

18.11.2 Tasks, Owners/Assignees and Dependencies

Task definitions will typically include the following information:

- Description of the works to be completed
- References to any associated documentation
- Name of the group/individual(s) responsible for completing the task
- Planned and actual start and end dates and times
- Anticipated duration of the task
- Dependencies between the task and other tasks (upstream and downstream)

18.11.3 Task Granularity – How Much Detail is too Much?

The level of detail needed will depend upon a variety of factors including; the skills of the person(s) completing the task, the average frequency at which the task is undertaken, the complexity of the task, the availability of relevant work procedures and/or technical documentation etc. Care should particularly be taken when assigning tasks to external contractors which may not have access to corporate knowledge repositories and process documentation.

In general work packages should only be broken down into separate distinct tasks where doing so aids understanding and/or it allows the completion of specific tasks within a work package to be tracked as key milestones or for compliance reporting i.e. it may be beneficial to break out the final systems testing task of a change in order to monitor when this is completed and to force the person(s) completing the change to acknowledge that this critical element of the works has indeed been completed.

18.11.4 Task Validation

It is impractical to assume that a single change manager will have the pre-requisite skills and experience necessary to be able to define every task required and the appropriate sequencing to implement every complex change. Consequently it is important that the change plan and individual task definitions be reviewed by technically competent subject matter experts in order to validate the implementation method prior to the change commencing.

18.11.5 Task Assignment

See the automatic assignment section of the incident management chapter of this book for details of automatic assignment processes which can be used within a change management context.

18.11.6 Gantt Charts and PERT Network Diagrams

Since the widespread use of MS Project became prevalent everyone knows what a Gantt chart is (even if they don't recognise the name). Gantt charts are a useful tool to visualise resource conflicts and task dependencies and allow sequencing to be juggled in order to try to condense delivery timelines and/or schedule a change backwards from a defined deadline.

The Program Evaluation and Review Technique (PERT) is a model for project management and complex change implementation invented by the US Navy in 1950's. PERT is a method of analysis used to model the tasks required to complete a given change project, especially the time needed to complete each specific task, in order to identify the minimum time required to complete the change.

PERT is primarily aimed at simplify the planning and scheduling of large and detailed changes. It is able to incorporate uncertainty in the sense that it is possible to schedule a change project without knowing the exact details and durations of all the activities. This event oriented technique is likely to

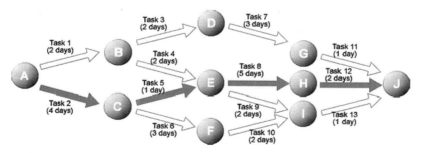

Fig. 18.5. An example PERT chart with the rate determining path highlighted

be of most use in complex schedule critical changes where cost is not a major factor but the overall completion time is.

Gantt charts and PERT analysis will not be appropriate for all change types but they remain valuable and powerful tools that every change manager should be conversant with if they are to fulfil their role effectively.

18.11.7 Scheduling the Job

Task scheduling is often a very frustrating process, with countless hours spent trying to align the diaries of the various service delivery teams in order to minimise dead time between dependent tasks and to prevent clashes and conflicts between mutually exclusive tasks and/or tasks which require the different service delivery teams to have sole access to a specific location or piece of equipment.

18.11.8 Combining Similar Jobs to Reduce Duplicated Tasks

It may be possible sometimes to combine planned changes with other jobs related to an asset (e.g. planned changes and/or routine tasks) in order to reduce the total amount of time needed to complete the works. These savings are typically realised by eliminating duplicated tasks such as data backups, power downs, restarts etc and help increase the overall availability of the asset and the service(s) which it supports.

18.12 Change Calendar

Also known as the Change diary, Operational Plan, Forward Schedule of Changes (FSC) etc.

The change calendar should clearly describe the current plan of changes to be implemented within the IT environment. It should clearly indicate those changes that have been formally approved and are scheduled for implementation as well as showing changes that are tentatively planned subject to approval etc. The change calendar should be closely tied in with the resource pool available to implement changes so that it can be used as an aide for task allocation etc. In addition to planned changes, the calendar may include details of repetitive routine operational tasks that are scheduled – this may facilitate the concatenation of work packages thereby enabling the removal of duplicated work tasks and therefore reducing the overall amount of system/service downtime needed. The details contained within the calendar should be capable of being filtered and/or sorted by:

- Service(s) affected
- IT Systems/Applications impacted
- Individual assets/Configuration items associated

- Physical location
- Skills required
- Change categorisation

The change calendar will typically focus upon far more than changes in isolation. Below, is a list of some of the types of information that may be included within the change calendar in order to improve the level of planning and control of the change management process:

- Approved change requests/Scheduled changes
- Tentative planned changes (Awaiting formal approval, equipment delivery, resource allocation etc)
- Agreed maintenance windows
- Hours of operation of the business
- Peak usage hours/Usage profile for services affected
- Corporate change freezes/Blackout periods
- Known business events (e.g. Start of a significant marketing campaign, end of a financial period, billing runs, stock counts etc)
- Resource availability information (e.g. Predicted staffing levels after authorised holidays and training course are considered)
- Statutory holidays (For all geographical regions as there are significant variations around the world – i.e. It may be possible to degrade the service capacity of a particular service when a significant proportion of its user base are on vacation)

18.12.1 "What if" Scenario Planning

One of the primary purposes of the change calendar is to enable change managers to evaluate the current situation and to test out potential implementation scenarios ahead of time. This scenario testing may highlight resource bottlenecks or risk hotspots which need to be avoided or dealt with. By juggling task sequencing and the high level phasing of changes it may be possible to mitigate business risk and achieve business milestones for change implementation without breaking the bank by incurring excessive levels of overtime.

18.12.2 Change Blackout Periods

There will be times when it is not appropriate to have any IT changes being implemented. In retail, this may be the seasonal rush or sale periods. In finance, it may be the run up to the end of the financial year. In manufacturing, it may correspond to periods of peak demand and output. Whatever the business drivers, it is important that the IT function responds to the organisation's need for stability and continuous service availability by halting all non essential change activity and focusing upon assuring service quality.

18.12.3 Release Selection

The change calendar may also be used to identify candidates for possible inclusion with a formal release cycle. The ability to see a schedule of similar change requests and/or changes affecting similar assets, systems, users etc may help to define potential synergies and task consolidation opportunities if they are managed as a bundle rather than individually.

18.13 Risk Management

Note: Sometimes referred to as impact assessment.

Risk management and in particular, risk assessment processes, have been common place within the environmental management and health and safety arenas for many many years. This proactive prevention based approach is completely relevant to the planning of IT change and should be implemented for all but the most trivial of actions.

18.13.1 Risk Assessment – as Easy as 'ABC'... Followed by 'D' and 'E'...

When talking about risk assessment we shall be using the term in a health and safety or environmental context. The phrase is also used within the IT security arena, and indeed the definition of some of the terminology and methods are similar, however the general practice used within the safety area is more applicable to general IT governance and service assurance than the slightly paranoid version used by security professionals. The method for assessing risk can be summarised in the following five stages. Each stage will require several iterations to be completed fully. Well as fully as any ongoing process can be...

Risk assessment in five easy steps:

- Identify the hazards
- Identify who and what could be affected
- Quantify the associated risk
- Define control measures to mitigate the risk
- Identify the level of remaining residual risk

18.13.2 Hazards

Hazards are often defined in terms of their end consequences, potential impacts or possible effects e.g. component failure, data duplication, data loss/theft, data corruption, poor response times, lost transactions, connection timeouts, virus infections, unauthorised access to corporate systems, intermittent errors, application errors, system locks/hangs, a degradation of system or service performance, a system or service outage etc. Although such effects may be worrying, they are best thought of the as the consequences of hazards, which themselves may include:

- Insecure systems (e.g. un-patched and/or poorly configured systems)
- Overly complex systems (e.g. the use of multiple middleware tools within a single integration chain)
- Single points of failure within the infrastructure
  - Physical e.g. a single server performing a specific function
  - Logical e.g. a single source of external data used to feed a process
- Shared resources i.e. a single system which takes part in multiple business processes and/or underpins multiple services
- Untried and unproven technologies/compatibility issues
- Under trained/Over confident/Inexperienced/Inattentive staff
- Environmental conditions – Excessive heat, humidity etc
- Poorly maintained hardware/systems
- Ineffective/inefficient procedures and working practices
- Incomplete tasks (related to changes and routine operations)

18.13.3 Risk

Risk can be considered as the potential something has to cause harm. The relative value of a specific risk can be compared against other risks by evaluating the way in which multiple factors combine according to the following 'equation':

$$Risk = Severity \times Likelihood$$

18.13.4 Severity

Severity is the level of harm/damage that would be caused if the risk were to be realised e.g. A motherboard failure would have a higher severity than a disk drive failure (Even if we don't yet make the assumption that the drive is part of a striped disk array) as the motherboard going down would be guaranteed to take out the entire system, whereas the disk failure could potentially just result in some data not being accessible.

$$Severity = Scope \times Level\ of\ disruption\ likely$$

18.13.5 Scope

The scope can be considered as measure of the extent of the damage or problem that could be caused if the hazards were to create an issue or incident. Scope may be expressed in terms of:

- The number of users and/or sites affected by the works
- The number of physical systems that need updating or amending
- The financial impact of the change (i.e. anticipated cost savings)
- The level of technical dependency upon the item being changed

18.13.6 Likelihood

Likelihood is a measure of the probability that the risk factor will cause harm. For the examples cited above, the motherboard failure would be considered less likely than the disk failure. This relative judgement is based upon the fact that the motherboard has no moving parts which could wear and fail and that practical experience shows us that drives fail more regularly than motherboards.

18.13.7 Common Risks Associated with IT Changes and IT Projects

Experience and post implementation reviews have highlighted the following areas as issues that should be reviewed as part of the formal risk assessment for a planned change:

- Communication
  - Internal within the implementation team
  - Between the implementation team and user base
  - Between the implementation team and third parties
  - Misunderstandings and miscommunications
- Information
  - Omissions in information provided
  - Inaccuracies in documentation
  - Document control
- Technology
  - Hardware failures/Software issues
  - Incomplete implementations of open standards
  - New or untried approaches to issues
  - System compatibility issues
  - Security policies that impact the selected approach
  - Third party vendor issues
- Data
  - Poor data quality (omissions, errors and duplication)
  - Lack of suitable data
  - Insufficient resources dedicated to data collection, cleansing and collation
- Assumptions
  - All assumptions are risky
  - Lack of validation of key assumptions
- Estimating
  - Insufficient time planned to complete specific tasks
  - Inappropriate resource skill levels defined for specific tasks

- Resources
  - Availability of suitably skilled resources
  - Motivation and morale of employees
  - Fatigue from excessive overtime etc

18.13.8 Controls

Controls should be considered as any act, provision, contingency or barrier that is intended to mitigate the identified risk by preventing it reaching its potential to cause disruption or damage. There are two primary types of controls that can be implemented; Physical and Procedural.

Physical Controls

Perhaps the easiest type of control to understand as they physically exist and can be seen by all involved. Examples of physical controls would include; Fault tolerance via hardware duplication, securing machine room access with locks and keypads, removal of floppy disk drives and USB ports from desktop machines, introduction of RAID striping to disk arrays etc.

Procedural Controls

Changes to working practices that ensure that identified hazards cannot cause issues. Examples of procedural controls would include; implementing back up procedures, splitting data entry tasks to have peer review of entered data, defining inspection processes to be followed etc.

Control Measure Implementation Hierarchy

When determining what controls to implement to reduce the residual risk associated with a change multiple controls should be selected according to the principles described below, if possible in the following order of preference:

- Avoid the risk completely by selecting an alternative lower risk approach
- Implement hardware redundancy/fault tolerance if possible
- Isolate the change from the live production environment until it is fully tested and validated
- Run current and proposed systems in parallel until you are sure that the change has worked
- Adopt risk aware working practices e.g. avoiding single man implementations where errors and omissions can readily go unnoticed and allow team working so that each persons activity is observed and checked by the next person completing a task
- Implement hot standby solutions in case problems are detected during the change implementation

- Complete full regression testing prior to releasing the change into production
- Perform data backups prior to implementing the change and test the associated restore procedures
- Alert system users to the potential issues and the actions to take to mitigate any known side effects
- Increase staffing levels on the help desk in the period following the implementation of the change to handle the potential increase in incident reports – This is not really a control but I have seen some organisations do this in the misguided belief that it is . . .

18.13.9 Effectiveness of Defined Control Measures

Unfortunately, the act of defining controls is not sufficient to mitigate risk on its own. Controls must be implemented correctly, vigorously tested and continuously monitored to ensure they are functioning correctly if they are to be effective.

18.13.10 Residual Risk

No action is without risk. The only people that don't make mistakes are the ones that don't do anything. Even if every conceivable control measure is implemented an element of risk will still remain. How this risk is described is largely an issue of personal preference, some will prefer a ranking system of trivial, low, medium and high. Others will relate more effectively with a numerical scale. Whatever the definition structure in place, the purpose of the residual risk rating is to make the business aware of the seriousness of the change and the fact that it could have a dramatic impact upon business operations.

Residual risk can be determined by evaluating the following 'equation':

$$((\text{Severity} \times \text{Likelihood}) - (\text{Control Measure effectiveness})) \times \text{External factors}$$

OK, so we've "done" risk assessment . . . let's put the damn thing out there . . .

18.13.11 Everything Changes . . .

Completing a risk assessment for a change is one thing. Using the risk assessment to mitigate risk is another thing entirely. Everyone involved within the change implementation must be aware of the risk assessment and what it means to them. The world won't stand still whilst the assessment is being conducted, nor will it stand still during the interim period between the assessment and the scheduled implementation start date. It is therefore vital that the assessment be validated prior to every task being started in order to ensure that the assumptions and controls defined still hold true and are still in place e.g. a memory upgrade to a server that is part of a load balanced pair will have minimal service impact providing the other server is up and running – but it may be a good idea to check that it is before pulling the plug...

18.14 Practice Makes Perfect - Dress Rehearsals and Testing

Wherever possible complex and/or high risk changes should be practised a number of times in a test environment prior to being implemented in the live production environment. These dry runs will enable the implementation team to validate the change plan (including task timings and sequencing) and will help to identify any additional controls that should be put in place to mitigate the risk from the change. The following questions will help you to evaluate your current test procedures for changes:

- Has the change been tested for compatibility and usability?
- Has the change been tested against all potential client types? How do we know what types of potential clients might be affected by the change?
- Have the tests used real life data and actual usage scenarios rather than bulk data loads etc?
- Was the test environment setup sufficiently similar to the real life production environment for us to draw a valid conclusion?
- Did the test environment include all dependent systems and processes?
- Was the testing sufficiently arduous and of long enough duration to identify potential side effects?
- Was the change completed in accordance with the change plan in the test environment or was the testing used to refine/develop the change plan? If so, were the steps needed to implement the change accurately captured?
- Did the change plan task sequence work logically? Did it become apparent that additional tasks need to be completed prior to implementing the change?
- Have any potential "gotchas" been identified during testing? Has this information been fed back into the change management plan?

18.14.1 Virtualisation and Testing

The wide availability of virtualisation tools has meant that many of the traditional barriers to change testing are no longer valid. It is perfectly reasonable to build a virtual environment that is the same as the environment to be changed and to run through the change implementation at leisure, observing its impact and refining the change implementation plan to minimise downtime etc.

18.14.2 Plan B (i.e. Back-out Plan)

In the event of the implementation team hitting an insurmountable problem during the change there needs to be a plan describing what is to be done to mitigate service impact and leave the IT environment in a usable state where possible. It should be remembered that it may not always be preferable to return the environment to the state before the change was initiated (e.g. in cases where the change is to replace a dead server etc there is little benefit in going back to a dead server where it may be viable to partially restore capacity or capability). The back out plan should tie in closely with any milestones or check points within the change plan and should have options defined within it to take different actions based upon which stages of the change plan had been completed when the back out plan was initiated.

- Has the back-out plan been tested and verified as fit for purpose?
- What level of contingency should be allowed within change plans to facilitate the implementation of the back-out plan?
- What pre-work and/or preparations are necessary to support the back out plan? Have these actions been included with the change's task list?

18.15 Change Control

The purpose of change control is to keep a watching eye on the progress of the change implementation in order to highlight potential slippages, overspends and show stopping issues sufficiently early to be able to avoid them and bring the change successfully to conclusion on time and within the agreed budget.

- Progress tracking/Task completion reports – The formal reporting of the current task status usually described in terms of the percentage of the overall task completed (either in terms of the work to be done or the time allotted).
- Periodic check point reviews – Meetings to review how the change is progressing and to identify any issues that have been identified that may potentially have a negative impact on the change.
- Plan versus Actual comparison – Day to day review of reported task data to identify exceptions and instances where the actual performance deviates from the agreed plan.

18.15.1 Ongoing Risk Assessment Activity

Every member of the implementation team must feel empowered to be able to raise a warning flag in cases where they identify something that could impact the change. Such events may include system failures, incidents, other changes, errors and omissions, assumptions that had not been sufficiently tested etc.

- Have additional risks been identified that require assessment and controls?
- Are the existing controls still in place and remaining effective?

18.15.2 When the Worst Case Scenario Happens...

The real test of a change manager or project manager only comes when their carefully constructed plan begins to crumble about their ears. The true measure of a manager is how they deal with a change when their back is against the wall. Getting an out of control change back on track is a difficult task and may require the allocation of additional resources and the implementation of additional controls. Having been in this situation too many times in the past, the only advice I will offer is to:

- Take a moment to take a step back and review the overall scene
- Communicate problems early to superiors so that it isn't such a nasty surprise
- Don't be afraid of calling a complete stop to the change activity – better to lose a day than incur two days delay having to undo something that was done incorrectly
- Formally update the implementation plan so that everyone is aware of the changes to the plan
- Regroup and reassign resources as necessary
- Remain vigilant, but remember that micro management seldom helps

18.16 The Benefits of 20:20 Hindsight

18.16.1 "We'd Like to Keep you in for Observation Overnight"

In a health care context, the more significant an operation, the longer the period allowed for recovery and recuperation. The recovery room is there to hold a patient under close observation until all concerned are happy to release them onto a ward. The same holds true for any IT infrastructure change. It is essential that sufficient resources are allocated after the fact to monitor the performance of the components of the infrastructure impacted by the change and to raise an early warning in cases where actual performance deviates from anticipated or expected behaviour. And yet it is common for change implementation teams to wash their hands of a change the moment it goes into production. In order to correct this behaviour it may be necessary to add post implementation monitoring and observation tasks to the change plan and to manage their completion as any other phase of the change.

18.16.2 Side Effects...

It is often very difficult to predict the potential side effects of a change in advance. The almost limitless number of combinations of software versions, patch levels and associated files, libraries and meta data settings, coupled with seemingly infinite hardware variations, model differences and configuration options mean that it is practically impossible to ascertain in advance the potential adverse effects of combining multiple elements of the IT infrastructure into a single cohesive system.

Proactive system observations may focus upon the following attributes and characteristics of the configuration items involved in a change as a means of identifying the early signs of potentially damaging side effects:

- Spikes or continuously high CPU load/utilisation
- Unusually high RAM usage (continuous or unexpected incremental growth therein)
- Response time issues (e.g. increases in page load times etc)
  - Conversely, processes which complete much quicker than they should are also indicators of potential issues. Rather than believing in a coding miracle, they usually just mean all the stuff that should be happening isn't.
- Degradation of system transaction times/Unexpected improvements (See above)
- Database and/or Disk contention
- Excessive I/O and/or Network traffic
- System locks (File and/or record level etc)
- System or application level alerts and/or errors
- Unusual physical signs
  - E.g. burning smells, smoke, funny noises, corrupted user interfaces etc

18.16.3 The Post Mortem/Post Implementation Review (PIR)

Post implementation reviews should be carried out for successful as well as problematic changes. The number and frequency of reviews will depend upon the size of the organisation and the nature of the changes being undertaken within a given period. The primary purpose of the post implementation review is to answer the following questions:

- How did it go?
- What did we do right/wrong?
- What can we learn from the experience to make things better in the future?

The tone and purpose of the review is all important. It is essential that the review meeting is not used to attribute blame for failures or errors during the change. Such a finger pointing exercise will do nothing to improve the change management process going forward and will just result in employees hiding mistakes and issues during subsequent changes for fear of being lambasted during a change review. The review must be conducted in an open and non-judgemental way with all involved in the change able to participate and contribute to the discussion.

The review meeting agenda is likely to cover the following areas:

- Evaluation of the defined change objectives to determine if the change was a success or not
- Review of any known side effects arising from the change activity
  - Including a formal review of any incident reports raised during or after the change activity that may be related
- Level of over spend or under spend against the change budget
- Comparison of actual task durations against the planned schedule
- Lessons learnt/Suggestions for improvement from the implementation team
- User feedback/comments related to the change
- The success, or otherwise, of the back-out plan (in cases where the change was aborted part way through).

18.17 Learning the Change Management Lessons of Industry

Depending upon your analyst, it is believed that poorly managed change management is responsible for between 60 – 80 % of all business impacting IT incidents within an enterprise. This figure explains why so much management attention and focus has been given to the whole arena of change management but does not, unfortunately, explain why this percentage has improved little over the past decade! There is a belief within IT circles that change management is hard. And because of this, management expect, and accept, a certain level of failure and pain associated with IT infrastructure changes. This self fulfilling prophecy leads to poor performance on the part of delivery teams and management alike. It must be remembered that the performance of subordinates is directly correlated with that of those managing them – if your teams performance is lacking then the first place to look is at yourself.

And yet in many industry sectors, change management is handled efficiently and professionally and without incident (if you pardon the expression). In the nuclear and pharmaceutical sectors for example, changes are equally prevalent, but in those examples, the industries have matured to a zero tolerance of change failure approach. Imagine the impact of a poorly upgraded cooling system at a nuclear power generation facility and contrast that with the impact of aborting a file server disk upgrade . . .

The pains associated with IT Change Management are well known. They can strike at the very heart of an organization causing slight user inconvenience or, in severe cases, total business paralysis.

If Change Management within the IT sector is to mature to a state comparable to that of the best examples in industry it is going to be necessary for IT professionals to look outside of their world and learn from the best practices and processes implemented in other sectors. There are some that still believe that IT changes are somehow unique and that the processes needed to implement them are specialist in nature. This section is intended to help break down this misconception and enable IT professionals to contrast their current approach to how change management is implemented elsewhere.

18.17.1 So how are Changes Treated in Non-IT Scenarios?

The physical nature or types of changes in non-IT scenarios are very different. However, the processes associated with their implementation share many similarities with their IT counterparts. The following change process areas will be considered and contrasted against common IT practice and ITIL processes:

- Change management culture
- Change planning
- Approvals and authorizations
- Design reviews
- Continuous monitoring
- Resource management and control
- Risk management
- Change control

Cultural Impact Upon Change Management

How an organization perceives a change determines the relative success of the implementation of that change. Organisations that rigorously tackle changes from a position of confidence in their success, are more likely successfully implement. This approach to change management is defined by the senior management team and their reactions to change related problems. It pervades the organization and becomes ingrained in the standard operating procedures and culture of the business. Where changes result in problems, they are vigorously investigated and the appropriate lessons learnt for the future. The business knows that change is inevitable and the success of the business is directly proportionate to its ability to implement change effectively.

Any tolerance of errors or failure within the change process enables employees to see that management, and hence the business, are not serious about change. Such an approach gives rise to a slip shod attitude, with near enough is good enough goals that become second nature and as a consequence become the normal way of operating.

Effective change management organizations recognize that every change is significant, irrespective of how seemingly trivial the change may appear to those on the outside. They baulk at the idea of arbitrary change classifications of minor, major and significant etc which are guaranteed to lull the unwary into a false sense of security and complacency. For they know that sometimes the apparently simple or mundane can have the highest risk associated with it. Repetitive changes or apparently isolated scenarios have a habit of causing the most critical of incidents if not treated with the same level of attention and analysis that seemingly more significant changes receive. The effective change manager is a student of chaos theory and recognizes and understands the multitude of interrelationships that exist between common and disparate systems that may give rise to a specific set of circumstances that raise the risk of the change beyond that which is usual.

This does not mean that changes cannot have standardized procedures associated with them as effective change management embraces process normalization and uses it to instil a consistent approach to change thereby delivering predictable results.

Avoidance of Change for Change's Sake

IT professionals are sometimes too focused upon achieving a change that they forget to consider why that change is necessary, and indeed if it actually is necessary. Every change must be considered from a business standpoint to ascertain if it is actually necessary. Continual upgrades and enhancements may very well generate IT activity but do they really add anything to the business? How many changes are implemented that the business has not requested? And of these unsolicited changes, how many deliver value to the business? After all, no one would willing undergo surgery without the hope of some form of benefit and yet IT departments are sometimes willing to conduct major surgery without any anaesthetic on little more than a whim.

It's all very well to claim that the business needs the latest and greatest version of something, but unless there is a specific risk associated with not upgrading, why should the organization incur unnecessary risk through the implementation of a change that it has not requested? If IT functions can learn to avoid unnecessary changes and focus their attentions upon effectively implementing required changes then they will be a lot closer to successful change management.

Level of Change Planning

The level and depth of detail used to model and plan IT changes is sometimes embarrassingly low. There is a general reluctance in some quarters to dedicate sufficient time and resources to this most critical element of the change management process. The old woodworker's adage of measure twice and cut once is as applicable to IT changes as any other. Only with effective planning can an organization be confident about the likelihood of success of a particular change. This oversight is usually blamed on the restricted amount of resource available and the mountain of changes required.

Non IT changes in comparison are often planned many weeks, months, or years, in advance with particular attention being given to the methodology to be employed as well as the desired end result. Plans focus upon the resource requirements, key milestones, contingency solutions and remedial action processes in the event of problems during the change itself. They will also identify go/no go decision points and intermediary acceptance criteria against which the change will be measured while it is in process. By focusing upon the method of implementation and carefully defining the entire change lifecycle it is possible to clearly identify change related risks and make the appropriate plans to eliminate them or mitigate their impact.

Role of Approvals

Traditionally, IT change requests undergo a formal approval cycle initially and then disappear into a void to be implemented in apparent isolation. This over simplification means that approvals can very soon become out of date in fast moving environments with a lot of change activity. An effective change management process will define multiple approval points through out the change lifecycle and will require the approvals to be received before the change is allowed to progress on its journey to completion.

Phased sign offs and split approvals ensure that the business is kept up to date with change implementation progress and ensures that current circumstances and conditions are considered during the implementation phase. It is also relatively common for non-IT changes to use the concept of condition based approvals i.e. an approval is given in advance subject to certain predefined conditions being satisfied at a predefined point in time during the process. This minimizes the time spent waiting for formal approvals to be processed during an implementation but ensures that change specific conditions are met to the satisfaction of the approving body.

Irrespective of what industry sector is performing a change, there are sometimes cases which do not go according to plan. However, the mark of a robust and resilient change management process can be considered as the way in which it handles non-conformity and adversity. Typical IT change processes have little or no in process checks or milestones to satisfy and consequently when things go wrong it is left to those implementing the change to use their initiative and try to rectify the situation to the best of their ability. Unfortunately this can sometimes result in actions that make matters worse or that have negative side effects to the business. The use of in-process approvals is designed to prevent making things even worse when the worst happens. In the event of a failure or error a predefined sub process is initiated to manage the deviation from plan. This remedial action process itself will include approval processes to ensure that all remedial actions are reviewed and approved in an attempt to get the change back on track without negatively impacting the business.

Design Reviews

Design reviews within IT are often neglected as there is an assumption that the only people with the skills needed to validate the design of a change are those that are sufficiently skilled to design it in the first place. In a market where skills are scarce it is impractical to duplicate skill sets and consequently there is no resource available to meaningfully review and verify a proposed technical change. Such an argument is of course ridiculous as specific skills shortages exist in every industry sector. The skills needed to perform an effective design review can be learnt and only require those reviewing a proposal to know enough to ask the right questions and to be able to validate the responses given logically and dispassionately.

An alternative used in some industries is the use of third parties to perform external verification of plans etc. Such an approach assumes that suitable organizations are available, that commercial confidence and data security issues are dealt with. The supposed impartiality of an external review ensures that plans are treated objectively and internal politics and business pressures do not cloud or impair the judgment of those completing the analysis. However, any verification service provided by a commercial provider will have the potential to be influenced by the cold commercial pressures of any customer-supplier relationship.

Irrespective of who conducts the design review, it is essential to ensure that it includes the validation of implementation plans as well as the actual change itself. The method of implementation not only can directly affect the potential success of the change but can also help determine the potential impact of the change on external systems etc and therefore the risk associated with it.

A secondary purpose of the design review is to ensure that extensive consultation within the business is completed. The formal notification of affected and interested parties ensures that every point of view is available for inclusion and that everyone is aware of the potential change. Ideally, details of all pending design reviews should be posted where they can be easily accessed by the business and reviewed on a regular basis to ensure the business is up to speed with current and planned developments.

Emergency change requests within the IT arena are often fast tracked without a formal design review in order to expedite their implementation. In certain circumstances such an approach can be considered as short sighted and liable to cause even greater issues than the incident the emergency change is intended to resolve. Emergency changes should still undergo a formal design review (even if this review is scheduled more rapidly than normal planned design reviews) and the review should be as detailed, or even more detailed, than a standard review in light of the fact that the business case, desired end point and implementation plan will have been prepared in haste. The review should be far from a rubber stamping exercise as it is the last line of the defense that the business has to protect it from unwise or ill prepared changes.

Continuous Monitoring/Real Time Post Mortems

Non IT change management processes do not wait until the dust has settled before conducting a review of events, nor do they restrict reviews to changes that were unsuccessful or that had problems. By reviewing every key stage of every change against plan, progress is measured and any deviation can be identified and addressed early. Only by being prepared to call a halt at the earliest sign of trouble can a change manager ensure that the change will run smoothly and that the process will be self regulating. Actual versus Plan variation is a measure of project control as well as planning capability and is the metric that the performance of individual change managers should be measured against.

Within IT, post mortems occur after the fact (and then usually only when things go wrong). By waiting until it is all over, the opportunity to prevent catastrophic failure is missed. If business impacting system failures are to be avoided it is essential that changes are monitored proactively and suitable actions taken at the first signs of trouble.

Post mortems by definition have negative overtones and can sometimes focus only on what went wrong. Post implementation reviews should focus on positive as well as negative aspects of an individual change and should be one of the mechanisms used to define and disseminate best practice within an organization.

Change Resources

Resource constraints are common in every industry sector and it is a problem that every change manager faces. The key is to ensure that sufficiently skilled personnel are assigned that are able to make value based judgments in real time. This is easier said than done and so industry has developed a series of control measures designed to assist the weary change manager.

The change plan should clearly identify the specific skills and qualification requirements needed to complete the change. This can then be cross referenced against a documented skills matrix and the appropriate resources assigned. Unfortunately, although there are numerous vendor specific formal certification schemes within the IT space, few are stringent enough to guarantee that a person holding the certificate is actually capable of completing the tasks required. Unless such certifications are backed up be skills audits and re-certification schemes then there is a danger that the person completing the change may have minimal knowledge or understanding of the version of software etc that they are modifying ... In all such cases, it is worthwhile for an organization to define its own skills database and grade employees according to their capabilities and skills/experience to try to ensure that changes are always completed by personnel competent and capable of doing the work.

Technical competence of those implementing changes is however only one piece of the resource puzzle. The skills element of a change may require additional personal characteristics to be leveraged. For example a change completed in isolation with little access to support resources may require someone with advanced troubleshooting or problem solving skills that are not necessarily found with a technical certification. Capability assessments including personality assessments and/or psychometric testing are sometimes used in industry to determine how likely an individual is to crack under pressure or how well they could lead a change team.

Risk Management is a Way of Life

Risk management is more than a paper exercise within non-IT industries. It is the systematic identification and ranking of potential risk and the planning to either eradicate the risk or mitigate its impact in the event of it causing harm. By evaluating the likelihood of a risk impacting a change, a cost benefit analysis can be undertaken for the control measures needed to address the risk. The design and implementation of suitable control measures is built into the change plan and is an inherent part of the change itself as is the proactive monitoring of the effectiveness of controls during the change implementation itself.

Contrast this against the world of IT changes where risk management is often just a box on a form for someone to tick. Back out and contingency plans are all part of risk management but they are not the complete story. All too often such plans are hypothetical in nature and fail the first time someone attempts to implement them.

Change Management/Control

Mature change management processes focus upon process completion and adherence to process methodology rather than purely managing by objective. It is understood that the trip is just as important, sometimes more so, than the final destination if unexpected side effects and new related issues are to be avoided. Rigorous real time monitoring and progress measurement is incorporated within the process to ensure everyone involved within a change is aware of how the change is going, what actions are in process at the current time and what actions are due to follow next.

Cost control is also fundamental to ensure that change related expenses do not exceed the agreed plan without appropriate approval for over spend being obtained. By tracking all of the time spent working on a change in conjunction with the materials and service costs incurred the change manager can proactively manage their total spend to ensure that the change is completed on budget.

18.17.2 That's all Well and Good but it'll Never Work in IT . . .

There are probably people reading this document that whilst applauding and supporting the concepts outlined have no intention of trying to adopt them within their IT operation. The reasons for this will be wide and varied but may well include some of the following points as they consider such measures:

- Overly bureaucratic (i.e. Sledgehammer to crack a walnut)
- Not responsive enough to satisfy the business
- Too time consuming as it would take too long to implement changes
- Inappropriate for IT changes as they are too complex to be handled this way
- Costly and impractical

Without exception, all such objections are driven by a failure to understand the basic premise of such an approach... It is more efficient and effective to implement all changes correctly and without incident than to waste time re-engineering a solution on site, investigating and rectifying problems and resolving incidents that arise from poorly managed changes. The method to ensure such an efficient change process is to focus upon up front detailed design analysis and incident prevention, underpinning these critical process steps and objectives with tight in process control and management.

It is somewhat bizarre that those people most unwilling to invest the time and resources necessary to do something properly are the very same people they seem happy to pay again and again to redo something and fix the problems with it that arise due to its poor initial implementation.

18.17.3 Conclusion

Industry can help IT management to re-learn some valuable lessons regarding change management processes and culture. Focusing upon what, why and how ensures that all potential risk is identified and can be designed out of the change, or controlled appropriately, at the planning stage. The cautious risk averse and systematic approach to implementing changes used by organizations in highly regulated industries can be adopted within an IT environment without extending change implementation times or introducing unnecessary levels of bureaucracy and cost.

18.18 Selling the Benefits of Change

The effective change manager must be a charismatic sales person as well as being a master of planning, scheduling, communication, risk analysis etc. It is not uncommon for changes to be heavily resisted by factions within the business if they are seen to negatively impact their level of influence, importance, job security etc. The benefits of change need to be identified and promoted amongst those who are apathetic to the change as well as those that are openly against it if it is to have a chance of success.

18.18.1 The Single Biggest Obstacle to Change is People's Resistance...

Resistance to change can manifest itself in many ways. There will be those people that openly criticise a change and try to over turn the decision. There will be people who moan and bitch behind the scenes and drag team morale down in the process. There will be people who smile and nod in the right places and have no intention of assisting in any way at all. There will be people who appear to be supportive and to participate in the change but try to subvert the progress of the change behind the scenes in a vain hope that it will be canned before it is implemented.

18.18.2 Identifying WIFMs ("What's in it for me"s)

The key to making evangelists out of skeptics is to make the benefits of the change overly personal. Identify how it will make their own personal and/or work life substantially better and low and behold they will start to listen. They won't concede the point just yet, but at least you have their attention and can start to win them over ...

18.19 Automated Provisioning – Change Management Nirvana?

The seamless integration between systems automation tools and change implementation tasks is considered by some to be the ultimate goal of the change management process. Automatically implementing the change after it is approved is often seen as a way of removing the potential for human error and delay. This may be partially true, however it must be remembered that any automated process is only as good as the people defining it and the data (both meta-data and transactional information) with which it has to operate. Since the majority of input data will originate from an individual or group, all that change automation is doing is removing one of the potential sources of human error, and in doing so it is also removing one of the opportunities for someone to identify errors earlier in the process and to correct the issue (or halt the change while it is addressed) before it is placed into production. I leave it to you, the reader, to decide whether you think this is a good thing or not. Examples of opportunities for task level automation include:

- User account set up
  - Granting Network access etc
  - Email accounts
  - Adding an email account to a distribution list
  - Corporate systems
- Access rights/permissions configuration
  - Application, module and functional level
- Software distribution/installation
  - Automatic install and uninstall
  - Content delivery

- File space extensions
- Password resets
- External service subscription/activation
  - Conference call login requests etc
  - VPN access
- Dynamic infrastructure configuration
  - Virtual resource allocation
    - Increasing the processing power (e.g. CPU numbers, speeds and assigned RAM etc) available to a specific virtual server instance to take account of increases in service demand

It is strongly recommended that the approval and risk assessment activities associated with automated changes be reviewed carefully to ensure that sufficient checks and precautions are present so that the automation of the change doesn't merely result in incidents, problems or outages being introduced into the IT environment quicker or more efficiently than before.

18.20 Which Comes First; the Change or the CMDB update?

This vexing question is discussed frequently within ITIL circles and, just as its equivalent within a chicken and egg context, is largely irrelevant. Irrelevant that is, providing the supporting systems are able to reconcile the discovered view of the physical world against the approved view and to flag exceptions for investigation and follow up. Now this works fine for discoverable changes i.e. things that can be detected by discovery toolsets, but less so for discrete changes that are undiscoverable e.g. application meta data updates etc. In these cases it is important to build a verification element into the change plan and to ensure that controls such as assignee independency (i.e. a fresh pair of eyes) are employed to validate that the change has been completed.

18.21 Change Management and Release Management

Change Management processes may operate on their own or in conjunction with a Release Management process. Where release procedures are in place, it is important for all changes that require a formal release plan to coordinate closely with the release team and to include them within the planning and change design phases.

Asset Lifecycle Management/Configuration Management

Also known as asset management, asset tracking, inventory management, equipment portfolio management etc.

Asset lifecycle management is the end to end process governing the way in which assets enter and exit the organisation. Configuration Management can be thought of as a subset of this process focused upon monitoring the condition and status of an asset (or Configuration Item in ITIL-speak), and its relationships with other assets within the environment. Configuration management is best thought of as the system by which the Configuration Management Database (CMDB) is maintained and managed (either manually or with automatic data feeds).

Traditionally ITIL focused configuration management processes do not go down to the level of granularity that many other industries/disciplines expect from the term. In general it is not used to track BIOS parameters, Card dip switch settings, INI file contents and the like . . . this level of information being considered too detailed to be tracked and recorded.

19.1 Process Objectives

The asset lifecycle management process should be focused upon the following core objectives:

- Extracting the maximum return from every asset for the minimum cost
- Extending asset life
- Understanding the relationships and dependencies within the IT environment
- Improving asset reliability and availability

19.1.1 Extracting the Maximum Return from every Asset for the Minimum Cost

The primary objective of the asset management process is to ensure that all configuration items are utilised to their best advantage, and are contributing effectively to the reliable operation of the business, whilst incurring the minimum expense possible.

19.1.2 Extending Asset Life

Extending the useful working life of every asset helps to ensure that the total cost of ownership is kept as low as possible. Assuming the changes related to the re-use, re-purposing and recycling of IT equipment are managed effectively then the cost savings from the deferred asset purchases and associated depreciation and/or lease payments can be significant. Proactive upgrades using relatively inexpensive components can dramatically enhance asset performance and capacity allowing the asset to handle increases in system usage and load without requiring the purchase of expensive replacement equipment.

19.1.3 Understanding the Relationships and Dependencies within the IT Environment

A detailed picture of service relationships, dependencies and impact models can significantly assist the IT function to mitigate some of the risks associated with the implementation of changes as well as ensuring that incidents are prioritised based upon their business impact. The increasingly dynamic nature of IT environments means that such models must be flexible enough to react to changes in circumstances. Ideally these models should have the ability update themselves based upon the findings of automated discovery tools and other system feeds.

19.1.4 Improving Asset Reliability and Availability

By analysing historic failure trends the IT function can begin to predict when future failures are more likely to occur. Preventive maintenance activities and proactive component replacements can then be planned in order to reduce the likelihood of an unplanned system outage due to a hardware failure. These actions can contribute to an increase in hardware reliability and consequently improve related service availability.

19.2 Common Issues

Common issues include:

- Asset location tracking i.e. finding out where stuff is . . .
- Asset and Component theft/loss
- Local stock piles/unofficial inventories
- Maverick purchases
- Unplanned and unapproved moves and changes
- Insufficient information available to make valid Repair vs. Replace decisions
- Lease penalties for non-return of like for like equipment
- Vast array of different configurations (Platforms, vendors, standards etc)
- Inconsistencies in data collection and reporting
- Data errors and omissions
- Under utilised warranties
- Massive volume of event management data leads to analysis overload
- Lack of useful performance information to determine actual asset usage/status
- Difficulty accurately predicting asset/component failure
- Over specification of equipment
- Under utilisation of equipment
- Asset reliability
- Asset degradation/Lack of planned preventive maintenance and upgrade
- Accidental disposal of leased assets, incurring punitive fines for non-return
- Environmental impact of IT Asset usage
- Safe disposal of assets

19.3 Process Flows

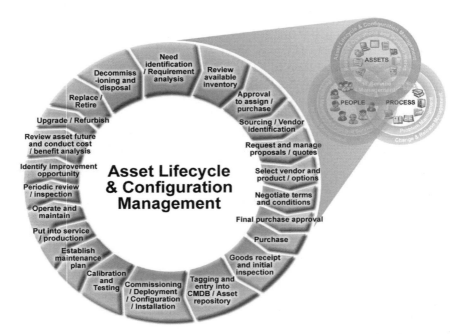

Fig. 19.1. High level overview of the asset management lifecycle

Key stages within the asset lifecycle include:

- Need identification to Purchasing
- Receipt to Installation
- Storage
- Commissioning/Deployment
- Routine usage (including ongoing maintenance)
- Inspection and test
- Periodic effectiveness review
- Modernisation/Refurbishment/Upgrade
- Reassignment/Re-purposing
- Retirement/Disposal

19.4 Key Players

Asset Users – People that physically access and use specific assets.

Asset Owners/Guardians – The persons or groups who are identified as having authority over, and responsibility for, a specific sub-set of assets and may decide how they are used i.e. their purpose, who may use them, their upgrade path and how the costs associated with them are to be distributed/allocated.

Purchasing – The procurement phase is integral to the lifecycle asset management process and requires purchasing executives to focus on more than just unit cost etc. Asset centric procurement ensures that the total cost of ownership, as well as non-financial measures are considered when selecting vendors and specific hardware models.

Configuration Specialists/Managers – Traditional configuration management roles are often little more than auditors of the current IT estate. However, in the future it is likely that the role will expand into the evaluation of technology advances, the definition of optimum configurations and the planning of how to efficiently migrate from the current state to the desired configuration.

Asset Manager – Individual with overall responsibility for the asset management process.

19.5 Process Metrics

- Number of units of specific asset classes, types by manufacturer, location, model, business unit etc
- Proportion of the IT estate that doesn't conform to optimised standard configurations

19.6 Asset Lifecycle Management and Configuration Management

Lifecycle management is the inclusive term used to describe all of the discrete activities associated with an asset during its existence. It covers every facet of the asset and every interaction it has with the wider IT infrastructure in general. Configuration management processes sit within the wider asset management process and cover the ongoing need to understand what you have out there at any given point in time. Configuration management should not be considered in isolation, but as part of a holistic asset management system focused at wringing every last drop of value out of an organisation's valuable assets.

19.7 The Configuration Item (CI)

"I am not a number - I am a free man!"

Number 6 (Patrick McGoohan), The Prisoner

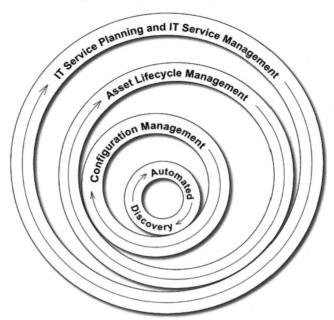

Fig. 19.2. Relationship between asset and configuration management

If one were to take ITIL literally, then pretty much everything within the IT arena from the pot plants, to the employees (not that it is always possible to tell the difference in some specialist IT departments) would be considered as separate configuration items. Whether the ITIL authors expect every member of staff to be bar coded and/or fitted with a RFID tag is unclear, however it is obvious that such broad brush statements do little to help those who actually have to implement such things.

Within this book you will find that the terms configuration item, device, asset, equipment, system, instance, hardware, application etc are used interchangeably. Such use of language should not inhibit understanding and hopefully the use of these synonyms will enable the text to flow appropriately within the relevant passages. Reaching for the trusty dictionary once more we find:

"Configuration – i) the arrangement of the parts of something, ii) (computing) the particular choice of hardware items and their interconnection that make up a particular computer system"

So extrapolating this definition we may define a configuration item as:

"Any element of a computer system and/or its underpinning infrastructure i.e. the physical and logical components that come together to deliver a capability that may or may not be leveraged as part of an IT service"

Put another way, configuration items are distinct instances of stuff. 'Stuff' being the fabric of the world within which we live, work and play.

19.7.1 Defining the Appropriate Level of Granularity

The sheer scale of the task of creating and maintaining a full and accurate record of every IT asset within the business is often daunting. For this reason, businesses often decide to initially focus upon a specific subset of their asset portfolio. The following criteria can be used to help with the selection of items to be included within this initial project:

- Categorisation based – i.e. restricting monitoring activity to configuration items of a specific asset class etc.
- Cost thresholds – i.e. the tracking of configuration items above a certain financial value
- Risk based – i.e. tracking configuration items that play a significant role within service provision and support

Although the above criteria may be used to identify an initial phase within a CMDB project, there is no reason that an organisation must ever make a record of every piece of IT equipment. Within the finance world, the term 'materiality' is used to define the relevant levels of journal entries, transactions and asset valuations that are insignificant to a company's overall financial position. Where differences in trial balances, P&L statements etc do not exceed this threshold they are ignored on the basis that it would cost too much to investigate and rectify the anomaly than to simply document the discrepancy and move on. Such an approach can also be taken with configuration items – What is the level of 'materiality' within your business for IT assets?

19.7.2 Common CI Attributes and Specific Characteristics

Having decided which configuration items to track and monitor, the next decision to be made is on the level of detail to record against each item. Tracking too much detail will incur an excessive administration burden, too little will deliver minimal benefit to the business. Everything from a teapot to an enterprise server can be adequately described by a dozen or so attributes, pretty much everything else is overkill. Twelve attributes? Surely that can't be enough? Well yes, it can - provided you don't start confusing your attributes with your relationships . . .

"Attribute – a property, quality or feature belonging to, or representative of, a thing"

The only minor problem is the fact that those twelve characteristics will be different for each different type of item. Beware of systems with hundreds of detailed attributes on a configuration item record. Such data overload will invariably be ignored by the people actually using the CMDB, as they will (rightly) assume that the quality of such data will be dubious at best, and will always fail to contain the one key piece of information that a person needs to solve a specific technical issue.

Core attributes may include:

- Classification i.e. what type of thing is it?
- Description i.e. which one of its type is it?
- Unique identifier i.e. what is the one thing that is specific to it and nothing else?
- Status i.e. what is its current circumstance/situation?
- Key milestones i.e. when did important stuff happen to it?
- Primary use/role i.e. what is it for?

These core attributes are applicable to practically all configuration items and provide the basic details that are necessary for many ITSM processes to function adequately.

19.7.3 Specific Characteristics – Getting Personal

However, sometimes it is necessary to go beyond these core attributes and add a few more pieces of data to improve the level of intelligence, or the impression of intelligence at any rate, within process automations and to aid with the decision making process undertaken by IT personnel. The following list outlines some of the most common types of asset specific data points that are used within business rules, workflow logic and process automation engines that underpin today's "expert" systems:

- Dimensions i.e. the physical size of the thing
- Capacity i.e. the amount of stuff that the thing can handle
- Configuration settings i.e. how it is currently setup
- Standards support i.e. the protocols and standards that it can use or be used by
- Versioning i.e. which versions of the thing is it and/or what version of things does the thing support, use, leverage etc
- Costs i.e. how much was it, and how much is it costing on an ongoing basis?

19.7.4 Dynamic Data Models

The pertinent details regarding a CI may vary throughout its useful life as its role and function changes. For example, someone working with a server that is used to run an application platform layer will be interested in the Physical RAM installed, the number of CPUs and their speeds etc, however over time this machine may become slow in comparison to newer models and may be repurposed (i.e. redeployed within another role) as a file server. At this point, someone working with the machine will be more interested in the number of hard disks (including their capacity, speeds and buffer sizes) as well as the number of disk controllers/IO cards installed. It is therefore necessary to be able to dynamically change the data schema for an individual asset or asset class over time in order to ensure that the current information requirements of the business can be satisfied fully.

19.7.5 Core CI Relationships

There is an old adage that one can judge the character of a man by the company that he keeps. The same can be said of a piece of IT infrastructure. The measure of the value of a CI is determined by its interactions with the rest of the environment and the various roles that it performs. Every asset can be considered to have its own unique sphere of influence. This influence will extend to, and impinge upon, a wide variety of systems and processes and may ultimately spawn numerous relationships and interdependencies with other entities within the wider business environment. Primary relationships tend to include the following items:

- Technical dependents – i.e. the physical dependencies (upstream and downstream) between the thing and other things
- Logical dependents – i.e. the processes, systems, applications and services which rely upon the thing
- Performance objectives – i.e. the levels of availability, responsiveness, output conformity etc that are defined within associated SLAs, OLAs and contracts
- People – i.e. the current owner, custodian and user(s)

19.7.6 Secondary Relationships

Secondary relationships is largely a misnomer as these links are sometimes every bit as critical to the business as those defined previously. However, such relationships are generally considered to be of less importance than the core relationships. Examples of secondary relationships would include:

- Location – i.e. where the CI can be found now, where its been and where it is yet to go
- Components – i.e. the things that go to make up the thing in question
- Contractual – i.e. what terms and conditions apply to this CI
- Organisations – i.e. the manufacturer, supplier, maintainer etc

19.7.7 Indirect Relationships

It is sometimes necessary to iterate across a relationship map, or hierarchy, in order to find things that are indirectly linked to a configuration item. Such relationship crawling enables the advanced analysis of complex problems that seem to have no linear or direct correlation between contributory factors. As well as this advanced analytical capability, indirect relationships are often used to determine implied relationships without having to incur the management overhead associated with defining and maintaining many many direct links. Examples of such indirect relationships that are often calculated automatically for use within back office processes include:

- Department/Team – i.e. the groups that the people related to it belong to
- Cost centre – i.e. the financial account codes associated with the people, location, departments or business units related to the thing

When considering the CI/Asset level data requirements for your ITSM solution, the following questions may help you to take a step back from the common crowded over laden data heavy asset related user interface and take a more pragmatic view:

- What information do you really need to record and maintain about each CI?
- Why do you believe that you need to store this information?
- Who will be using the specific information? Are they likely to trust the stored data or will they gather it afresh each time they need it?
- How will they be using the information? i.e. Is it a part of a calculation? Does it aid decision making? etc
- Who will be responsible for maintaining the data point and how will they do this?
- What is the cost/benefit of collecting and maintaining this level of data?
- How can the data be stored and/or presented to ensure those that need the information can get to it as efficiently as possible without negatively impacting those system users that do not need to know the data?

19.7.8 CI Classification

For details regarding categorisation concepts and potential pitfalls etc please refer to the Incident Management section of this book where the advantages and disadvantages of various approaches to ticket categorisation are discussed in depth. The concepts outlined there are equally applicable to configuration items as they are to incident reports – well kind of anyway.

19.7.9 CI Lifecycles/Status Models

Just as different types of incident will require a different lifecycle and process flow, so will configuration items. Software applications will have a different status model to physical hardware items such as servers, and servers will have a significantly different lifecycle to PDAs. Each element of the infrastructure will undergo its own journey through its own specific lifecycle at its own rate and may initiate smaller sub-lifecycles during specific phases of their existence as required. For example, a server may transition from procurement to commissioning to production etc and during that high level process flow may experience numerous modernisation cycles where its capabilities are reviewed and upgraded whilst it continues on its way to its ultimate decommissioning and disposal . . . Equally an asset may have sub-statuses defined to give the wider IT community additional information as to the current situation, for example an "In production" status may have sub-statuses of "Backup in progress", "Database being re-indexed", "Routine Maintenance ongoing" etc to ensure that other system users are aware of the likely cause of any short term performance degradation that is experienced.

19.7.10 Cookie Cutter Fun – The CI Catalogue

The CI catalogue enables the asset manager to define a series of templates. These templates define a standard configuration which may be requisitioned and purchased before being implemented via a change request. The purpose of such a catalogue is two fold; i) it enables the user community to see what has been approved as acceptable to purchase/deploy and ii) it enables the current infrastructure to be compared against the idealised model held within the catalogue.

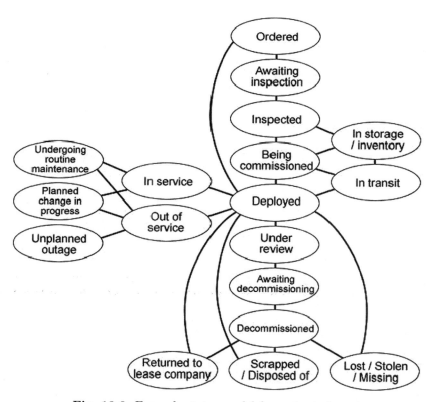

Fig. 19.3. Example status model for a physical asset

19.8 The Configuration Management Database (CMDB)

19.8.1 I am Spartacus ... no, I am Spartacus ...

Recently, every ITSM solution vendor has put their own particular spin on the CMDB story. Hailed as the 'single view of the truth', the 'heart of your ITSM system' or the 'manager of managers', CMDBs are perhaps the most over hyped aspect of the ITSM market at this time. ITIL's lack of definition of the nature and purpose of the repository goes some way to explaining why so much confusion has arisen. Object orientated architectures, cross asset class support, federated data sources, dynamic relationship models and intelligent reconciliation engines add to the marketing noise and do little to improve the comprehension of the average IT manager on the street.

19.8.2 A Filing Cabinet by any Other Name would Hold as Much!

In essence the CMDB is a repository to hold information regarding the IT environment and the ITSM processes which support it ... Countless column inches within the trade press, a plethora of vendor whitepapers and hundreds of hours of presentations at sales meetings and user forums have been used to discuss the perfect CMDB design. And yet this pre-occupation with achieving the optimum CMDB architecture is often used as an excuse for inactivity. The objective of the CMDB is to efficiently and effectively support and underpin IT service management processes – nothing more, nothing less. You could spend months defining the ultimate CMDB architecture – then again, you could start improving services instead ...

19.8.3 The Emperor's New Clothes

Just as the little boy in Hans Christian Anderson's classic fairy tale saw, the current CMDB phenomenon lacks any real substance or innovation. It is a rehash of pre-existing concepts and products to bring an illusion of freshness to the marketplace. As one sales executive remarked to me when his corporate marketing machine unleashed its own particular brand of CMDB related propaganda into the world, "Didn't we already have a CMDB?". The answer of course was "Yes", but don't let the marketing folks hear you say that! By asking this single question, this sales person had seen through the marketing hype and cut to the very heart of the matter. If only the rest of the industry could be so perceptive, then we could actually get on with having meaningful dialogues regarding the proactive improvement focused use of ITSM related data ...

Chances are, if you have implemented a software solution to manage you IT support issues, that you already have a CMDB of sorts. Whether or not it can meet your current and future business needs is another story. But you probably already have something that could lay claim to the title of "CMDB" if you wanted to.

19.8.4 Data! Data! Data Everywhere...

There are very few green field sites in the world that have no incumbent ITSM solution or IT related tools in place. There will inevitably be multiple silos of information around the organisation, holding similar data about the same configuration items. This is why CMDB vendors talk of federated data models where legacy systems retain ownership and control of their data but are leveraged by the central master CMDB to give a holistic view of the world. The theory being that the central repository does not have to replicate the data that is distributed throughout the infrastructure, instead it merely stores pointers to the remote datasets and details of how it is to be accessed (including any real time translation or transformation processes necessary). Real time transactional integration engines then connect to the remote information silos as required and return a combination of local and federated data points to the end user seamlessly when requested. Like I said, that's how it works in theory.

Perhaps the classic hypothetical example of data federation is an ITSM system which manages the day to day operation of IT assets in parallel to an ERP system which maintains the fixed asset register entries for the IT assets and calculates the depreciation, book value and residual value on a regular basis. In the event of a terminal failure of an IT asset or component, the ITSM system is able to automatically connect to the ERP system in real time and determine the current financial value of the item, the availability of appropriate spares within inventory etc, and can then use this data point as part of its "repair or replace" business logic to provide real time decision support information to the asset manager. Unfortunately, few commercial systems are at this hypothetical level yet. Federated data models are a much talked about, but seldom delivered, functionality at present. One should particularly beware of vendors claiming to deliver federated data layers which are nothing more than a series of point integrations that enable a user to drill down into an external data source from within the native user interface. Launching a hardware vendor's customer support site and navigating to the configuration of a specific piece of hardware is a good trick, but is it really a federated database?

The cynics amongst you may remember the previous marketing campaigns from the major ITSM vendors which asserted that multiple silos of information, or disconnected islands of data, were a very bad thing indeed. In fact, these vendors spent many years trying to force unnecessary data consolidation upon unwilling customers that one has to wonder if they have all recently suffered from corporate amnesia, or perhaps dementia. Maybe, but It may also be that they have all decided that if they can't beat them then they may as well join them...

19.8.5 Having One's Cake and Eating it...

"Federation – a loosely coupled collection of separate entities which co-operate with each other, and operate together, for mutual benefit whilst retaining overall control locally"

Federated data models allow incumbent legacy systems to continue to function as before, minimising the risk to the business from having to rip and replace numerous systems at once. They also enable the organisation to avoid sometimes difficult internal discussions regarding the ownership of data and who has the right to update it. Many vendors dodge the issue of maintaining federated data by stating that a request for such an update is passed to the administrator or owner of the external data for them to review and implement. In reality, such a labour intensive process is highly likely to be unworkable and so organisations are faced with a choice; either they live with data quality and data consistency issues or they invest in transactional middleware which can support the application of sufficient data validation and business logic testing to inbound update requests before automatically performing amendments to the federated repository.

19.8.6 Trusted Sources and Data Confidence

Not every piece of data relating to the same configuration item will be consistent and correct. Different data sources will have different levels of data quality, and within a specific data source the level of data quality may fluctuate significantly. Determining the level of confidence that one has in a particular subset of data from a particular data source is often a difficult task, based upon incomplete information and gut feeling rather than detailed information. The following factors should be considered when evaluating data quality:

- The age of the data i.e. the amount of time since the data was collected/last updated
- The level of control in place regarding updates i.e. data validation routines, restricted access etc
- The mechanism used to update data i.e. manual data entry versus automated data capture and input
- The number of people or systems that are permitted to update/modify the data source
- The particular competence of the system populating the repository i.e. is it a generic discovery tool reporting upon an uncommon operating system or is it a native vendor supplied tool that should have better access to the details of the O/S in question.

Unless a sufficient level of confidence in contributing data sources can be established, and defined within robust business logic and automation rules, then the reconciliation process will remain as labour intensive as before.

19.8.7 Populating the CMDB

Given that a CMDB can be thought of as a filing cabinet, unless it is filled with information it is nothing more than an empty cupboard... Now a filing cabinet that is crammed full of valuable records is one thing, but an empty one is something else completely! So it is essential to populate and maintain the CMDB. The following steps will help you on the way to making your filing cabinet potentially useful:

- Identify data sources
- Rank data sources for trustworthiness
- Determine which data points from which sources are going to be considered as the master
- Perform data cleansing (e.g. de-duplication, corrections, applying defaults for omissions etc)
- Integrate with data sources/Extract required data
- Define import methodology and schedule/frequency
- Establish and implement data validation rules
- Import data into the single system
- Consolidate data and/or reconcile multiple datasets to form master
- Define data synchronisation requirements
- Periodically refresh external data sources with master data
- Periodically re-import changes from source datasets and reconcile
- Define controls to maintain master data
- Enforce controls

19.8.8 Leveraging the CMDB – i.e. using it . . .

There is little or no point in having a CMDB unless it is used. The more the CMDB is used the greater the return will be upon the resources expended in its creation and ongoing maintenance. Every single process within the ITSM arena has the potential to touch the CMDB to access information or to use it to store information related to specific instances of the process inputs and outputs. In short, the CMDB should be an embedded part of every IT process and should be used by every member of the IT function on a daily, if not hourly basis.

Given its pivotal role it is perhaps interesting to see some vendors claiming to be able to overlay a shiny new CMDB on top of an existing brown field site. How can such an approach pay dividends unless every system used to manage ITSM processes is plumbed in to the central source of asset data? Surely the level of real time bi-directional integration required and the associated professional services effort needed to actually realise such a vision would make the payback or break even period for such a project unworkable . . . Or are such claims merely a thinly veiled disguise to hide the need to rip and replace your underlying infrastructure? Caveat emptor!

19.8.9 Common CMDB Related Issues

The following list describes some of the most common problems encountered when implementing and using a CMDB:

- Too many configuration items being tracked i.e. level of granularity being set too low
- Poor data quality (Errors, omissions, duplicates etc)
- Overly complicated data models with excessive numbers of asset classes and relationship types being modelled.
- Numerous disparate data sources with different levels of data quality
- Consolidating reports across distributed and/or object orientated data models can be troublesome
- Gaining consensus within the business regarding who should be the owner of particular elements of the data landscape

19.9 Meet the Parents ... It's all Relative

"The foot bone's connected to the leg bone,
The leg bone's connected to the knee bone,
The knee bone's connected to the thigh bone,
The thigh bone's connected to the back bone,
The back bone's connected to the neck bone,
The neck bone's connected to the head bone,
Oh, hear the word of the Lord!"

Dem Dry Bones, Unknown

Relationships are important. Relationships have always been important. Recently, IT management has become convinced, helped largely by a concerted marketing campaign from some of the biggest vendors in the business keen to foist their latest and greatest relationship visualisation toolsets upon the unsuspecting IT executive, that relationships are all important. Placing too much of an overt focus on the relationships and dependencies between the configuration items that support business services can have a detrimental effect upon the overall quality of service delivered ... How so? Concentrating solely upon mapping the relationships between physical elements of the infrastructure may leave other factors that contribute to service quality out in the cold. External factors such as network load/congestion, shared resource consumption, contention between multiple business services, demand spikes, personnel availability etc. can all have a significant impact upon service delivery and overall service quality. It is important to bear in mind that it is not necessary for a machine within a defined dependency hierarchy to go down for a service to be impaired beyond use.

Assuming that service dependency modelling is done as part of a holistic approach to IT service management then it can be a useful tool in the resolution and prevention of business impacting events and issues. When configuration item relationships are used to describe more than mere linear binary dependencies, they become even more powerful and enable the IT organisation to prioritise incidents in real time according to the risk of service interruption or impairment.

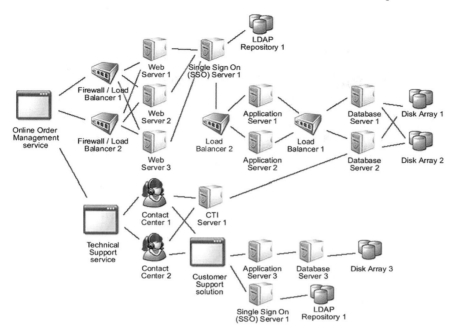

Fig. 19.4. Example relationship map for a business service

19.10 Elements of a Relationship

Naturally for a relationship to exist their must be two or more parties involved. At the lowest level this is sufficient to define a link. But in order to be truly useful, relationships must be supplemented with additional data points such as:

- Relationship type
- Ratio
- Uniqueness/Exclusivity
- Direction
- Initiation date/time
- Expiration date/time
- Impact effect
- Weighting factors
  - Parameter
  - Contribution

19.10.1 Relationship Type

A description of the nature of the relationship between the parties involved. The following list outlines an example of some relationship types that may be found within an IT environment:

Entity type 1	Relationship type	Entity type 2
Configuration Item 1	. . . is dependent upon . . .	Configuration Item 2
Configuration Item 3	. . . acts as hot backup for . . .	Configuration Item 4
Configuration Item 5	. . . forms part of . . .	Item Group 1
Individual 1	. . . is a member of . . .	Team 1
Individual 1	. . . is the primary user of . . .	Configuration Item 6
Individual 2	. . . is the manager of . . .	Team 1
Configuration Item 6	. . . is situated within . . .	Location 1
Business service 1	. . . utilises . . .	IT System 1
Individual 3	. . . is a user of . . .	Business service 1

19.10.2 Ratio

A description of how many parties of each type may be involved in the relationship. Typically, relationships are 1:1, 1:n, n:1 or n:n where n is any number. Relationships involving more than two parties may leverage the concept of a relationship group to manage the additional links or instead the relationship object itself may be capable of understanding that there are more than two elements to the relationship. An example of a 1:n relationship would be the link between a team lead and their employees (except in cases of matrix management obviously). A load balanced application dependency chain on the other hand may have multiple n:n relationships between the relevant pieces of infrastructure and software that go to make up the service.

19.10.3 Uniqueness/Exclusivity

There are two types of exclusivity that can apply to relationships:

- Mandatory uniqueness
  Some types of relationship may only be able to be made once and may never be amended. For example the relationship between a piece of hardware and its original manufacturer is an exclusive relationship – the equipment can only be initially built once and by one organisation.
- Historical exclusivity
  Some relationships may only be in place between one set of objects at any point in time. The institution of marriage is a case in point. Excluding polygamy and bigamy, a marriage must only exist between two parties at any point in time. People can be married multiple times but not during the same period.

19.10.4 Direction

Many relationship types have a directional element to them. For example "X is the manager of Y" has a very different meaning to "Y is the manager of X"! It is therefore necessary to clearly define on which side of the relationship each related entity resides if the true meaning of the link is to be preserved.

19.10.5 Initiation and Expiration Date/Time

Without start and end dates, relationships become stateless. This restricts their usefulness significantly as there is no means of identifying the scope and status of the relationship model at any point in time and prevents it being compared against historic or future versions. The completion of initiation and expiration dates for a relationship also enables one to determine whether the relationship is current (present), historic (past) or planned (future). Planned relationships should be managed carefully to ensure that the predicted link is actually in place, via suitable validation mechanisms, when it becomes due...

19.10.6 Impact Effect

The impact of one entity within a relationship upon the other entity, or entities, is something that is often over simplified. The nature of the impact of a failure on one side of a relationship may be linear, non-linear or based upon a combination of other external factors. Linear impacts describe scenarios where the impact upon the related item is directly proportional to the level of failure on the other side i.e. a system failure on one side can be considered to cause an automatic system failure on the other, similarly, a performance degradation of 50 % would be seen to reduce the performance of the related item by half. In today's IT environment it is relatively uncommon for large production systems to have single points of failure and as such a total failure of a single element of a service dependency chain is likely to have a negative impact upon service capacity and performance without taking the service down completely. Put simply, the impact effect describes how the capacity or capability of an entity is linked to the capacity or capability of those entities to which it is related.

19.10.7 Impact Calculation Rules

A series of business rules may be defined against each relationship record to define how each party to the relationship may affect the other under a series if predefined circumstances and/or scenarios. Such rules can come in a variety of forms:

- An algebraic expression to calculate the relative capacity of each entity into which characteristic data from both sides of the relationship may be substituted before performing the evaluation
- A sequential series of rules, or test cases, that have a corresponding capacity rating assigned against them in the event of a match or pass. The rules are tested in sequence until a pass is identified and the corresponding capacity value is set
- A banded approach which defined ranges within which asset parameters of characteristics may be in order to consider the asset capacity to be at a certain level

19.10.8 Weighting Factors/Contribution to Capacity

The following list describes some of the asset attributes that are sometimes used within impact effect calculations:

Parameter	Contribution to the relationship
Disk capacity	Megabytes of free space
Processing power	Total CPU capacity
Memory available	Available RAM
I/O throughput	Number of connections and speeds

19.11 Configuration Management

Configuration management in an ITIL context is all about knowing what you have and how it interacts with your other stuff. Minor details such as where it is, what it's for, how much it's costing you, who is responsible for it etc seem to be optional extras in the land of ITIL. The ITIL configuration management process covers the identification, recording, and reporting of IT components, including their versions, constituent components and relationships. The basics of configuration management, according to ITIL, are as follows:

- **Planning** - Defining the purpose, scope, objectives, policies and procedures relating to Configuration Management. *I.e. Deciding what you want to do about Configuration Management and writing it down...*
- **Identification** - Selecting and identifying the configuration structures for all the infrastructure's CIs, including their 'owner', their interrelationships and configuration documentation. It includes allocating identifiers and version numbers for CIs, labelling each item, and entering it on the Configuration Management Database (CMDB). *I.e. the Administrative task of logging asset details...*
- **Control** - Ensuring that only authorised and identifiable CIs are accepted and recorded, from receipt to disposal to ensure that no CI is added, modified, replaced or removed without appropriate controlling documentation. *I.e. Maintaining a paper trail for all activities involving assets...*
- **Status accounting** - The reporting of all current and historical data concerned with each CI throughout its life cycle e.g. tracking the status of a CI as it changes from one state to another. *I.e. Keeping records to be able to demonstrate how and when things changed...*
- **Verification and audit** - Audits to verify the physical existence of CIs and check that they are correctly recorded in the Configuration Management system. *I.e. Checking that the records are correct and recording the fact that you checked...*

Configuration management can, and should, be much more than a record keeping exercise. In addition to the traditional defined ITIL role, configuration management teams can increase their contribution, and therefore their value, to the business by beginning to perform the following tasks:

- Impartial analysis of technical advances, product innovation etc and its usefulness to the business
- Determining the number and types of standard configurations needed within the infrastructure
- Technical definition of standard configurations for the various operational areas of the business
- Analysis of the currently deployed IT environment to determine the level of compliance with the target configuration model
- Identification of the changes necessary to move existing equipment towards the relevant standard configurations
- Development of rationalisation plans and proposals
- Status reporting on progress towards a rationalised configuration model

19.12 Automated Discovery

Automated discovery tools work in a variety of ways to discover and identify IT devices (either by passively monitoring network traffic and extracting machine details from the packet headers or by proactively broadcasting messages across the network and waiting for devices to respond). Having discovered and identified a target device, the discovery tool then attempts to collect data about the system. This auditing activity can be achieved using remote commands such as MSI, SNMP etc or via a dedicated client agent application that is installed upon the discovered machine to interrogate the system configuration before transmitting the results back to a centralised server.

19.12.1 Horses for Courses . . .

There is currently a vast array of different discovery tools available within the market. Not all discovery solutions perform the same function and this should be remembered when evaluating various tools in order to ensure that one compares apples with apples. Although all discovery tools do share some common functionality it is the differences that are more interesting. The three main types of discovery tool available today include:

- Configuration discovery
- Topology discovery
- Security discovery (Systems administration/Vulnerability testing)

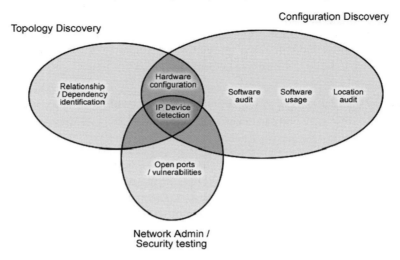

Fig. 19.5. Relationship between various automated discovery toolset types

19.12.2 Configuration Discovery

Configuration discovery tools perform periodic audits of the hardware configuration and the installed software on a target machine. The level of detail and accuracy of information gathered will vary from vendor to vendor and will often depend upon the operating system running on the target machine. For this reason it may be appropriate to use multiple discovery tools within an environment to ensure that all of the required data is captured accurately.

19.12.3 Topology Discovery

Topology discovery can be thought of as the dynamic identification of interdependencies between networked configuration items to form service relationship models and dependency hierarchies. Topology discovery tools typically use a combination of network traffic analysis and client application configuration details to build a map of data flows between solution components.

19.12.4 Security Discovery (Systems Administration/Vulnerability Testing)

Vulnerability scanners use a variety of broadcast protocols to interrogate network devices, probing for open ports and other security related issues.

19.12.5 Frequency of Discovery Sweeps/Audits

Management must temper their unnatural desire to run discovery sweeps continuously if they are to prevent them negatively impacting the wider IT environment. Realistically, the frequency of discovery sweeps should be based upon the anticipated level of change expected and may be different for different portions of the infrastructure e.g. mobile machines or machines in public places should be audited more frequently than machines located in a secure server room. When defining an audit schedule the following factors should be considered:

- Network impact (due to the associated data volume and the number of network trips) of conducting the audit (particularly for agent-less discovery solutions) and transmitting the results back to the central server
- Processing capability of the discovery server (i.e. is the server able to deal with the backlog of results that it needs to process)
- Frequency of change within the IT environment (i.e. there is little to be gained from auditing an area which changes infrequently every hour)
- The needs of the business i.e. what is the IT function trying to achieve from its automated discovery activity

19.13 Reconciliation – Turning Data into Information

"Reconcile – to make, two apparently conflicting things, compatible or consistent with each other"

Reconciliation within an IT context can be considered as the process of comparing one set of data against another in order to identify unique records (i.e. additional records or missing records), to enhance one set of data with information from another or to determine instances where the details of a record have changed (i.e. differences). In other words, IT reconciliation is a high tech game of snap where each player has literally thousands of cards . . .

It should be noted that reconciliation does not necessarily have to be between a CMDB dataset and a set of automated discovery results. Reconciliation may also be used as a part of the following scenarios:

- The enhancement of discovery data with financial and contractual information by reconciling the CMDB data with a data feed from an ERP system
- A comparison of the current situation against a predefined target situation e.g. a future 'blue sky' view of the environment after a planned major series of changes have been implemented, in order to track progress
- The assignment of person related information (e.g. user, owner, custodian etc) against hardware data e.g. by reconciling an application usage log containing IP addresses and usernames against a list of machine specific IP addresses.
- The enhancement of discovery data with additional and/or more reliable technical data points from a specialist, or niche, discovery toolset

Reconciliation is typically a two phase process involving two datasets, a master/source and a target. Initially a target record is matched against the master/source dataset to find the corresponding entry. This matching can be done using a series of ranked pairing criteria e.g. machine name, serial number, IP address, MAC address etc, or a combination of such attributes to find a unique match. The match may be done by a direct logical test or by formatting or manipulating the data (e.g. converting both sides to uppercase text to eliminate any case sensitivity issues etc) prior to performing a comparison. Where a match is found, the two records are usually tagged with a unique identifier to allow easier reconciliation on subsequent reconciliation runs. After matching, the two records will be compared and a series of logical checks performed. These checks will be defined as business rules and may compare attributes and/or associated child records e.g. installed software, associated components etc in order to identify differences or exceptions.

Reconciliation processes in all but the smallest of IT environments will involve many hundreds of thousands, if not millions, of queries, checks and validations in order to complete fully as fundamentally every row in the target dataset must be compared against every row in the master data source. Naturally, features such as data subset identification, intelligent querying logic, multi-threaded matching engines and pre-reconciliation indexing and sorting tasks may reduce this burden somewhat but the workload will remain significant. The level of processing power necessary and the timeline for a reconciliation run to finish should not be under estimated. For this reason it may be advisable to dedicate specific hardware to perform this function in order to ensure that the normal operation and usage of the system is not impaired.

19.13.1 Manual Reconciliation (Walk Around Audits, Inventory Checks, Stock Counts etc)

Even the most sophisticated automated discovery tools are unable to answer some fundamental asset related questions. Where is the asset located? Who is using the asset? What is the asset being used for? This basic information is often inaccessible to discovery tools and it is necessary to physically visit locations, interview users or custodians and record this data manually. The results of this auditing activity can then be imported into the service management solution and reconciled against the CMDB to update these CI attributes.

19.13.2 Exception Handling

Where the reconciliation process identifies discrepancies between the external results and the baseline data then an exception report is usually raised. Exceptions are typically one of three types; an expected item not being present, an unexpected item being found or a difference in an attribute or characteristic of a known item. The exception handling process then applies a series of business logic against the exception and takes the appropriate action. The level of manual intervention and the process to be followed for each exception type will vary from organisation to organisation but the following options are commonly found:

- Initiate an investigation (via an incident report)
- Initiate a change request to return the asset to the previous state
- Allocate available software inventory against the asset
- Initiate a purchase cycle to legitimately buy a software license in order to restore license compliance
- Initiate a change to remove the offending software
- Update the CMDB with the revised details
- Update the base record set with additional data points from the matched records
- Perform a virus scan to ensure that the change is benign
- Log the exceptions to a report, put the report in a file, put the file in a cabinet and forget it . . .

19.14 Asset Lifecycle Management – From Soup to Nuts . . .

"Which creature in the morning goes on four feet, at noon on two, and in the evening upon three?"

Riddle of the Sphinx, Greek Mythology

Thankfully, we don't have to undergo the trials of Oedipus to recognise the fact that the passage of time has an effect upon all things, from men to their machines, a natural lifecycle exists which governs and predicts the various stages of existence with uncanny accuracy.

A basic asset lifecycle may include the following phases:

- Need identification/Requirements analysis
- Procurement
- Goods receipt
- Inventory management
- Storage and transportation
- Commissioning
- Normal operations
- Re-definition of role and/or function
- Upgrade/Modernisation
- Decommissioning
- Disposal

19.14.1 Need Identification/Requirements Analysis

Long before the shiny new server is finally delivered; it is nothing more than a glimmer in the eye of some techno geek. But before even that, it is a set of requirements from the business. The role of the asset manager is to review these requirements against existing capabilities to determine if they can be satisfied using the current infrastructure or if new equipment is needed.

19.14.2 The Black Art of Hardware Sizing and Selection . . .

Much to the annoyance of anyone attempting to size a box for a particular business application scenario, software and hardware vendors are often vague about the likely capacity and performance characteristics of their offerings. Phrases such as "The performance metrics given are based upon laboratory conditions and should be used for indicative purposes only - actual performance may vary" are commonplace and it is left to the IT function to make an educated guess based upon past experience, peer suggestions etc . . .

Pitfalls to avoid:

- Over specification of hardware beyond all realms of reason
- The selection of new technology because it's "cool"
- Neglecting to account for peak usage spikes sufficiently
- Equipment with limited upgradeability
- Failing to include projected volume/usage growth in the design

19.14.3 Procurement

Despite IT budgets being cut significantly in recent years, total expenditure on IT hardware, software and services is still considerable in the majority of organizations. Whilst the corporate purchasing function implements formal procurement processes and procedures for larger capital purchasing decisions, routine and replacement purchases are usually left to local IT function. Unless a formal procurement system is used in conjunction with approved supplier and standard configuration listings, costs can spiral out of control and the IT estate can quickly become awash with maverick purchases of unauthorized equipment and multiple unsupported, or unsupportable, configurations.

The procurement process tracks requests from initial purchase requisitions, through formal multi-stage technical and financial approval cycles, to placing the formal purchase order with the vendor. Upon delivery, the process may govern the logging of goods receipts (including partial shipment support and returns of faulty or damaged goods etc), asset tagging and serialization, invoice matching and reconciliation against orders as well as formal cost allocation across multiple cost centres.

The procurement process should enable the IT function to:

- Leverage corporate purchasing agreements more effectively
- Rank and rate vendors according to multiple key performance indicators such as price, delivery times, quality (e.g. delivery punctuality, completeness and product conformance to requirements) and invoicing accuracy
- Significantly reduce the amount of off-contract/maverick purchasing within the business, reducing business risk and improving the quality of products and services procured
- Negotiate improved rates and terms with external suppliers based upon actual vendor usage and performance data
- Automate routine purchase requests based upon inventory usage and other external events to facilitate just in time equipment and material sourcing

19.14.4 Goods Receipt

Typically IT asset management systems fall short at the critical stage of the process where the wheels touch the road i.e. when the goods are actually received. Goods receipt procedures should be implemented in order to ensure that the business receives what it has paid for, at the quality it expects and that it is recorded and entered into the configuration management database (CMDB) correctly. The goods receipt process must be flexible enough to handle the following use cases/scenarios; complete shipments, partial receipt, multi stage receipt cycles (i.e. including the use of inspection and holding areas etc), inbound inspection, tagging and return processes.

19.14.5 Inventory Management

Effective stock control and inventory management is an essential element of a holistic lifecycle asset management system. Inventory systems provide asset managers with a detailed picture of asset allocation and geographical/operational distribution. This ensures that the utilization of valuable IT assets can be maintained through proactive dynamic assignment according to business needs and equipment availability. Only then can an appropriate return on investment on an asset by asset basis be assured, guaranteeing the lowest possible total cost of ownership and maximizing the return to the business. Implementing robust inventory management procedures will help the IT function to:

- Minimize unnecessary expenditure on costly IT assets that already exist within the organization
- Reuse/Re-issue surplus and returned equipment before it becomes obsolete
- Reduce stock levels and associated storage costs etc to the minimum needed to provide the required level of service to the business

- Track the location and condition of mission critical components of the IT infrastructure
- Maintain adequate stock levels of consumables and commonly requested spare parts to minimize service down time in the event of a failure etc
- Plan and predict asset usage (including the reservation of equipment) against specific projects and/or cost centres to ensure that equipment utilization is maintained and excessive overhead avoided
- Control the issue and return of all assets effectively (including loan equipment)
- Avoid incurring storage costs for excessive and/or obsolete inventory items

19.14.6 Storage and Transportation

We are fortunate that most IT equipment and related consumables are non-perishable. With perhaps the exception of printer cartridges and screen wipes, IT equipment can be left on the storeroom shelf for an indefinite period and there will be a reasonable chance that, when sometime in the future we pull it down and blow the dust off it, that it may still actually work. That is, until we subject it to the rough and tumble of the delivery man... Technology advances have meant that it is no longer necessary to 'park' hard drives before transportation but the opportunity for fatal damage still remains. Most people have experienced a dead on arrival (DOA) delivery and the corresponding frustration and delay. Careful packing helps but it is somewhat inevitable that a small percentage of equipment will not be working when it arrives at its final destination.

19.14.7 Commissioning

Commissioning is the process of configuring a new piece of equipment in order to make it usable and useful to the business. Unless a high end server is commissioned correctly it may become little more than a very expensive heater contributing to nothing more than the ambient temperature in the machine room. Commissioning typically includes; software installation, configuration of the environment, installation of additional hardware components, driver setup, performance tuning, load testing, application of security policies etc

19.14.8 Normal Operations

Under normal operating conditions with all IT equipment working satisfactorily, you could be mistaken for thinking that the life of a configuration manager would be nice and quiet. In fact, there are several ongoing activities that must be attended to, including:

- Performance monitoring
- Utilisation measurement
- Rationalisation planning
- Migration planning

19.14.9 Performance Monitoring

Configuration managers are often charged to keep a watching brief on the day to day performance of the configuration items under their control. Whether this be through the use of end to end transaction monitoring tools or server based statistics, the objective of the exercise is to identify the first signs of a downward trend in performance and to initiate proactive actions to prevent users being affected.

19.14.10 Utilisation Measurement

Understanding the level, frequency and profile of usage a particular asset experiences on an ongoing basis helps the configuration manager to plan for demand expansion and/or to investigate the possibility of sharing the resources of the asset with another process, service, function or role. The goal for every piece of equipment is to make it as utilised as possible, thereby increasing the level of return from it, without jeopardising overall system integrity or reliability.

19.14.11 Rationalisation Planning

Just as every procurement professional is continually looking to reduce the number of suppliers used by an organisation, progressive asset or configuration managers will continually attempt to reduce the inherent complexity of their IT infrastructure by reducing the number of hardware and software vendors, platforms, architectures and technologies deployed throughout the environment.

19.14.12 Migration Planning

It is rarely practical to implement significant infrastructure changes in one step. The configuration management team will often need to work closely with change managers to help determine the current status of major changes. By comparing "as is" snapshots of the environment against "as should be" descriptions, deltas can be identified and the relevant plans made to migrate from the current situation to the desired state.

19.15 Preventive Maintenance

Note: Also known as Routine operations or IT operations.

Preventive maintenance activity is aimed at minimising the likelihood of service impacting events by proactively performing routine operations tasks necessary to prevent system issues on a periodic or condition based schedule. IT operations can be thought of as performing the equivalent role of a maintenance team e.g. checking oil levels, greasing nipples, tolerance checking etc within a manufacturing environment. I.e. the preventive actions necessary to keep the IT machine ticking over and to prevent performance significantly degrading due to normal wear and tear. . .

19.15.1 Condition Based Scheduling

With condition based scheduling the period between maintenance tasks is not fixed. Instead, pre-defined characteristics or attributes of the asset are monitored to determine when the next maintenance activity is required, just as a car service becomes due after a specific number of miles have been completed. IT related maintenance conditions may include the number of

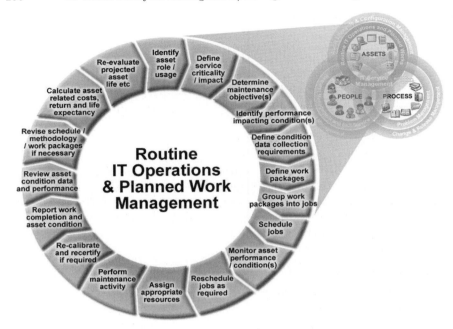

Fig. 19.6. High level process overview for preventive maintenance

hours of continuous running, number of transactions completed, amount of file defragmentation detected, volume of data stored etc.

The following list of questions will help identify the preventive maintenance requirements of configuration items within the environment:

- Have proactive maintenance tasks been identified for all business critical IT assets?
- Has risk assessment identified potential risks that need to be controlled proactively?
- Is condition based or periodic task scheduling being used?
- If condition based scheduling is selected, how is the condition data being collected and analysed in order to determine when the preventive action is required?
- Is the frequency of preventive tasks optimised to deliver maximum benefit for minimum cost?
- How often is the effectiveness of the preventive maintenance plan reviewed and amendments made?
- Is the successful completion of preventive maintenance tasks tracked and monitored?

19.15.2 A Manager of Managers...

The trouble with much of the routine activity that goes on within an IT department is that no-one knows what the other guy is doing. In fact it is very common for no single person to have a complete picture of all that is in process. Niche tools have evolved over time to simplify the performance of routine tasks. However none of these tools, with perhaps the notable exception of elements of the Microsoft Operations Management (MOM) framework which is slowly starting to provide some level of cross-discipline visibility, allow users to have a holistic view of the IT operations activity.

If a single view of the planned routine operations could be generated it would help with many ITSM processes including change scheduling, impact analysis and incident diagnosis to name just a few. Such a holistic manager of managers would need to tap into the scheduling engines of the following toolsets in order to generate a picture of planned activity on an asset by asset and service by service basis:

- Patch application
  - Package distribution, automated installations etc
- Database maintenance
  - Archiving, statistic recalculation etc
- Vulnerability testing – sweeps
- Antivirus software – scheduled low level scans
- Automated discovery toolsets - audits
- File level operations/Storage management
  - Backups, disk defragmentation etc
- Batch transfers/ETL processes
  - Data synchronisation, reconciliation etc
- Report generation/Bulk print runs
- Back office transaction runs
  - e.g. Billing calculations etc
- Document management tools/Search engines
  - Content crawling, index generation etc

19.16 Ongoing Viability Assessment

Note: Sometimes referred to as an asset effectiveness audit.

A viability assessment can be considered as a periodic review of key infrastructure components (including hardware, software and systems) to determine when they have reached the end of their useful life and how to make best use of them going forward. Such an assessment may be completed individually on an asset by asset basis or on a group of similar assets. The key question to be answered by the assessment is "Is it worthwhile continuing to use and maintain the asset in its current role?"

In order to come to a conclusion the following factors should be considered and weighed up against each other before making a final recommendation:

- Cost/benefit analysis
  - Maintenance contracts
  - Remaining leasing costs
  - Preventive maintenance costs
  - Power consumption (direct and indirect)
- Availability of suitable spare parts
- Availability of required technical knowledge/skills to be able to support the asset effectively
- Recent reliability and availability metrics
- Current performance and capacity
- Upgrade potential
- Physical size (i.e. machine room space required)
- Power consumption/Heat generation contribution
- Risks associated with changing the current configuration

Recommendations regarding the asset may include:

- Continue using it within its current role
- Downgrade its role to less business critical functions
- Upgrade the asset to increase its capacity and/or performance
- Replace the asset with a more up to date alternative
- Adjust its preventive maintenance plan to improve reliability etc

It must be remembered that it is relatively common for seemingly obsolete and redundant hardware to be used beyond its recommended life for mission critical functions within even the largest organisations due to the perceived risks associated with changing. The old adage "If it ain't broke, don't fix it" is often cited as a reason for such technological inertia when in fact it is more likely to be due to the fear of the effects of change . . .

19.16.1 Estimating the Projected Remaining Useful Life

The remaining useful life of a configuration item can be determined by comparing the current utilisation and spare capacity of the asset against the projected future load required by the business. Useful life estimations should take account of the potential to increase capacity (be that processing power or storage capacity) through upgrade as well as the potential to use the asset within different, less demanding, roles or functions in the future.

19.16.2 Defining an Upgrade Path

Before deciding to upgrade a configuration item, the following questions should be considered and reviewed:

- Is it technically possible to upgrade the asset?
- Is it economically viable (based upon cost benefit analysis)?
- For how long is it anticipated that the upgrade will extend the useful life of the asset?
- What are the risks associated with performing the upgrade?

19.17 Stop the Upgrade Merry go Round – I Want to Get Off!

There is no rule written in stone that states that you must always upgrade applications to the latest and greatest release. Fortunately, IT management is less prone to jump in feet first at the request of the software vendors than it once was and the pain associated with the early adoption of new releases is less of an issue than it used to be. Every upgrade should be reviewed in terms of the anticipated business benefit versus the likely risk associated with the implementation of the upgrade.

19.18 Decommissioning

When IT budgets were plentiful, decommissioning was often limited to putting a screwdriver through a disk drive before throwing the equipment into a skip. Now those days of plenty are long gone and organisations can no longer be as wasteful with their valuable IT assets as perhaps they once were. Embarrassing high profile cases of corporate data loss have also meant that businesses now understand the need to ensure that sensitive information is diligently removed from all machines before they finally leave the organisation.

The decommissioning process should address the following questions:

- Have all transferable software licenses been returned to the organisation's software pool (after uninstalling them from the machine to be disposed of)?
- Is it worthwhile keeping key hardware components as spares for remaining equipment e.g. power supplies, fans, memory etc?
- Have all salvageable components been removed and entered into inventory?
- Has all useful data been backed up and transferred onto the replacement system?
- Have security policies regarding data cleansing been implemented fully?

19.18.1 Lease Returns

Where the equipment that is being decommissioned if due to be returned to the supplier under the terms of a lease agreement it is important to ensure that it is in as near a comparable configuration to its original condition as possible. The terms and conditions or lease contracts vary considerably and therefore it is important that the specific requirements of the agreement are adhered to if punitive penalties are to be avoided. It is fair to say that many leasing companies anticipate significant levels of defaulting on equipment returns and sometimes inflate penalty fines to recover monies they were unable to realise when the lease contract was signed. Seemingly attractive lease rates may have a nasty sting in the tail for the unwary IT manager and it is therefore critical that full end to end asset lifecycle management practices are implemented effectively.

19.18.2 End of Life Planning

It is rarely practical to simply turn off the tap when it comes to removing or replacing key IT infrastructure components. End of life planning should address issues such as user lock outs, cut over activities, parallel running, data backups, production data migration, network traffic redirection, IP address reassignment, license reclamation and support contract cancellation etc.

19.19 Cradle to Grave is no Longer Enough...

19.19.1 Environmental Impact and Safe Disposal

Environmental regulations, such as the Waste Electrical and Electronic Equipment (WEEE) regulations in the UK, are becoming more and more common around the world and are beginning to require businesses to take a more responsible approach to the disposal of IT hardware than previously. Some of the hazardous material lurking within your desktop PC:

- Antimony trioxide – Used as flame retardant within desktop cases
- Arsenic – Found within older Cathode Ray Tubes (CRT) inside aging monitors
- Cadmium – Used in circuit boards and semiconductors
- Chromium – Used in steel as corrosion protection
- Cobalt – Found in steel carcasses for structure and magnetivity
- Lead – Found within Cathode Ray Tubes (CRT) inside monitors
- Mercury – Used within switches and housings
- Polybrominated flame retardants – Found in plastic casings, cables and circuit boards
- Selenium – Found in circuit boards as power supply rectifier

19.20 RFID and Asset Management

Radio Frequency Identification (RFID) technology is slowly making its way from the lab into the main stream. Major retailers are beginning to use it in production environments as a tracking mechanism for pallets of goods etc within warehouse operations and the level of usage of the technology will only increase going forward. RFID as a technology has a variety of uses including:

- Asset identification i.e. barcode replacement
- Location tracking
  - Passive monitoring (short range fixed readers)
  - Active monitoring (RFID radar (currently limited to approximately 100 meters in range))
- Localised data storage i.e. tag based data stores
  - Equivalent of a log book to record servicing activity etc.
  - Store of information regarding current configuration settings etc.

RFID is sometimes hailed as the magic pill to cure all of asset management's ills. And yet it is often used a nothing more than a high tech replacement for printed barcodes. Such implementations gain little from the use of RFID and one has to wonder what benefits the businesses implementing RFID in such a manner are expecting to realise.

Asset location detection using RFID is not yet capable of finding the position of an asset to the level of accuracy of RTLS or GPS, nor does it have the range of other real time locationing systems. Passive readers can be effective at tracking asset movements from room to room or building to building but fail miserably to identify machines being moved from rack to rack, or blades moving from slot to slot within a server room. Since physical security measures and network discovery tools are reasonably effective at identifying/preventing unauthorised server moves between distinct locations, RFID currently occupies a "nice to have" spot within the minds of IT executives but lacks sufficient compulsive arguments to make it a "must buy" at present.

Given that using RFID as an asset identification tool only is a waste (as bar-coding gives the same functionality with less cost and all that is saved over manual operations is the time taken to key in a serial number or unique identifier and the potential for human error that is associated with this). It remains to be seen how this technology will be applied more fully within the IT asset management space...

19.21 Linear Assets and IT

Linear assets differ from traditional discrete assets in so far as they are continuous in nature. This means that it is often necessary to use spatial data to reference a specific element or segment of a connected system rather than a unique identifier. Examples of linear assets within an IT context include; network segments, cable runs, virtual environments spread across multiple pieces of physical hardware, distributed application architectures, load balanced web farms etc

19.22 Don't Forget to Play "NICE"ly Children

In the future, configuration management teams will operate in a manner similar to the UK's National Institute for Clinical Excellence (NICE) – This government body reviews the effectiveness and economic viability of clinical treatments for medical conditions and determines which treatments are to be provided free of charge to the UK population under the auspices of the National Health Service (NHS). The body comprises of numerous experts from all fields of the health care profession who meet to review the relative merits of one treatment against another. The purpose of the organisation is help ensure that the NHS's scarce financial resources are used effectively and that the general population derives the maximum benefit possible from the expenditure.

Future configuration teams will spend their time reviewing systems and solutions currently deployed/in use, identifying best practice and approving/authorizing hardware and software configurations for the organisation as well as determining the appropriate availability/distribution strategies. This sort of approach will reduce duplication of effort, diverging technology streams etc and will open the door to improved purchasing leverage as well as increases in reclamation and recycling processes.

Software License Management

Also known as software license management, compliance management, software asset management.

20.1 A Common Understanding of Software License Management

Software License Management is a relatively new discipline within the IT Service Management arena and as such it has yet to be fully embraced by the analyst community or general marketplace. This lack of a common vocabulary and/or definition of the elements of a holistic License Compliance strategy mean that it is essential to come to a clear understanding of what is included within the scope of a Software License Management solution.

Software License Management can be thought of as the combination of a set of IT Service Management tools and disciplines/processes to ensure that an organization is in complete control of the usage (including the re-use (re-cycling) and re-deployment), distribution and disposal of its valuable software assets. It should be noted that Software License Compliance is not solely a technical issue and will require significant investment in business processes and procedures that underpin a corporate wide software usage policy if such an initiative is to be successful.

True Software License Management can be achieved through the careful and focused implementation of a combination of ITIL disciplines. Many vendors have created a stand alone bundle of functionality and labelled it as a dedicated software management solution. Instead it is recommend that you, take time to step back and review the way in which software is used, managed and tracked from a process perspective within today's modern IT environment. There are numerous touch points that such a solution will have within an organization and ensured that your IT service management solution has the required functionality and flexibility to meet the specific needs of your business.

20.1.1 Potential Benefits of Effective Software License Management

The potential benefits of implementing an effective Software License Management policy and approach can be very significant. These benefits are not only realized financially (although this is where the primary drivers predominantly come from) but also through improvements to the robustness and resilience of the entire IT infrastructure. The non-exhaustive list below highlights many of the key areas where benefits can be achieved.

- Prevent the illegal use of software
    - Avoidance of non-compliance fines and associated negative publicity
    - Identify the level of corporate exposure due to pre-existing unapproved software usage
- Reduce software purchase costs
    - Eliminate over-buying
    - Avoid costly enterprise wide corporate agreements
    - Realize bulk purchasing discounts
    - Deploy only that software that is actually required
    - Downgrade casual users to standard versions and/or freeware viewers
- Leverage existing software license investments more effectively
    - Recycle previously purchased software internally
    - Redeploy installed, but unused, software to users that need it
- Reduce software maintenance costs
    - Only pay maintenance on software that is actually in use
- Improved purchasing control
    - Negotiate improved terms and conditions with software vendors at initial purchase and subsequent contract renewal
    - Leverage existing corporate purchasing agreements to their best effect
    - Eliminate maverick buying
- Identify potential security risks
    - E.g. Discovery of peer to peer file sharing systems that could expose sensitive and/or proprietary data
- Reduce/Mitigate the risks associated with implementing planned changes
- Reduce the number of incidents associated with unapproved software conflicts
- Increase the supportability of the environment
- Improved internal cost allocation based upon actual usage

20.1.2 Challenges Associated with Software License Management

Unfortunately, Software License Management is not without its challenges. The following listing outlines some of the more common reasons for under performance or project failure.

- Vast array of licensing models and definitions
  - Named users, Capacity based licensing, Concurrent usage models, Modular based access rights etc
- Identification of installed software is not yet an exact science
  - System fingerprinting and file comparisons are not fool proof
- Use of browsers/generic clients to access systems
  - Usage is connection based rather than dependant upon physically installed files/applications
- Multiplexing systems (I.e. gateways, consolidation tools etc)
  - End to end process integrations may include multiple software license usage steps
  - System to system touch points may not be clearly visible
- Closing the stable door after the horse has bolted
  - License agreements may state that simply installing the software is sufficient to be responsible for licensing
- Insufficient leverage of the Software Asset Repository by the rest of the business
- Audit frequency and coverage for mobile workers and/or disconnected systems
- Practicality of locking down user environments to prevent unapproved software installation
- User resistance to policy enforcement
- Entitlement chains – maintaining proof of ownership chains etc.

The use of a strong software asset management solution will go some way to mitigating these factors. However, it should be recognized that a successful implementation incorporates far more than merely tool selection and implementation. It is necessary for the software license usage policy to have high level sponsorship and for this commitment to be communicated to all levels of the organization.

20.2 Steps to Software License Management

Before embarking upon a software license management project it is essential to look beyond the tool selection process and understand the many other external factors that contribute to the success or otherwise of such an initiative. The following task list outlines some of the main steps necessary to successfully implement such a project.

- Define and agree software usage policy
  - Senior Management sponsorship
  - Clearly defined responsibilities/accountability
- Identify procedures and processes necessary to support the policy
- Develop and publish procedures/processes
  - Initial promotional campaign
  - Part of new starter induction program
  - Ongoing awareness program/reminders
- Define purchasing policy related to software assets
- Identify approved software vendors and software items that may be purchased
  - Various levels of requirement/capability will need to be defined
  - Define where standard, professional and enterprise versions of software are appropriate to be deployed
  - Define alternative cost effective products (including freeware) for common requests
- Identify IT Service Management tools needed to support procedures, processes and policy
- Embed/Model defined processes model standard management tools
- Identify/select and deploy Software Asset Discovery and Usage Monitoring tool(s)
- Define frequency for automated discovery/audits
  - Dependent upon the way in which software is utilized/deployed
  - Different areas/software types will have different audit frequencies
- Collate/Import data into central Software Asset Repository
- Review existing purchasing data to determine what has been purchased centrally/legitimately
  - Approved purchase cycles/central rollouts
  - Locally sourced purchases
  - Software that has been purchased as an individual expense item
- Review existing repositories of software license information
- Review terms and conditions of known software purchases to identify usage models and licensing restrictions
- Import/Load data into the central Software Asset Repository
- Reconcile known/authorized software assets against discovered software instances
- Implement a rogue software license amnesty to try and obtain proof of purchase for locally sourced licensing
- Identify corrective/remedial actions and define compliance plan
- Implement corrective actions
  - License purchases
  - Software removal
  - Provision of alternative software

- Educate the user population about the software usage policy
- Achieve initial Software License Compliance state
- Proactively monitor effectiveness of policy at predefined frequencies
- Identify errors/omissions and breaches of the software license management policy
- Implement remedial actions as required
  - User education/training
  - Disciplinary action
  - Machine lock downs
  - License purchases
  - Software removal
  - Provision of alternative software
- Report level of compliance to senior management
- Conduct periodic review of discovery data and identify trends within software usage/deployment
- Maintain communication channels/Reinforce messaging/Re-educate user base as required
- Feed software usage/deployment data into the purchasing cycle for (re)negotiating enterprise level agreements with software vendors
- Feed software usage/deployment data into the review cycle for the design of standard system configurations/builds
  - Automatic provision of freeware file viewers etc to minimize demand for licensed software
  - Identification of freeware alternatives to widely used licensed software
  - Definition of version by version user requirements and user profiles to prevent over spend on professional or deluxe editions of licensed software
- Implement software reclamation procedures as part of standard IT asset disposal process
  - Identification of unused old (defunct) versions of software that can be upgraded to the latest/required version of the software
  - Identification of unused comparable products that can be used as part of vendor led software replacement/displacement programs

20.3 Elements of a Software License Management Solution

As discussed previously, a successful solution will consist of several elements all working together to support the defined business processes and underpinning policy. These elements will include:

- Discovery tool(s)
  - Physical Inventory

- o Software installation
- o Software usage/utilisation

Tools designed to identify the physical assets that are connected to an organization's network at any point in time. In addition to determining what hardware is actually out there (and potentially where it is physically located) the discovery solution will also determine what logical software assets are installed and how often they are used (Note: The level of information associated with software license usage will vary greatly depending upon which discovery tool is used and should be treated as nothing more than an indicative guide).

- Usage monitoring tool(s)
  - o Client based activity monitoring
  - o Server based usage monitoring
  - o Web application usage tracking
  - o ERP license usage monitoring

Tools designed to track the actual level of usage associated with individual software instances and/or user accounts (for client server based solutions). Advanced solutions may also be able to identify user actions/usage profiles that indicate specific modular level license usage for large client server implementations.

- Software Asset Repository

A central repository for all software related information. Typically this will form an integral or federated part of the overall CMDB but may be a standalone store for organizations that have not yet consolidated their IT Service Management infrastructure.

- Integrations

  - o Financial systems
  - o HR systems
  - o Change and Release Management system
  - o Incident/Problem Management system

The ability to integrate seamlessly with external systems is a critical success factor for the implementation of a Software License Management solution. Unless there is a free flowing data stream between the component parts of the solution the system will become out of date and will not realize the return on investment that it should.

- Software Deployment tool(s)

Automated deployment and installation of requested software using subscription based client agents and a centralized hub based distribution network enable the automation of the provisioning piece of the software license management story.

- Entitlement management

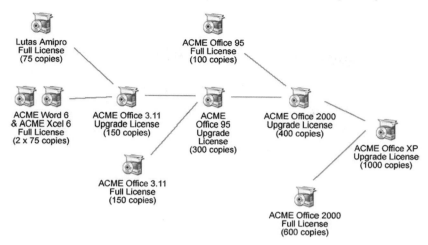

Fig. 20.1. An example software license entitlement chain

The ability to trace back through the historic procurement chain to identify which upgrade licenses depend upon which upgrade licenses etc right back to an originating standard license. The entitlement chain should be locked to prevent multiple licenses being based upon a single originating license if true license compliance is to be maintained.

20.4 Features and Functionality of an Effective Software Asset Repository

In order to implement the defined software license management policy the supporting tools need to be flexible and comprehensive enough to model a wide variety of license contracts in order to ensure compliance and provide the capabilities necessary to proactively manage the deployed software portfolio. The Software Asset Repository will consist of the following components and/or functionalities:

• License lifecycle support

The ability to track and manage software license instances through the purchase requisition phase, procurement, stock item, deployment/installation, usage, return to inventory, redeployment, retirement, upgrade etc. The system should be capable of keeping an audit trail for each deployed item of software (where required by the business) in order to demonstrate compliance and good corporate governance.

• Contract management

Tracking and management of contract associated costs (including cost allocations to financial centers etc) and terms and conditions of usage. The contracts system acts as the fundamental point of reference for all users of the system and defines the duration of the contract, the people involved as well as proactively managing the re-negotiation process giving the purchasing function the information they need to be able to agree the best possible commercial terms.

- Discovered vs. Authorized reconciliation

The reconciliation process is intended to enable the system to identify discrepancies between actual software physically deployed within the environment and the known/approved software recorded within the configuration management database (CMDB). Where discrepancies are identified, workflow should route cases to the relevant areas to allow a formal investigation to be undertaken (if required) and the relevant remedial action to be implemented.

- Proactive management of licenses (e.g. Renewal notifications etc)

The system should monitor time based metrics associated with contracts (and associated contract hierarchies) and proactively alert defined roles within the organization where notification thresholds are met so that they can initiate the appropriate actions to ensure that contracts are managed in a timely manner.

- Inventory management

  o Virtual storerooms/stockrooms for unused software licenses
  o Management of issues and transfers etc
  o Automatic re-order levels

A fully featured stock management solution is required to handle the volume and complexity of software license transactions commonly implemented. The system should be capable of handling upgrades, software bundles (productivity suites etc), exchanges and re-issues.

- Cost tracking/cross-charges/charge backs

The primary driver for the majority of software license management initiatives is financial. Because of this it is critical that any solution selected to support such an initiative be capable of tracking and allocating costs accurately in accordance with the organizations financial system and policies.

- Request management and self service

An investment in a central software asset repository will not deliver the level of returns expected unless it is being continuously used and updated. Request management functionality enables employees to request software and have those requests reviewed, approved and managed in a consistent and efficient manner.

- Purchasing

  o Purchase requisitions (including approvals etc)
  o Purchase order integration
  o E-commerce integration
  o Receipt handling

- Reporting solution

  o Compliance/Status reporting
  o Exception reports
  o Trend analysis

The ability to extract useful information from the system is a critical factor. It is essential that the solution support open standards for data mining and provide the capability to deploy management reports to the web to allow access from anywhere at any time.

- Integrations with:

  o Financial systems
  o HR systems
  o Change and Release Management system
  o Incident/Problem Management system

20.5 To Serialize or not to Serialize ...

One of the major areas of confusion regarding software license management revolves around how logical instances of software assets are modeled/represented and handled within the management solution. There are no right and wrong answers to this question and because of this many implementation projects waste considerable amounts of time and resource pondering this very point.

As there are numerous options available to system administrators regarding how they will treat, track and manage individual instances of software within their organization, it is imperative that they carefully evaluate each carefully before determine the most appropriate course of action. These software modeling methods typically include:

- Software instances treated as an inventory item
- Software instances treated as a serialized asset
- A hybrid solution where software can be treated as both an inventory item or as a serialized asset

The following section will outline the advantages and disadvantages of these various approaches.

20.5.1 Software Instances Treated as an Inventory Item

In this scenario a central inventory item is created for each type of software (e.g. MS Office 2003), these inventory items are held within a virtual storeroom, or network of virtual storerooms depending upon the accounting needs of the organisation. This inventory item is then available to be reserved, transferred and logged against, or associated with, physical assets (i.e. computer equipment) using traditional inventory and storeroom management functionalities. In many ways the software instance is treated like an attribute of the asset upon which it is installed, this allows management reporting to identify how many instances are deployed and how many are held in stock thereby being able to demonstrate compliance.

This methodology is particularly useful, and appropriate, for software types that are issued to the majority of IT assets e.g. operating systems, office automation suites, core internal applications etc. It provides a means to manage software deployments without requiring an excessive amount of management overhead in order to maintain and track compliance. In addition to these benefits, the software license management function are able to take advantage or traditional inventory management functionality such as integrations with purchase requisitioning processes, automatic reorder levels, stock reservation systems etc.

It doesn't however typically give organizations the level of granularity necessary to proactively track and manage software usage and/or utilization that is required for high value software instances (e.g. High-end Drafting/CAD solutions etc). Where an organisation is keen to ensure that its high value software assets are being utilized effectively, it is necessary to be able to proactively monitor their usage and subsequently move software assets from machine to machine and user to user as the needs of the business dictates.

20.5.2 Software Instances Treated as a Serialized Asset

In this scenario, individual instances of software are created as logical assets within the configuration management database (CMDB) and are typically uniquely identified using their license key and/or a combination of the original purchase order reference and serial number. These assets can then be related to physical assets (i.e. computer equipment) in a hierarchical structure in order to clearly identify where the software is installed at any point in time. When not in use these logical software assets can be transferred to virtual software storerooms and held in stock until such time that they are deployed once again.

There is a significantly greater level of system administration associated with this approach as each individual instance record must be uniquely identified and assigned. This added burden is offset by the enriched functionality available when treating a single software instance as a fully fledged asset. Software assets can be traced from machine to machine and user to user easily.

Companies can easily demonstrate exactly who was using the software at any given point in time and can therefore demonstrate license compliance more effectively. But where this approach really starts to pay dividends is in cases where an organization want to maintain a restricted pool of high value software assets that are utilized as required (e.g. within an outsourcing or project orientated environment). Such a model requires total control of assets to prevent duplicated installation and parallel usage if license compliance is to be assured.

20.5.3 Hybrid Solution where Software is Treated as either an Inventory Item or a Serialized Asset

Offering the best of both worlds it is recommended to use the most appropriate methodology to the type of software being managed. Doing this allows you to easily manage large software roll outs (e.g. such as operating systems etc) whilst maintaining the level of control necessary for high value software assets.

21

Service Level Management

Proactive monitoring of IT service delivery to ensure previously agreed targets for responsiveness, quality and availability are consistently met.

As business begins looking upon IT as a service provider more and more, it becomes essential that the relative level of goodness, or quality, of that service be clearly understood. If IT services are to be managed effectively it is vital that unambiguous measures be implemented to verify that performance is within previously agreed tolerances and that where delivery fails to meet defined user expectations that appropriate remedial actions be taken to restore and compensate. Threats from outsourcing and internal competition between service delivery groups mean that it is imperative the IT function not only delivers value, but more importantly is seen to deliver value to business.

Service Level Management processes enable IT organizations to clearly define their service offerings and service characteristics in order to ensure that requesters understand what is on offer and what will be delivered as well as understanding the minimum input requirements placed upon themselves. By empowering service delivery managers to establish useful business focused service delivery metrics that define and measure the actual quality of service provided as well as the time taken to deliver those services, they can begin managing IT for the benefit of the organisation in general.

21.1 Process Objectives

The service level management process should be focused upon the following core objectives:

- Ensure service delivery performance is within defined and agreed limits
- Prevention of SLA breaches
- Identification and monitoring of Key Performance Indicators
- Provision of information to the service design function to enable service quality to be improved

21.1.1 Ensure Service Delivery Performance is within Defined and Agreed Limits

The primary goal of the service level management process is to help assure user satisfaction by ensuring that IT services are consistently delivered in accordance with the agreed terms and conditions as described within the service definition or service catalogue. It should be noted that the consistent delivery of services within agreed service levels does not guarantee end user satisfaction. There may be cases where the user population is unhappy with the service levels that have been agreed between their management team and the IT function and such instances should be referred back to the service delivery management team and/or process owners for them to communicate these concerns with the business. Where appropriate, the agreed service levels can then be redefined and an increased series of service level objectives can be implemented.

21.1.2 Prevention of SLA Breaches

By proactively identifying instances where a SLA breach is likely ahead of time, the IT service management system allows IT management to take the necessary precautions and preventive actions (e.g. assignment of additional resources, escalation to a team with additional technical skills, implementation of detailed progress monitoring controls etc) in order to avoid a SLA target being missed. Care should be taken that the activities initiated to prevent a SLA breach do not have a detrimental effect upon any other services and service levels.

21.1.3 Identification and Monitoring of Key Performance Indicators (KPIs)

Key Performance Indicators help an organisation define and measure progress toward organisational goals. Once an organisation has analyzed its mission, identified all its stakeholders, and defined its goals, it needs a way to measure progress toward those goals. Key Performance Indicators are those measurements. KPIs are quantifiable measurements that reflect the critical success factors of an organisation. Many things are measurable. That does not make them key to the organisation's success. When selecting KPIs, it is important to limit them to those factors that are essential for the IT function to reach its goals.

21.1.4 Provision of Information to the Service Design Function to Enable Service Quality to be Improved

Service delivery performance metrics captured as part of the SLM process may be very useful within other areas of the business. The use of SLA data in conjunction with SPC tools such as control charts enables service improvement teams to identify historic trends and to determine if a particular process is under control. Only when a process is brought under control can real sustainable improvements be made – attempting to improve an erratic out of control process will inevitably lead to spurious results that may undermine the improvement activity completely.

21.2 Common Issues

Common issues affecting Service Level Management include:

- SLA definitions that drive inefficient or unproductive behaviour
- Unrealistic SLAs defined/agreed without consulting the teams responsible for delivering the service
- Complex SLA definitions that are not clearly understood by the implementation groups
- Too much focus on individual tickets
- Lack of aggregated view of performance as a whole
- Excessive numbers of alerts/notifications cause people to ignore them

- Unnecessary over performance against SLAs
- Diverting resources to an SLA which is already a lost cause
- Micro management by the numbers
- Elements of service delivery being outside of the control of implementation groups (e.g. outsourced service providers etc)
- Large number of SLAs with different requirements mean that agents are unsure of what is expected of them
- Usage of SLA metrics to rank individuals de-motivates, erodes team spirit and leads people to deliberately conceal issues and search for sneaky ways of hitting targets
- Systems and/or processes that allow users to cheat/falsify measurements and metrics
- SLAs that fail to take account of the changing priority of an issue
- Escalating issues too early/too late
- Excessive administrative burden associated with SLA data capture, analysis and reporting

21.3 Process Flow

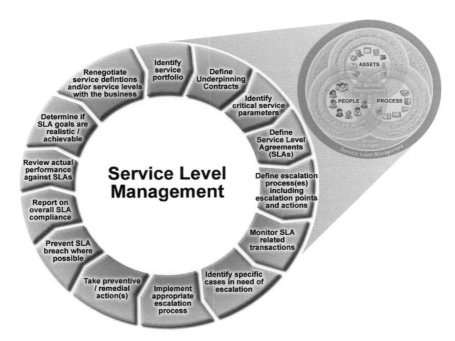

Fig. 21.1. High level process overview of Service Level Management

21.4 Key Players

Service users/subscribers – Anyone who knowingly or unknowingly accesses, consumes or uses a service.

Service/Support Agents – Personnel tasked with providing the service and supporting users trying to utilise it.

Delivery Group(s) – Functional teams responsible for the delivery of the service within the agreed parameters.

Service Delivery Managers – Management position responsible for the end to end delivery of one or more services. The service delivery manager is typically focused upon delivering a service in accordance with the agreed specification whilst keeping overheads and cost of delivery as low as possible.

21.5 Process Metrics

Metrics to measure metrics? Be off with you sir!

21.6 SLAs, OLAs and UPCs – Jargon that Helps?

ITIL suggests that each service level agreement (SLA) is supported by one or more operational level agreements (OLAs) and that the SLA itself acts as a representation to the business of the specific terms and conditions governing service delivery performance as laid down within the under pinning contract (UPC). So what does all this mean?

It could be argued that in many organisations SLAs etc are nothing more than an IT equivalent to the inspection and test function within the Quality Assurance department of a 1970's production facility. Why the 1970's? Well this was the period of the quality (r)evolution when inspection and test ruled the quality roost . . . Over the following decades, the quality management function became less preoccupied by layering quality on after the fact and started to deliver improvement when it began to function on the basis of prevention. How long will it be before IT follows suit?

21.6.1 SLAs – A stick to Beat the Delivery Team with or a Tool for Service Improvement?

ITIL defines a SLA as:

"A written agreement between an IT Service provider and the IT Customer(s), defining the key service targets and responsibilities of both parties. The emphasis must be on agreement and SLAs should not be used as a way of holding one side or the other to ransom. A true partnership should be developed between the IT provider and the Customer, so that a mutually beneficial agreement is reached, otherwise the SLA could quickly fall into disrepute and

a culture of blame would prevent any true service quality improvements from taking place."

Unfortunately many organizations never get past the first line of this definition and walk smack bang into the prophecy laid out towards the end of the paragraph. This is particularly true in poorly defined outsourcing environments (especially at the lower end of the spectrum where services are charged on a purely transactional basis).

SLAs have a habit of being used and abused by both customers and delivery teams alike in order to justify short term exceptions to process and procedure. However their use as a means of avoiding having to pay for what is delivered is probably less common than many in the outsourcing community would have you believe. Such penalties are often waived in return for 'free' extensions to contract scope and other such exceptional items which should by rights be subject to a formal renegotiation. SLA breaches in effect become negotiation tokens for the customer purchasing executives to leverage when they need something that they forgot to include in the original contract . . .

21.6.2 Kicking them when their Down – Rolling SLA Periods

Given that many people really do use SLAs as a means of imposing pain upon suppliers, it is only right to describe perhaps the most vindictive use of SLAs in use within outsourcing contracts today. If you're going to inflict pain you may as well get the biggest bang for your buck as they say. Not

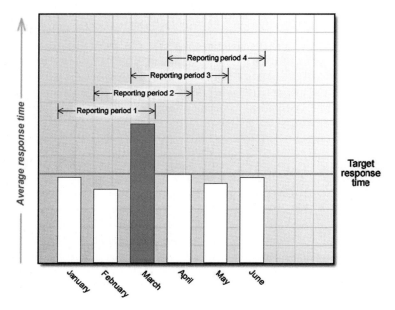

Fig. 21.2. Rolling SLA reporting periods and their effects

content with penalising someone once for a misdemeanour, the concept of rolling SLA periods allows you to potentially inflict multiple penalties for the same service failure. Put simply, the SLA calculation period is set to a duration longer than the reporting period e.g. the SLA is calculated over the preceding quarter but reported upon (and therefore liable to incur penalties on) on a monthly basis. The effect of such a heinous contract arrangement is to make the service function have to 'carry' poor performing months over an entire quarter – thus making momentary blips in performance far more significant and costly. Advocates of the rolling SLA period will claim that it provides an incentive for service consistency, and of course it does! But, you can't help feeling that it is really just the contrivance of a cunning purchasing executive who wants to wring every last cent of post sale 'discount' out of the deal...

21.7 Elements of a Service Level Agreement

The following list outlines the core elements of a traditional time based (i.e. responsiveness focused) SLA:

- Objective(s) of the SLA
- Focus of the SLA
- SLA reporting periods
- Validation triggers
- Monitoring frequency
- Escalation process
    - Escalation thresholds
    - Escalation actions

21.7.1 Objective(s) of the SLA

All too often, SLAs are written and approved without anyone seeming to take a step back and ask what it is that the business is trying to achieve through the definition of a particular SLA. Although all SLAs claim to do all of the following it is not always the case in practice. Unless the objectives of the SLA are clearly defined and supported by the terms laid out within the agreement then it will always fail to fully meet the needs of the business. In general, SLAs tend to be drafted with several of the following goals in mind:

- Compliance with contractual terms
- Increased user confidence (and therefore, hopefully, satisfaction)
- Monitoring the performance of specific groups, individuals or sub-contractors
- Identification of process improvement opportunities (i.e. black holes, bottle necks, erratic process steps etc)

- To set user expectations appropriately regarding the level of responsiveness etc
- Improvements to system/service reliability and stability
- To enable non-performing parties to be penalised
- To satisfy an in-house or external auditor/consultant
- To generate operational data to be analysed as part of preventive action initiatives
- To demonstrate performance and increase the perception of value of the IT function within the business i.e. to increase IT visibility

When considering the objectives of a SLA, the following questions should be kept in mind at all times:

- What is it that the SLA is supposed to be doing?
- Will the SLA help improve/guarantee/assure the quality of service delivered?

21.7.2 Focus of the SLA

The focus dictates what it is that the SLA is actually monitoring. It should define the type of thing (e.g. incident records, service requests etc), and the distinguishing features of the things to be tracked (e.g. incidents of a specific categorisation, service requests from a specific user group etc) by the SLA. Care needs to be taken to ensure that the SLA only measures what it needs to and does not include additional unrelated records as these may skew the reported compliance metrics and cause unnecessary and/or unwanted escalations.

21.7.3 SLA Reporting Periods

It is important to clearly define the specific reporting periods for the SLA. Typically SLA metrics are based upon traditional calendar measures (i.e. daily, weekly, monthly, quarterly etc) but some organisations are starting to rationalise this and focus their SLAs more closely on the periods of particular importance to the business e.g. month ends, quarter closes, peak sales periods etc.

21.7.4 Crossing Reporting Thresholds – What's in and What's out . . .

If the SLA is to give a fair and accurate picture of performance then details of how tickets crossing the boundaries of a SLA reporting period should be handled need to be defined. The three corner cases that need to be addressed are as follows:

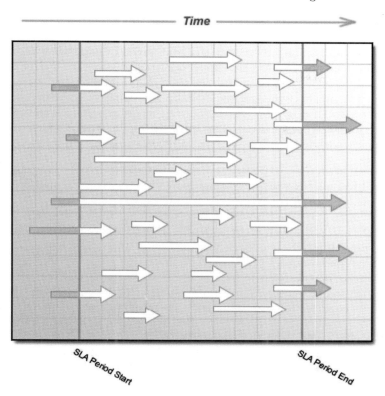

Fig. 21.3. Tickets in process and their relationship with SLA periods

- The ticket's SLA started before the reporting period started and finished during the current period
- The ticket's SLA started during the current reporting period and the ticket is not ready for closure at the end of the period
- The ticket's SLA started before the reporting period started and the ticket is not ready for closure at the end of the period

It may be possible to exclude these corner cases from the SLA calculation in cases where the percentage of such tickets is relatively small in comparison to the bulk of the work being completed i.e. a long duration SLA reporting period with many short duration tickets being raised and closed during the active period. However, all exclusions should be treated with extreme care as unscrupulous service delivery managers could take advantage of such agreements and artificially keep issues open longer than necessary to ensure they fall outside of a specific reporting period e.g. at year end when bonuses are being calculated for example.

21.7.5 Validation Triggers

SLA triggers determine when that the SLA should begin being measured/ tracked for a specific ticket. These triggers start and stop the clock or counter and are typically evaluated upon ticket creation, modification (e.g. status updates, assignments etc) and periodically according to a defined schedule (e.g. every hour for example). Validation triggers are generally condition based business rules which are evaluated by substituting the current values of ticket data into a predefined logical test or arithmetical equation and then evaluating the results.

- SLA Initiation i.e. when performance against the SLA should begin to be tracked. It should be noted that having passed this trigger/rule once is sufficient to start the SLA being monitored but failing the rule is not sufficient to stop the SLA clock by itself. Such a trigger would be for SLAs governing situations which must be dealt with in accordance with due process, irrespective of whether or not the initiating event is still relevant e.g. A security intrusion investigation where the ongoing analysis etc should continue to completion even if the intruder is no longer present. Alternatively it could be for something more mundane such as the monitoring of a process step when a ticket first enters a specific status value but not on subsequent entries into the status.
- Ongoing tracking i.e. conditions under which the SLA should be monitored continually. The classic example of such a trigger would be a SLA that is to be tracked only when a specific business service is unavailable or a piece of hardware is out of service. The moment service is restored then the tracking of the SLA is ended.
- SLA termination i.e. when the monitoring of the SLA should cease. A trigger, or set of conditions, which define when the management system can stop monitoring the SLA as it can be considered that the objective has been met.

21.7.6 Monitoring Frequency

The monitoring frequency is the rate at which the SLA is evaluated. The rate has to be sufficiently frequent to ensure that all escalation thresholds are identified when they become due with minimal delay or lag. However, it is important not to check too often for breaches etc as this will incur an unnecessary processing burden and may require a dedicated machine to be provided to manage SLA monitoring if wider system performance is not to be affected. There are two main methods of defining when SLA rules are evaluated to see if an escalation threshold has been crossed:

- Event based monitoring – i.e. evaluating the SLA conditions when specific events occur e.g. file creation, record updates, closure of related tickets etc.

- Periodic/Scheduled checks – i.e. checking the SLA every X seconds, Y minutes or Z hours/days until such time that the SLA is no longer valid or that its objective has been met.

21.7.7 Escalation Process

The escalation process defines the actions that are to be taken during the lifecycle of the SLA. These actions may be focused upon raising the awareness of the issue in hand or they may be targeted at assigning additional resources etc. Whatever the specifics of the actions defined by the business, they will be part of a formal escalation process or flow that lays out when actions are to be initiated and what those actions are to be.

21.7.8 Escalation Thresholds

Also known and escalation stages, escalation points or escalation process steps.

The escalation threshold defines when an action, or sequence of actions, is to be initiated in relation to a specific case that is being tracked against a SLA. Thresholds are typically based upon one of the following two mechanisms:

- Time based
  Time based thresholds are either defined in absolute or relative terms. Absolute thresholds are set at a defined period after an event (usually when the SLA is triggered) and do not typically change throughout the ticket lifecycle i.e. the escalation date/time is set in stone and does not alter in accordance with changing circumstances.

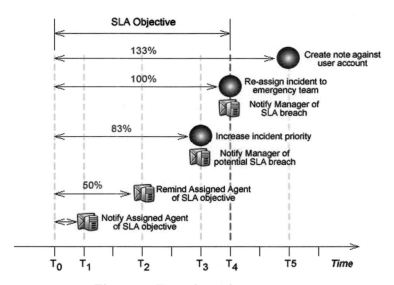

Fig. 21.4. Example escalation process

Relative thresholds are usually defined as a percentage of the SLA target or objective. By setting a percentage of the time elapsed since the SLA was initiated and recalculating the escalation date/time every time the SLA conditions are checked the SLA can react to changing circumstances e.g. re-prioritisation of incidents in light of changing business requirements etc.

- Rule based
  The SLA threshold is based upon a characteristic of the underlying record and/or is dependent upon the numbers of records associated with it or their characteristics. For example, a SLA may monitor the number of times an incident is re-assigned, in the event of the ticket being passed from pillar to post the SLA could identify this and ensure that the relevant people are notified to put a stop to the buck being passed yet again. Alternatively, a SLA may monitor the number of incidents being related against an outage record and automatically escalate the outage to a classification of "major incident" or similar when sufficient numbers of reports have been received from the user population.

It is worth noting that escalation thresholds may continue after the objective of the SLA has been passed or breached. Such thresholds can be used to trigger remedial actions etc beyond the formal breach of the SLA in order to ensure that the process completes and the underlying issue is eventually closed off.

21.7.9 Escalation Actions

At each escalation point an action or a series of actions may be defined. These actions are intended to make people aware of the underlying case and to promote the speedy resolution of the issue in hand. Common types of escalation action include:

- Notifications (i.e. alerts (usually via email) that are send to a defined series of recipients based upon role, relationship to the issue, location, time of day etc)
- Setting the value of a specific field on the underlying records e.g. raising the priority or severity of an incident record as more and more people become affected
- Creation of a new associated record e.g. bulletin board announcement etc
- Relate the underlying ticket with another record e.g. the assignment of a technical trouble shooter to investigate an issue that has dragged on without resolution

21.7.10 Starting the "Stop the Clock" Function

Many service delivery managers are utterly convinced that it is inevitable that there will occasionally be situations where the service delivery team is unable to fulfil their function due to circumstances beyond their direct control. In such cases it may be appropriate to suspend any associated SLAs to prevent the service organisation being negatively impacted by the effect that the delay would have on its delivery performance metrics. Such circumstances may include; times when the service function is awaiting information from the user, periods when a third party system or infrastructure component e.g. WAN links etc is unavailable, user availability to complete resolution testing etc. Irrespective of the drivers behind the need to suspend an ongoing SLA, the following questions should help ensure that the relevant issues are considered to ensure that the integrity of the SLA system is maintained:

- Who has authority to "stop the SLA clock"?
- Can the clock be stopped unilaterally by the support team or is the consent of the affected party, or parties, required?
- Can the clock be stopped at any point during the SLA timeline or are there periods when stopping the clock is not permitted e.g. 5 minutes before breach on the last day of the SLA reporting period?
- What criteria must be met to permit the clock to be stopped?
- What evidence of these criteria must be maintained to demonstrate compliance to the terms of the SLA?
- Is stopping the clock seen as last resort or a necessary tactic in order to meet SLA objectives?
- Does stopping the SLA clock impact the status of the underlying ticket?
- What impact does "stopping the clock" have on escalation processes that are already in process? Are they suspended/cancelled?
- Are suitable reports regarding the use of this functionality available to ensure transparency and to prevent it being abused?

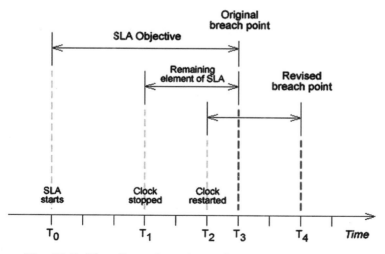

Fig. 21.5. The effects of starting and stopping the SLA clock

21.7.11 Resuming the SLA after "Restarting the clock"

Having stopped the clock, it is only fitting and right that one would potentially want to restart it again at some point.

- Who is able to restart the clock? Do all parties have to agree to the clock restarting?
- Can the clock be restarted automatically when certain criteria are fulfilled e.g. receipt of an email from the requester etc?
- Is the remaining SLA recalculated on a pro-rata basis against the proportion of the original SLA that was used? Or is it recalculated based upon the circumstances when the clock is restarted? What are the rules regarding this recalculation?

21.7.12 Stand Clear of the Doors when the Train is in Motion...

Circumstances and priorities change on an hourly basis within most IT shops and it is vital that the systems that underpin and support the service delivery process are capable of reacting to the current needs of the business. It is therefore desirable for the support system to automatically adjust the SLA objectives of a specific ticket in response to changes in priority, impact, scope etc whilst the ticket is in process. Such an alteration of the SLA focus and/or target may necessitate the usage of a different escalation process or it may just require the escalation date/times to be updated to take account of the revised timeline for dealing with the issue.

21.8 Dynamic SLAs

21.8.1 Closing the Stable Door before the Horse has a Chance to Bolt...

Wouldn't it be nice to avoid all of the recriminations, finger pointing and penalty fines associated with a major SLA breach? Providing the SLA objective is reasonable and achievable there is no reason why it should ever be breached (excluding the impact of major incidents, acts of god, unforeseen events etc). At the very least, such a breach should never come as a surprise for the service delivery team as they should be constantly aware of their performance against the SLA and their likely close position at the end of the current SLA period...

21.8.2 No Crystal Ball Required

Every IT outsourcer who is keen to avoid incurring SLA related penalties (and I use this tautology deliberately in this case) dedicates considerable resources

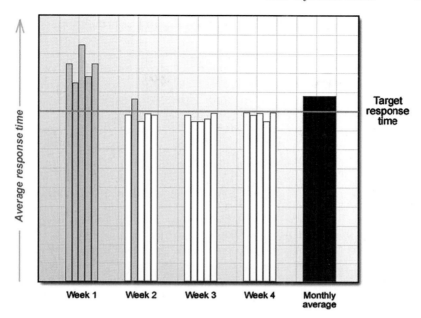

Fig. 21.6. Traditional static SLA

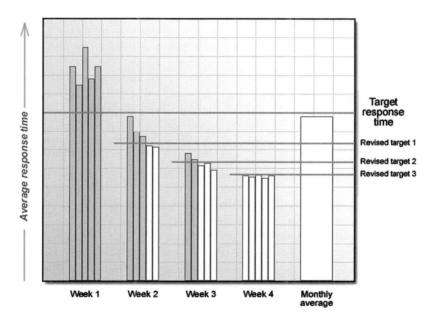

Fig. 21.7. Dynamic SLA

to the forward projection of current service delivery performance to determine whether or not it is likely that they will breach a SLA objective. It is not uncommon for large outsourcing contracts to have as many as two or three people dedicated to the creation of service delivery predictions on a daily basis. These predictions will typically be based upon a series of scenarios and assumptions to give worst case and best case measures of the probability of SLA compliance. Contrary to popular belief, such calculations do not require the power of a super computer and are usually undertaken by a service delivery manager with a working knowledge of MS Excel. However such activity is time consuming and could and should be undertaken by the ITSM solution as part of its background processing – this is after all why we use IT in the first place. When determining if an SLA breach is likely or inevitable, the following steps are completed:

- Calculate the current performance against the SLA
- Estimate likely performance for cases that are currently in progress
- Select an appropriate service usage profile/model
- Use the usage profile to determine likely level of service usage within the SLA period i.e. estimating the number of instances over which the remaining delivery effort can be shared to increase or decrease the overall SLA performance
- Extrapolate SLA performance forward to the end of the current SLA period
- Evaluate whether a breach is likely
- Calculate an adjusted SLA objective/target necessary to ensure compliance or to minimise the level of over delivery against the SLA
- Determine if a SLA breach is inevitable based upon the adjusted SLA target
- Repeat the process periodically throughout the SLA period

21.8.3 Predictive Models for Service Usage

Even the most complicated of service usage behaviours can be approximated to one of six basic profiles.

Predictive models not only allow the service level manager to extrapolate current delivery performance forwards to determine whether or not SLA objectives will be satisfied, they can also be used to identify discrepancies between the actual demand profile experienced and the anticipated distribution of service demand. Such discrepancies may be an early indicator of a change in service usage behaviour and/or may also help to identify external demand generation factors (e.g. a successful marketing campaign, disruption of a competitive service, an increase in the user population from an acquisition etc) which may be radically altering the way in which users consume a particular service offering.

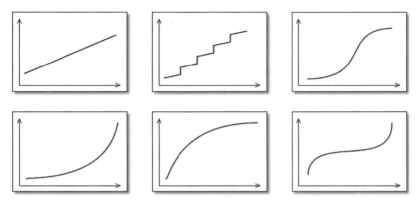

Fig. 21.8. Models for predicting service demand

21.8.4 Who Needs a Predictive Model Anyhow?

The level of accuracy of prediction models can be very accurate, but they may not be necessary for organisations with very stable demand characteristics. Such organisations may decide not to dynamically model demand but to use historical values instead.

21.8.5 The Dangers of Diverting Resources to a Failing SLA

Anyone who has played the board game Risk is likely to be aware of the dangers associated with committing all of ones resources to a specific short term goal. Focusing on a single SLA objective may leave you exposed on different fronts and unable to react quickly enough to changing circumstances. Every arm chair general knows that the key to the game is to win the war, not just the battle.

Constant tinkering (as redirecting resources based upon short term objectives has to be seen as nothing more than tinkering with the process in question) may mask underlying systemic issues and prevent management from identifying process related issues that require corrective or preventive action as early as they may do so otherwise.

21.9 The Three Pillars of Service Quality Measurement

Most service level management processes focus upon the following areas:

- Responsiveness
- Availability
- Quality of Service

The relative weightings of these measurement categories would typically be 7:2:1. This bias toward responsiveness based measurement is primarily due to the historic lack of suitable tools to measure availability or QoS related metrics with the necessary level of accuracy needed by the business. As monitoring solutions come of age, IT functions are addressing this imbalance and are slowly changing the way in which they look at service performance and are consequently altering this service quality measurement ratio. In the future, when the principles of service assurance are more commonly adopted as a philosophy within IT, it is predicted that the ratio may shift to something closer to 3:3:4.

21.9.1 Responsiveness

Traditional responsiveness SLAs track how long it takes to do something. Most responsiveness SLAs are based upon the assumption that people don't like to wait when the have requested assistance. This is true. But people are often prepared to wait a little longer if they are sure that they will get the result the desire every single time. Response time on its own is not a sufficient measure to determine service quality.

21.9.2 Availability

Availability metrics monitor the proportion of possible time that something is online or available to use. The theory being that services should be available on demand as often as possible in order to be able to serve users needs when they need them to be served.

21.9.3 Quality of Service

Historically, quality of service measures within an IT context have been based upon the time taken for a specific IT system or application to do something for an end user, be that to login, open up a customer record, return a set of search results or to commit a transaction etc. Such metrics have been selected because they are relatively "easy" to monitor, capture and analyse. However, system responsiveness is not the only measure of service quality. The following list describes some additional metrics that could potentially give an even better indication of the perceived quality of a system:

- The accuracy and usefulness of searches i.e. the proportion of time that users select one of the top 5 or 10 records from a search results list.
- The number of times an automated assignment is inaccurate i.e. the frequency at which automatically assigned tickets are re-assigned to a different individual or group
- Proportion of tickets that are incorrectly closed i.e. the service function deems they are complete before the actual issue is resolved

- The percentage of times that an application warning message box is closed instantaneously i.e. the user considers the warning irrelevant or irritating. Such behaviour is symptomatic of a system that is out of step with the needs of its users and the business...

21.10 Pulling it all Together – Aggregated SLAs

All too often service level management tools concentrate upon individual tickets. All manner of bells and whistles go off as a single ticket approaches its breach point. Such high profile noise, naturally attracts the wrong kind of attention i.e. over enthusiastic managers who want to save the world one ticket at a time... In the grand scheme of things, an individual ticket is usually only important to the individual(s) related to it. Management should concentrate upon the overall system performance and should have sufficient trust in their teams to leave the process, and the people who work the process, to deal with the inevitable statistical blips that will invariably crop up along the way.

Aggregated SLAs focus upon the overall performance of the system and take account of statistical variation (either naturally by the nature of the extended period under review or mathematically through the exclusion of upper and lower percentiles of ticket data). Such an SLA may state that X% of incidents received within a period of Y days are to be resolved within Z hours of receipt. Or it may even be even easier that and state that X% of incidents received within a period of Y days are to have an average resolution time of no more that Z hours. Why is the second example easier to meet? Because it uses an aggregated average rather than an aggregation of a maximum value, example one could be breached by the poor performance of a single ticket, example two is likely to require a more concerted and consistent show of incompetence...

- Is there a sufficient volume of data to be able to calculate meaningful averages etc?
- Is it appropriate to exclude upper and lower percentiles to discount/ eliminate the extremes of process variation?
- How are cases that extend past the reporting period thresholds handled?
- Can the aggregated SLA be inappropriately skewed by a small number of extreme results?
- Does the value of the aggregated SLA fluctuate significantly over time? i.e. Is the underlying process out of control/behaving unpredictably?

21.11 Agreed Service Levels – Resisting the Temptation to Over Deliver

If you are fortunate enough to have sufficient resources to be able to meet or exceed all of your service commitments then please feel free to ignore this section completely. However, if you work in the real world then you will be continually forced to make value judgements regarding resource allocation and the selection of which subset of the user population to disappoint or upset next.

Few IT functions, if any, monitor the level of over delivery against agreed SLAs. Every minute that is 'wasted' by resolving a particular incident type early could be used against a different issue with a more aggressive or challenging SLA objective.

- How often are you thanked for beating a SLA? Never? How often are you spanked for missing a SLA? Do you enjoy it? So why do you permit your teams to waste time over delivering against 'easier' SLAs?
- Do you regularly over deliver some IT services whilst failing to meet SLA objectives for others?
- Are IT staff instructed to complete each assigned task fully before moving on to the next?
- How often is current SLA performance monitored and fed back to the team? Is this often enough?
- Are ongoing SLA projections calculated to determine likely performance?
- Are team task prioritisations fixed in stone or are they dynamic enough to be able to respond to changes in demand and IT team performance?

21.12 Service Quality Perception and the Sample of One . . .

Vocal minorities can have a disproportionate effect upon the standing of the IT function unless they are handled effectively. Their concerns, legitimate or otherwise, must be addressed promptly if they are to be prevented from tarnishing the fragile reputation of the IT team within the wider organisation. Unfortunately however, IT is often the last to hear of the niggling gripe that has been the subject of endless hours of water cooler discussion regarding the lack competence or focus within the IT function.

Individual users tend to have a fairly limited view of the overall performance of IT and may have their view unfairly clouded by the way in which their own particular cases are dealt with. The following action plan may act as a more appropriate alternative to getting your scariest DBA to take the disaffected user into a darkened room and putting the frighteners on them:

- Identify – Work out whose mind needs changing
- Contact – Reach out and go to them directly
- Empathise – Understand the users pain and frustration
- Deliver – Do whatever it takes to make it right
- Educate – Help them to see how their issue fits into the picture
- Include – Get the user to help you to improve
- Convert – Create a walking talking advertisement for IT

21.13 Traffic Lights

A roll up of roll ups ... and we're not talking wacky baccy here! Then perhaps maybe we are ...

It is common for senior management to want to see the current status of a service or customer account represented in a single graphical representation, most frequently these senior managers request a simple traffic light approach where green is good and red is not. However, the people asking for such indicators often have little or no understanding of how such a ranking could or should be created. They will sometimes talk in broad terms of a hierarchy of SLAs, performance metrics and thresholds and walk off to an important meeting before they are forced to explain themselves further ...

IT services may have multiple SLAs and other performance metrics associated with them. The creation of a single service indicator requires considerable thought based upon the relative weighting of the SLAs, penalty thresholds and the relative time remaining within the current reporting period(s). In an ideal world, the composite SLA indicator should be based upon the current performance, the time left remaining within the SLA period and the likelihood that the underlying SLAs will be met. More usually the traffic light is based upon a statistically flawed combination of performance data that does little to help senior management understand the current level of risk exposure that their organisation is facing.

Automating the calculation of a composite SLA may also have its challenges as different SLA measurement and reporting periods may need alignment, or where this is not possible, the SLAs may need to be calculated on a pro-rata basis and combined in accordance with a predefined algorithm. Combining SLAs which measure different types of service parameter is also interesting, as comparing time based metrics with event frequencies and the like requires careful thought and the application of banded comparisons.

21.14 Developing Meaningful Metrics that Help Improve Service Quality

When defining service metrics it is important to have a clear understanding of what you want to measure and why you want to measure it. The generation of metrics for their own sake will do little to improve the situation and may be counter productive. It is always best to try and put yourself into the position of the service user and determine what would make you unhappy with the service. If you can then put a quantifiable metric against this service element, along with a threshold (or thresholds) that define when the service is unacceptable, then you are well on the way to defining a useful measurement. Ideally, the usefulness of each measurement should be validated with a sample of real users in order to see if your view of their wants and needs corresponds to theirs.

- Are the metrics clearly defined, measurable and useful to those doing the job? Are people asking for the metrics to be provided? If not, why not? What are the real people in the field using to manage their work on a day to day basis?
- Are the metrics focused at the end user experience? Are process efficiencies being sought in contradiction to the quality of the user experience?
- Do the metrics measure productive activity rather than just monitoring activity? Do the metrics encourage sub-optimal behaviour?
- Can the metrics be fudged, or subverted by the service delivery teams? i.e. Is there the possibility that people can cheat?

21.15 Management by Numbers is a Self Fulfilling Prophecy – People Cheat!

It is practically impossible to implement any ITSM process that is totally secure and tamper proof. There is no such thing as a child proof safety cap for the ITIL jar. Every system can be unduly influenced to some extent in order to deliver the metrics that management desire by the wily middle manager with an eye on their bonus. The following suggestions may help to combat such behaviour, but it remains the job of management to continuously review the system, the metrics that measure the system and their effectiveness/usefulness on an ongoing basis.

- Avoid placing too much emphasis on any single metric – always base rewards upon a combination of factors (ideally factors which may conflict with each other so that focusing on one area will have a detrimental effect on the other)
- Remove manual inputs wherever possible - using system generated times etc will help avoid low level cheating, however it should be noted that any system that utilises the local machine time is open to abuse if the local clock is not locked down
- Use impartial third parties to collect data where necessary – I have seen examples of satisfaction surveys being sent out by the delivery teams, they decided who received them and they worked with the end user to get the result that they needed ...
- Prevent undue pressure being exerted upon the users – User satisfaction survey results should be confidential unless the respondent agrees otherwise. I have seen cases where users reporting less than the required level of contentment have been harassed by service desk staff and management in an attempt to get them to retract their comments and improve the rating given. All it meant was that these users refused to participate in the programme in future ...
- Use sensible analytical models and avoid knee jerk reactions – Statistical blips are part and parcel of the infinite variation of ITSM processes. Persons reviewing performance data must be educated in basic statistical techniques in order to prevent them making ill informed judgements based upon the data they have in their hand

Release Management

To say there is a common understanding within IT circles of what the release management process covers would be slightly optimistic. Despite over almost 18 years of ITIL exposure the industry still has dramatically different views of what this particular process is actually for. There are four generally accepted release management models/definitions in use today:

- Change implementation process
  Release management acts as the conscience of the IT function by acting as the final gateway to the production environment and is often considered as the last line of defence against unintentional side effects and errors. Change management processes are used to deliver a finalised and tested change into a pre-production environment along with a set of tools and/or procedures for migrating the change (or replicating it where migration is not practical) into the live production environment. Acting as the final gatekeepers, the IT operations team take the completed change and associated work package and implement it fully in accordance with the defined release process.
- Software development management process
  The release management process governs the software development cycle from the identification of requirements, to the identification of code modules requiring update, creating branches in code lines, coding, refactoring/code optimisation, smoke testing, consolidation of development streams, packaging of code changes into a release, installation/implementation development, quality assurance plans, compatibility testing, documentation, patch/update delivery etc.
- A means of coordinating a bundle of related change requests
  Releases are used to describe groups of related changes that need to be managed in a coordinated manner (similar to the distinction used between programme and project management).
- A process for implementing changes that affect significant numbers of assets and/or users
  Changes that are to be implemented on multiple user systems in parallel such as operating system upgrades, application deployments etc are often treated as releases. Such rollouts will typically be broken down into manageable phases in order to minimise disruption, network load, training demand, support spikes etc.

The reasons for this lack of consistency are probably due to the overly general nature of the ITIL documentation regarding release management. According to ITIL, release management is like change management but different, it is related to software development but it isn't and leverages a definitive software library (DSL) – whatever that is...

22.1 Project Management and Programme Management – an Analogy

The relationship between Change Management and Release Management shares many parallels between that of Project and Programme management disciplines. "What's the difference between a project manager and a programme manager/director?" you may ask... About £50k on their base salary in today's job market! Now this is obviously trivialising the differences between the roles, but I think it important to recognise that there are considerable areas of overlap which both functions perform.

Programme management's role extends the day to day goal/objective orientated methodology of project management and attempts to orchestrate numerous disparate projects into harmonious co-existence and synergy, whilst avoiding discord and conflict. Effective programme management will:

- Identify shared objectives between projects and sub-projects
- Facilitate communication and collaboration between isolated implementation teams
- Highlight potential conflicts and inefficiencies
  - Similar resource requirements or skills needs
  - Sequencing and/or scheduling issues
  - Potential areas of duplication
- Act as an arbitrator in cases of conflict or difference of opinion
- Ensure overall organisational objectives are included/accommodated even where they may conflict with the short term goals of an individual project
- Suggest areas where different project teams may work together for mutual benefit

Similarly, release management must orchestrate multiple changes in order to ensure the objectives of the business are satisfied efficiently and effectively.

22.2 Process Objectives

The release management process should be focused upon the following core objectives:

- Efficient and error free implementation of changes to assets and processes
- Minimising the level of service disruption

22.2.1 Efficient and Error Free Implementation of Changes to Assets and Processes

The primary purpose of the release management process is to predictably transform the known current situation into the desired situation via a series of predefined steps and/or actions. The success of a release can be measured in verifiable terms by comparing the defined objectives of the release against the actual status and attributes/characteristics of the related configuration items etc. involved in the change after it has been implemented.

22.2.2 Minimising the Level of Service Disruption

The release management process wherever possible should follow the guiding principle of the Hippocratic Oath i.e. "...never do harm...". Minimising the level of service disruption during the planning and implementation of the change, as well as attempting to ensure that there are no related incidents caused by the change itself helps to ensure that the business is not negatively impacted by release activity.

The more observant amongst you will probably have noticed the startling similarities between the above objectives and those defined for the change management process. This is deliberate. Release management may be thought of as an extension to Change Management and as such the two processes will share many of the same objectives and goals. For the purposes of brevity, the remainder of this section of the book will try to focus upon the distinctions between the disciplines rather than repeat the similarities.

22.3 Common Issues

Common Release Management issues include:

- Lack of visibility of all changes that are planned or ongoing within the environment
- Insufficient or inaccurate detail regarding change tasks which make identifying potential synergies difficult
- Unclear lines of reporting and undefined seniority hierarchies between projects and project leaders
- Poor release process definition/Unclear process scope
- Release scope creep – the elephant continues to grow and grow...
- Size and complexity of the release is not understood due to poor understanding of what is out in the IT environment, where it is and how it will be impacted
- Poor packaging – incomplete instructions, untried methodologies, missing files/elements of the release package
- Design modifications being applied as the change leaves the door
- Changing circumstances between release phases
- Extended release schedules that mean that a release becomes obsolete before it has been fully deployed
- Difficulty ensuring that the release has been deployed to every end node for which it was intended

22.4 Key Players

Recipient(s)/Beneficiaries – The people who are directly impacted by the release and are intended to receive benefit from it.

Implementation Group(s) – The groups or individuals tasked with performing specific actions/tasks as described within the release plan.

Change Manager – The individual with overall responsibility for a specific set of changes within the release who prepares and validates the implementation plan, schedules resources and monitors the progress of the implementation.

Release Manager – The individual with overall responsibility for a release who coordinates the change resources and monitors the overall progress of the release.

22.5 Release? More Like a "Controlled" Escape!

In an ideal world, changes are consistently released in a careful and controlled manner into the awaiting IT environment where everything is ready for them to ensure that the business suffers minimal disruption and is able to take advantage of their designed benefits immediately. In the real world, changes escape through gaps in the IT fence in dribs and drabs, wreaking havoc and causing confusion. Those that are caught in the act of absconding are controlled to some extent, but the fact that they are largely already on their way when controls are applied means that the illusion of control is often a more accurate description.

22.5.1 Types of Release

Just as there are different types of change request, there are multiple different release types. These include:

- **Scheduled maintenance releases**
  Continuous release cycle scheduled at predefined intervals that is associated with a specific application, system or process. By agreeing in advance a schedule of maintenance updates, application and system owners can group system improvements and bug fixes into manageable chunks of work. This also enables the support function to talk to the end user community in a more meaningful way i.e. "Yes, we know that is an issue and it is currently scheduled to be addressed in release x in March" etc
- **One off/Ad hoc/Project based releases**
  An unplanned release that is scheduled as required in response to external events and/or newly identified business requirements. Ad hoc releases may be bundles of related changes or a single change that has an extended implementation scope.
- **Incremental releases**
  Releases focused at extending the capabilities of an existing system, application or process. Such releases are usually fuelled by the natural organic

growth of a system over time, or may be to add features and/or functionality that were omitted from a previous release due to resource constraints
etc. Incremental releases are often intended to build upon a previously
laid foundation and as such may not include all files, data etc to deliver a
standalone application on their own.

- **Consolidated releases**
  In cases where different incremental releases have been deployed across an
  environment it may be necessary to re-establish a common baseline. Consolidated releases are sometimes used to do this and may apply multiple
  incremental releases on top of an initial roll out release in order to ensure
  every end node is brought up to the same level.

22.6 Release Management as ITs Last Line of Defence

Whilst the release management team is the last group to physically touch
a series of changes this does not relieve any of the responsibility of those
who conceived, developed and packaged the release in the first place. Release
activities are nothing more than a mechanism for rolling change packages out
into the organisation. The change management team should never be allowed
to forget this and attempt to abdicate their responsibility for the quality of
their changes to the release function – it is after all their sole purpose in life...

22.6.1 Multiple Environments Help Minimise Mistakes

In my early days as an implementation consultant it was still common for
application changes to be developed and implemented on the live production system. This was obviously a less than ideal practice, however it did
certainly focus the mind and ensure the adrenaline was flowing. Nowadays
it would be unheard of for such a gung ho approach to be permitted. And
rightly so. Reductions in real terms of hardware costs and the improvements
in virtualisation technology mean that there is no reason why a multi phase
release approach shouldn't be used. Large enterprise systems typically have
the following server hierarchy as a minimum:

- Development
- Test/Acceptance Testing
- Pre-production
- Production

It is also not uncommon to have a dedicated training system to be used in
parallel with the pre-production environment for business with high volumes
of staff turnover e.g. call centres etc which need to be able to train up new
starters on a continuous basis. However many environments are used within
the release management process, the following question remains valid:

- Are the Test and Pre-production environments sufficiently similar to the
  production environment to be useful?

22.6.2 Packaging

Although the term is used heavily within an automated software distribution and deployment context, "packaging" is equally valid within any release scenario to describe the bundle of deliverables that are to be passed to the person or group tasked with rolling out a specific release in order to enable them to put the change(s) into place. The 'package' should consist of the following:

- Packing list i.e. an inventory of what is included in the release
- Deliverables (Files, executables, data etc)
- Automation and monitoring tools (Scripts etc)
- Implementation instructions
- Validation procedures and anticipated results
- Acceptance criteria

Perhaps the most critical of all of these elements is the validation procedures. Without detailed validation criteria, the release team will be unable to ascertain whether or not the change has been applied correctly and will be forced to unleash the change upon the waiting world without really knowing if it has succeeded or failed. The validation procedures should include instruction on how to perform the tests as well as details of the acceptance criteria for final release.

22.6.3 Acceptance Criteria

In rigid release management scenarios, there are in fact two acceptance processes. One when the release package is delivered from the IT function to the IT Ops or release team – this is to verify that the component parts of the release package have been provided and that the associated documentation is sufficient. The second acceptance phase is the formal acceptance and sign off that the change applied in the pre-prod environment is ready for final deployment into production. It is important to remember that the release team's role is not to perform a technical evaluation or operational review of the proposed change. The release team must operate on the basis that formal change management process and due diligence has been completed and understand that their role is to take the outputs of such deliberations and make their transition to the live environment as slick as possible. It is therefore necessary for release teams to separate the "why" from the "what" and focus upon the "how" – this is often easier said than done. The cardinal sin for a release team is for them to believe that they know better than the change team and to arbitrarily modify or amend the nature of the change on its way out of the door.

- Release process acceptance related questions
  - Are the criteria for accepting a change into pre-production clear, concise and unambiguous?
  - Do all members of the accepting team have the pre-requisite skills and experience to be able to make a value judgement as to the acceptability of the proposed change package?
  - Does the release acceptance plan require all possible variations of client O/S versions etc to be tested/validated? If not, what risk controls will be implemented to address untested configurations?
  - Is the release team able to distance themselves from the change sufficiently to remain objective?
  - Is it possible to validate the change in a pre-production environment? If not, what additional control and/or testing is planned?
- Final go/no go decision points
  - Does the applied change behave as described within the release plan?
  - Were the implementation instructions valid?
  - Is the release team comfortable that the change(s) can be rolled out into the live environment as required by the business?

22.6.4 Release Management as a Whistleblower

Every member of the release team must be confident that they have the right and authority to stop a release leaving the door if they have a concern about the stability, security or reliability of any of the content of a specific release package. Such power should be used sparingly if it is to be valued/respected and must always be backed up with demonstrable and objective evidence rather than opinion and personal style preferences.

22.7 Software Development Releases

The processes and best practices associated with software development are beyond the scope of this book, however I would heartily recommend that any readers who are involved in these activities take the time to read and inwardly digest the contents of "Code Complete" and "Rapid Development" by Steve McConnell. For me these books represent some of the best practical guidance on the subject that can be found anywhere and should become a regular reference point for anyone involved in software development in any capacity.

22.8 Common Release Strategies

It could be argued that there as many release strategies as there are releases. But that would make for a very long chapter and wouldn't necessary help too much, therefore we will restrict ourselves to some of the most common approaches to deploying releases within an IT environment:

- Parallel running/Dual operation
- Stepped/Staggered implementation
  - Regional
  - Operational units
  - Job role
  - Condition based e.g. Age of equipment etc
- Big bang
- Shelf update/On demand
- Pilot schemes
  - Low hanging fruit vs. Toughest nut to crack

22.8.1 Parallel Running/Dual Operation

As the name suggests, the replacement system or application version is run in parallel to the incumbent. Effectively using two separate systems to do the same job may require data to be entered into both systems manually or where this is unacceptable/impractical such a release strategy may require the development of an interim integration between the two systems to ensure that those user not yet migrated across have access to data/work input on the new system and vice versa. The length of time spent in parallel operation will depend upon the amount of time needed to migrate every user over as well as the level of confidence/comfort that the business has in the replacement system.

22.8.2 Stepped/Staggered Implementation

The purpose of a staged implementation strategy is to ensure that the delivery team don't bite off more than they can chew in one go. By focusing limited resources on a limited scope deployment the theory states that success can be guaranteed. Unfortunately, overly extended deployment strategies that have too many steps are often canned before they achieve any real momentum as the business becomes impatient for the promised benefits, consequently phases 5 and 6 may become phase 'never'...

22.8.3 Big Bang/Damp Squib

Creationist theory aside, the big bang approach turns even a modestly sized deployment into an event. As with every major spectator event there will be those sitting on the side lines hoping to see it fail miserably. Such is the nature of things. Preparation is critical for such an approach and it is vital that the deployment team take time to do their due diligence prior to the big day, rehearsing contingency plans etc if all is to go well.

22.8.4 Shelf Update/On Demand

The release is not formally pushed to the business, instead the IT function waits for the business to come to it and applies the release as and when it is requested. Such an approach minimises initial disruption but may take significantly longer to complete. Release teams should also be aware that news of a particularly useful release will spread like wild fire within the business and the initial trickle of requests for upgrade etc may very well turn into a raging torrent which could flood the unsuspecting IT organisation if it isn't careful to proactively manage demand so that supply can keep up.

22.8.5 Pilot Schemes/Proof of Concept Deployment

The trouble with pilot implementations is that they are often inconclusive. It is essential that the success criteria of any pilot be clearly defined in unambiguous measurable terms. When deciding on where to pilot there are usually two schools of thought – either you pick a nice soft target to get a quick win under your belt, or you select the hardest most inhospitable environment possible on the basis that if you can get it in there, you can get it in anywhere...

So we know the plan, all we need to do now is pull the trigger...

22.8.6 System Cutover

When moving from one system to another the following high level task check list should be used as a guide to ensure that all of the major bases are covered:

- Set the date and inform user base
- Perform backups of both systems
- Incrementally transfer legacy data to the new system noting checkpoints for all major datasets
- Test import routines and data validation models for in progress data as well as closed/historic records
- Suspend users/User lock outs
- Transfer of "in process" issues and data deltas (based upon known checkpoints etc)
- Validation of transfers – Sanity check all interim data transfers
- System re-instatement/Return replacement system into production
- Unlock users on the new system
- Notify user population
- Monitor initial activity very carefully

22.9 Release Activities

22.9.1 Pre-release Activities and Planning

There is an old adage that states that "failing to plan is planning to fail". Nowhere is this truer than in the area of release management. The size and complexity of release activities mean that planning is of paramount importance. The following non-exhaustive list describes some of the pre-release activities that should be put into place before embarking upon a significant release:

- Pre-requisite identification
- Baseline levelling/Pre-requisite enforcement
- Support ramp up and education
- Inventory and/or content pre-positioning
- Implementation team training/skills certification and verification
- Communication/Awareness campaign

Pre-requisite Identification

Identifying the minimum criteria for a release to succeed is an important step to complete before the rollout begins. Pre-requisites are often thought of as minimum technical specifications necessary for a specific piece of software to run. In addition to hardware requirements, the pre-requisites should include any software dependencies and user skills needed for the deployment to be a success.

Baseline Levelling/Pre-requisite Enforcement

How often have you been on a training course where some of the attendees clearly didn't read the pre-requisites? Such an oversight invariably leads to time being wasted with the instructor covering background information that the attendees should already know. It also often results in the attendees without the necessary background knowledge seeing the course material as more complicated than it really is and sometimes results in them switching off completely. Just as within an education environment, release management needs to enforce pre-requisites firmly if the release is to run smoothly.

Support Ramp Up and Education

The first port of call for user problems should be the support team. Therefore it is essential that they have been given the opportunity to get up to speed with the content of the release prior to the first support call being logged.

Inventory and/or Content Pre-positioning

Every year, there is a shortage of one or two specific toys in the shops at Christmas time. Such shortages may increase short term demand but they also invariably lead to many people being disappointed and may harm long term sales of the items concerned. In order to ensure a major release is not hampered by such logistics issues it is wise to try and predict demand and to ensure sufficient stocks of equipment, training materials etc are located where they are needed before the rollout begins.

Implementation Team Training/Skills Certification and Verification

There is an assumption within some IT teams that the bodies on the street will be able to work it out, whatever it may be, as they go along. Now this may be true to some extent, as IT implementation teams have had to become resourceful and multi-skilled over the years to compensate for such poor management practice, but it will always lead to sub-optimal performance and unnecessarily high re-work rates. It is far better to instigate a simple formal training plan and process for all persons actively involved in the deployment in order to help ensure that the release is delivered consistently and to a high standard. Such a training programme need not be overly onerous as it can itself demand a certain level of pre-requisite knowledge etc, however it should be done to close the loop and ensure that best practice and practical field experience are shared across the release team.

Communication/Awareness Campaign

Many people do not like surprises. Even nice surprises can irritate and upset some people. Therefore it is always (well usually anyhow, it is after all the exceptions that prove this rule) better to let people know that a significant change is on its way. Such communications should not be too long and complex, a short consistent series of sound bites utilising existing communication channels works best.

22.9.2 Activities Required During the Release

Releases can be "ongoing" for a considerable time and therefore it is essential that their progress is tracked and monitored to ensure that all is going to plan and that the business receives the benefits it is expecting. The following list outlines some of the release management activities that are often performed during a release deployment. It should be noted that these activities should be thought of as in addition to, not a substitute for, proper change control procedures.

- Monitoring of the level of completion/progress
- Exception handling for failed implementation nodes i.e. rework
- Implementation team performance and morale monitoring
- Ongoing messaging/communications
  - Status reporting etc

Monitoring of the Level of Completion/Progress

The day to day monitoring of progress may be conducted at the change level rather than the task level if such metrics exist. In their absence, the release manager must consolidate and aggregate all task performance reports in order to give an overall picture of how the release is progressing.

Exception Handling for Failed Implementation Nodes i.e. Rework

In the real world, releases seldom 'hit' all of the desired end points in their first hit – machines are turned off, disconnected from the network, with users on business trips, vacations etc. Equally, not every end point that is 'hit' will respond as desired. It is therefore necessary to determine how such exceptions should be handled. Some organisations have dedicated rework teams to follow up after the main deployment phases whose primary role is focused upon finishing off the job in hand. Other organisations prefer to schedule a final mopping up phase where all those end points know to have been missed or failed in previous phases are redone. Whatever the process, the fact that release management invariably needs to accommodate less than 100 % coverage models remains.

Implementation team performance and morale monitoring

Extended deployment cycles, especially those involving long periods away from home, can have a detrimental effect upon individual focus (i.e. attention and conscientiousness etc) and morale. It must be remembered that the success of the release is largely in the hands of those tasked with getting down and dirty with the pieces of tin and as such it is important to ensure that the implementation teams are looked after adequately.

Ongoing Messaging/Communications

Just as people like to know that a change is coming, they also like to be kept in the loop regarding progress and how it is going...

22.9.3 Post Release Activities and Planning

Just as a subset of all changes implemented will undergo a formal post implementation review (PIR), a sample of releases should also be reviewed in order to determine how the release management process is performing. In addition to this process level activity the following release level tasks should be completed:

- Mopping up activities
- Incident analysis i.e. post implementation observation

22.10 When should a Single Change be Treated as a Release?

It is important to remember that not every change will need to be handled as part of a release. In fact, it is likely that the majority of changes will be managed independently. When determining whether or not a specific change should be deployed using the release management process the following criteria should be evaluated:

- Implementation duration - Implementations that continue over extended periods may be best handled as releases
- Number of machines/systems/users affected – Changes impacting large numbers of end points will benefit from being handled as a release
- Geographical locations affected
- Complexity of change

Taking all of the above into consideration, the change manager (in conjunction with the CAB) may decide to involve the release management team in the deployment of the change into production.

22.11 How should the Contents of a Release be Selected?

A planned release may be extended to accommodate additional similar changes in certain circumstances. Intelligent change managers will sometimes try and get their changes included within the scope of an existing release in order to delegate responsibility for the final delivery phase. Changes may find their way into a release in a variety of ways:

- The change may be nominated for inclusion within a scheduled release during the formal change approval process
- Individual changes may be invited to participate within a release by the nominated release manager

- Spin off changes associated with changes already within a release may be included due to their heritage

In most cases the assigned release manager will have the final say as to whether or not a suggested change is included within the scope of their release.

22.12 Does a Release have to be "Finished" to be "Complete"?

Just as the painting of the Forth and Golden Gate bridges is never truly completed, many releases will never be 100 % finished either. The continual evolution of the IT landscape, the relatively short useful lifespan of modern hardware, the continuous patch and security alert software cycle and the rate at which organisations change mean that releases may not be finished before they are defunct, obsolete or superseded. However, the IT delivery team needs to be able to move on to their next challenge and hence it is necessary to artificially close out releases to make way for the next wave of change. The following list outlines some of the ways in which this arbitrary end point can be determined:

- Defined completion level i.e. the release will be consider completed when 95 % of systems within scope have been upgraded
- Duration limited i.e. the release activity will continue until the 31st December and will then be considered complete for example
- Conditional complete i.e. the release will continue until all end nodes are upgraded or until such time that a newer release covering the same functionality is identified
- Fixed volume of work i.e. the release will be deemed complete after y deployment cycles have been run, irrespective of the number of end node failures identified

Availability and Capacity Management – The Black Sheep of the ITIL Family

Availability and Capacity Management differ from other ITIL disciplines in so far as they focus upon intangible attributes of a particular service or asset rather than upon the handling and processing of definite instances or requests.

Availability can be thought of as percentage of possible time that something (e.g. a service, system or asset etc) is in a suitable condition and operating to an appropriate level of performance to be utilised by its user community after agreed exclusions (e.g. planned maintenance windows etc) have been excluded. Availability is typically negatively impacted by unplanned events such as incidents, outages etc as well as planned events such as changes scheduled outside of agreed maintenance windows etc.

Capacity can be thought as the absolute or relative volume of activity that a particular thing (e.g. a service, system or asset etc) may be able to facilitate or support when in operation. Capacity may be expressed in a wide variety of ways including the following:

- Transfer rate of data that can be passed to the thing or retrieved from it
- Volume of data that may be held/stored at any one time
- Number of concurrent users, connections, processes, threads etc
- Rate at which transactions are handled e.g. X submits per minute

Capacity fluctuates frequently in response to a wide variety of factors including:

- Other systems and processes utilising resources associated with a specific capacity measure
- Unplanned events such as hardware failures, system outages etc
- Demand exceeding the defined usage volumes, uneven usage profile/ distributions etc
- Planned events such as routine operations, preventive maintenance etc

So given the interdependent and embedded nature of these things, is it any wonder that the task of managing availability and capacity with any degree of certainty is amongst on of the most challenging challenges in the ITSM arena.

23.1 Sphere of Influence and Sphere of Control

So many of the factors that directly impact and affect availability and capacity are outside of the spheres of influence and/or control of those charged with managing such things as to make the associated management roles practically impossible. In many ways the roles of availability manager and capacity manager are bogus. At best such roles should be described as 'planners' or 'coordinators' as this more accurately reflects the possible impacts of personnel performing these functions. If capacity and availability management are to add any value to the mix they must be included upfront in the service design process. Only then can they have a chance of delivering what the business really needs. Attempting to ladle high availability requirements or significant capacity increases onto an already baked service definition is unlikely to produce cordon bleu results without incurring exponential cost increases . . .

23.2 Availability Management

A key service quality metric for many IT services is the amount of time that the service is available to use when its users expect that it should be available to use. Availability management is the discipline tasked with ensuring that a particular service continues to deliver within the pre-defined operational/functional envelope (i.e. within agreed response times etc) for the proportion of time that the business has agreed with the service delivery function.

23.2.1 Process Objectives

The availability management process should be focused upon the following core objectives:

- Clearly understand and define the business requirements regarding service availability.
- To plan, measure, monitor and continuously strive to improve the availability of the IT Infrastructure, services and supporting organisation to ensure these requirements are met consistently.

23.2.2 Common Issues

Common availability related issues include:

- Misalignment between expectation of the business and the level of service availability provided by IT
- Inadequately defined service catalogue
- Poorly defined availability profiles which do little to assist with the scheduling of changes etc

- Unrealistic SLAs defined/agreed without taking service availability profiles into account
- Changes that overrun pre-defined maintenance windows and negatively impact the service availability
- Over specification of availability requirements leading to unnecessary cost
- Communication issues between functional disciplines
- Insufficient focus and/or time and resources given to availability planning

23.3 Capacity Management

Capacity Management is a process used to manage the capacity of an IT service to ensure that it meets current and future business requirements in a cost-effective and efficient manner. As the usage profile of an IT service changes over time and the service itself evolves, the amount of physical computing processing power, data storage requirements, staffing levels needed to deliver and support the service also changes. If it is possible to understand the demands being made currently, and how they are likely to change over time, then the planning for growth or shrinkage becomes easier and less reactive i.e. painful. If there are peaks in, for example, the processing power consumed by the service at a particular time of the day, capacity management processes would propose analysing what is happening at that time and to request changes in job scheduling etc to maximise the utilisation of the existing infrastructure.

23.3.1 Process Objectives

The capacity management process should be focused upon the following core objectives:

- Clearly understand and define the business requirements regarding service capacity.
- To plan, measure and continuously monitor the available capacity of key elements of the IT Infrastructure to ensure these requirements are met consistently.

23.3.2 Common Issues

Common capacity related issues include:

- Poor coordination between resource consumers leading to periods of peak demands colliding
- Unpredictable demand profiles/usage patterns
- External events (such as marketing campaigns etc) that generate additional demand for services

- Lack of anticipation of service uptake/growth
- Hardware, software or technical architecture constraints that make scaling a solution difficult
- Exponential increases in the volume of data required to be accommodated, used and leveraged
- Legal requirements to store historical information for extended periods
- Reliance upon event management systems data to learn of capacity issues after they have already become an issue

The Current State of the ITSM Solution Market

Before I start explaining my particular take on the current state of the IT Service Management market I would like to explain the incestuous nature of the space to those not immediately involved. There are in fact very few large players in the market and it is very common to see the same faces with different business cards periodically, indeed if one stays with a particular vendor for long enough many of the old faces become new faces once more as they return to the fold... The limited number of large enterprise customers for such solutions and a typical technology refresh rate of between three and five years also means that many people end up competing with friends and acquaintances for accounts that they themselves have previously sold the outbound incumbent system under a different banner. This brings its own challenges but that, as they say, is a different story.

Given the cyclical nature of the industry I am keen to point out that this book, and in particular this section, is not based upon any single vendor in particular. Any similarity between the practices described herein and my current and former employers is accidental and is completely unintentional and should not be taken as anything more than the general observations of a world weary ITSM practitioner who has had to nurse the emotional and physical scars of many many successful ITSM implementation projects over the years. Not only have I been there, I have bought the T-shirt and worn it out multiple times. I have been fortunate to see the market from a wide variety of angles ranging from application support, to development, to consulting, to product management, to marketing, to programme management and sales. Each role has brought with it a new set of perspectives with which to view something that I mistakenly believed I knew already.

And so without further explanation or excuses I will now outline my current thoughts on the state of the ITSM market...

24.1 General Industry Trends

The following series of lists outline how, in my opinion, movements within the general marketplace have had an impact upon ITSM solutions and ITSM implementations.

Tool requirements have increased...

- Paper based systems
- Spreadsheets and Access databases
- Custom built tools
- Commercial development toolkits and template solutions
- Commercial off the shelf (COTS) tools/Out of the box (OOTB) applications
- Open source projects?

Solution sets have evolved...

- Niche products from specialist players
- Integrated solution suites (Loosely coupled collections of point solutions)
- Modular plug and play solutions with common technology
- Unified platforms for ITSM built around ITIL compliance
- Extensions to core platform via integrations with point solutions

License models are changing...

- Perpetual licenses
- Term licenses/Rental
- On demand/Usage based pricing
  - Subscription based
    - Users/Assets
    - Processes
  - Transactional
    - Ticket volume
    - Asset numbers
- Value based pricing (Shared risk and return)

System architectures continue to develop...

- Client-server
- n-tier extracted architectures
- Web enabled
  - CGI emulation of fat client interfaces
- Web architected
  - True thin client implementation
  - Static html/server based processing
- Rich Internet Applications (RIA)/Web 2.0
  - Dynamic interactive user interfaces

Business models have changed...

- IT as an in-house/Non-competitive cost centre
- Non-core commodity outsourcing e.g. printer maintenance etc
- Infrastructure and Support outsourcing
  - Abdicating control and responsibility
  - Chasing promised cost reductions
- Competitive outsourcing
  - Multiple vendors being played off one another
- In-sourcing IT to deliver business value and competitive advantage
- Teaming with outsourcers/Symbiotic mutually beneficial partnerships
  - Linking the success of the outsourcer to the success of the customer

Hardware is becoming more and more sophisticated...

- Hardware was proprietary and rigid
  - Minimal configuration capabilities
- Interface standards emerged
- Hardware reliability and complexity increase
  - Rip and replace black box components that are nigh on impossible to maintain with a soldering iron
- Plug and play devices
- IP enabled network aware hardware
  - Shared resources
- Self diagnostics and self healing equipment
  - Remote monitoring units as part of the asset
- Self maintaining intelligent assets
  - Multiple sensors to monitor performance
  - Intelligence built in to ensure that they operate efficiently
  - Connectivity over the web to send and receive data
  - Self updating firmware
  - Proactive alerts to request assistance

24.1.1 Consolidation Within a Mature Market

In recent times there has been a considerable amount of merger and acquisition activity within the ITSM space. Larger vendors have been acquiring niche solutions to round out their solution suites. And in one or two cases, some of the largest players have joined forces in an attempt to dominate the space. Such activity is only to be expected in a mature market such as this. The big three players at the moment are (in alphabetical order) CA, HP and IBM. BMC is following close on their heels but lacks the breadth of offering and financial clout of these majors...

24.1.2 Just because it is a Market Leader doesn't Mean that it is the Best Solution for you...

Branding is key. Just as CFOs don't get sacked for buying SAP or Oracle, CIOs like the career protection and warm cuddly feeling that comes from buying from the 200lb gorillas of the ITSM market... This is not to say that these vendors don't provide good solutions, by and large they do. However, smaller vendors may provide equally good (or in some cases better) solutions but fail to be selected due to the power of brand and market presence.

24.1.3 The Good, the Bad and the Ugly

There are literally hundreds of vendors offering solutions within the ITSM space. These vendors range from small one man bands operating off their kitchen tables to huge monolithic organisations with hundreds of thousands of employees spread across the world. Each vendor has positive and negative points and individual organisations must take care to evaluate potential suppliers across a wide range of criteria in order to be sure that they select the right vendor for them.

24.1.4 ITIL is the Price of Admission not the Game Itself

What ever the size of the vendor, it is important that off the shelf tools should go beyond a cookie cutter template approach and deliver real value to customers. Real features and functions that can be used to deliver real benefits are what is called for. If a vendor cannot articulate how their solution underpins good ITSM practice then they really do not deserve your business. It is not just a case of "What?" anymore, suppliers need to be capable for explaining "How?" and "Why?"... The tool selection is but one piece of the ITSM story and vendors must ensure they can position their offerings in context with the wider ITIL based initiatives to improve service delivery, reduce operational costs and increase customer satisfaction.

24.1.5 ITIL Compliance should be More than Just Ticking the Boxes...

Sadly within many ITSM solution vendors there is a disconnect between their customers needs and the engineering, product management, marketing and field functions which mean that the products they develop do not always include the features and functionality needed to manage IT services in the real world. Instead, it is common for commercial solutions to give the appearance of process capabilities beyond their scope by adding appropriately labelled fields to user interfaces with little or no thought as to why or how they could be used in practice. This 'deception' is then compounded by the impartial external certification bodies who take such capabilities on face value and do little more than a cursory examination of the solution before proclaiming to the world that it is capable of supporting an ITIL based ITSM system.

24.1.6 Innovation is Dead, Long Live the Analysts

Good management is systematically stifling innovation and preventing new and interesting software products coming to market. It is hardly surprising when the costs associated with developing, releasing and marketing enterprise level software solutions are considered that vendors want to ensure they have a reasonable chance of success before investing in a new release. In order to remain competitive, large corporations continue to play a game of cat and mouse with their competition and with the marketplace in general. Enterprise level solutions are organically grown based upon long term market trends and the views of the analyst community (who themselves get their ideas from looking at the market upon which they commentate). With such an introspective view of the world it is hardly surprising to see that ITSM products have not changed dramatically in almost a decade. Where innovations have come, it is from small niche players at the periphery of the sector being consumed by the big players and having the relevant functions and features added to their core offerings.

Walking around ITSM related tradeshows has become quite a depressing experience in recent years with there being few new or exciting developments to see. I truly believe that the industry is ready for a significant change in the way in which ITSM is practiced and defined.

Crystal Ball Time . . . The Future of the ITSM Space . . .

25.1 If ITIL is Only the Beginning, Where or What Next?

Perhaps ITIL v3 will be the shot in the arm that the ITIL guidance set needs. Or perhaps another standard such as CoBIT will come to the fore and take its place. Maybe the IT industry will look outside to the world of quality management for systems such as Six Sigma etc. Or maybe a completely new series of best practices will be developed that can take the IT world forward. Whatever the future has in store, the IT Service Management marketplace will continue to exist in one form or another until such time that computers become the appliance based commodities of the science fiction movies. In the world of science fiction, computers seldom, if ever, crash. Applications integrate seamlessly with one another. And no-one, but no-one, ever calls the help desk to find out why their life enhancing gizmo isn't working properly . . .

But then again, perhaps ITSM will become an irrelevance as the business world embraces the business process automation and management markets (BPA and BPM) because they believe that maybe just maybe these new fangled tools will be the elusive magic pills that finally deliver up to their hype. Nah . . .

25.1.1 Potential Future Trends in (IT)SM

Is the following happening now? No. Is the following going to happen anytime soon? No. Might the following happen someday? Maybe. Should the following happen? Yes, absolutely!

25.1.2 Back to Basics . . .

Process rationalisation is needed to restore clarity and increase understanding. In order to rationalise ITSM and ITIL, the industry must take a long hard look at what it does now and more importantly why it does it. In essence everything within ITSM comes down to one of four things:

- We react to input from our customers...
- We perform planned activities...
- We use and maintain resources...
- We strive to improve...

25.1.3 Everything Else is Just a Variation Upon a Theme.

Incidents, service requests, complaints, requests for information, questions etc – These are all inputs from customers. All issues, be they of any type, need to be proactively driven to conclusion through the systematic application of a relevant and appropriate process.

Changes, releases, planned maintenance, routine operations activity etc – These are all just packages of work that we plan and perform.

Employees, assets, applications, systems, infrastructure etc – These are all resources which we use to deliver, all resources need to be managed, maintained and tracked if they are to be utilised effectively.

SLAs, KPIs, OLAs, Business intelligence, Performance dashboards, Problem management, Satisfaction surveys etc – These provide the rationale and the mechanism for making things better. Prevention is the only objective worth coveting. Preventive action and systemic improvement to deliver true service assurance will be the factor that separates the good from the excellent in the future.

25.1.4 But won't Common/Shared Process Models Mean that Everything will become the Grey Gooey Gunk of Nano-technology Nightmares?

The ability to support infinite variation does not necessitate a enormous expert system supporting an infinite number of processes. A series of four carefully designed process models with the relevant supporting infrastructure (e.g. dynamic state models, context sensitive process flow amendments/diversions, data driven user interfaces, scripting based data input guidance, role based system intelligence etc) would be sufficient to not only support current ITSM best practice but would provide the platform from which those benefits could truly begin to add value to the wider business world.

So much for the blue sky vision...How might we start on a journey to get there?

25.2 Cross Discipline Approaches Continue to Blur Towards a True Consolidated Service Desk (CSD)

The concept of the consolidated service desk is one that has been around for quite some time but has not really materialised within the mainstream. There

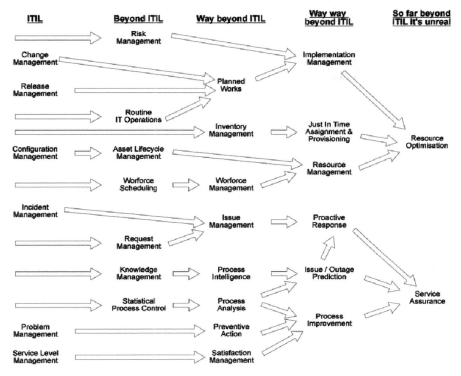

Fig. 25.1. Service management process convergence

are many reasons for this but the biggest by fair is the inherent corporate politics associated with such a change. In order for a true CSD to be implemented, multiple business functions must come together and agree to work within a consistent first line framework. Since this is seen by many functional heads as a watering down of their personal influence and power it has been resisted strongly. Self service portals may prove to be the Trojan horses needed to break this impasse as they are often used to provide a common front end to multiple back office systems.

The consolidated service desk of the future should address as a minimum the following types of request in addition to IT related enquires:

- Facilities
  - o Moves, Repairs, Clean ups etc
- Human Resources
  - o Benefits (e.g. Health care, Assistance programs etc)
  - o Training
  - o Personal details updates (Changes in circumstance etc)
- Finance
  - o Payroll enquires, bank detail changes etc

- Business support functions
  - ○ Sales support
  - ○ Legal/Contracts
  - ○ Operations

25.3 Applying (IT)SM Principles to Every Asset Class

Many of the principles outlined within this book are equally applicable to non-IT equipment and services as they are to IT hardware, software, network infrastructure and IT services. The processes used to investigate non-conformance, undesirable and/or unexpected behaviour are similar irrespective of what it is that is causing the issue. Similarly, the processes used to instigate changes to the status quo share many common elements across the board. By extracting these high level process flows and supplementing their overall model with context specific extensions, process detours/diversions and system enhancements, organisations will be able to rationalise the way in which they handle the management of every type of asset within their business.

25.4 The Line Between Internal and External Support Processes Continues to Blur Further...

The needs of internal and external customers are often very similar. In fact, in the future it is likely that the definition of what, and who, is a customer will change significantly. Service management processes and service offerings will adapt to handle a wide variety of 'customers'. These parties will all have their own requirements of the service organisation and service management processes will have to have the inherent flexibility to provide infinitely variable solutions to requests in a controlled and consistent manner. The 'customers' of tomorrow will include:

- Employees
- Customers
- Prospects
- Partners
- Suppliers

25.5 Convergence of CRM and ITSM Concepts to Define True Service Management

It would be incredibly arrogant to assume that the IT service management world had nothing to learn from other areas. The CRM space in particular has fostered a significant amount of ingenuity and development over the past decade or so. Mature CRM solutions have many features and functions which would be extremely useful within an IT context. The following list outlines just some of the CRM functionalities that could and should be applied to the world of ITSM:

- User profiling
- Expectation management
- Demand modelling
- Product/Service configuration tools
- Campaign management

25.5.1 User Profiling

User profiles define subsets of the user community according to their role, skills, level of IT literacy, common requirements, propensity to make mistakes/ask for assistance etc. By profiling the user community the service organisation can make intelligent predictions regarding the level of demand for their services from specific groups and can use this information to create focused educational and informational content to try and alleviate spikes in their workload. Profiling may also be used as part of release strategy to mitigate risk and ensure that sufficient support staff is made available in the appropriate locations during a roll out.

25.5.2 Expectation Management

Expectation is everything to the end user. Incorrect or misaligned expectations can lead to user dissatisfaction. The proactive setting of user expectations based upon current workload volumes, projected demand profiles, ongoing clear up rates and durations, staffing levels/shift patterns etc can significantly reduce the volume of follow-up/chase call backs and, if done routinely with accuracy, will promote a professional, in control, persona for the support organisation.

25.5.3 Demand Modelling

Demand modelling enables the support organisation to predict what level of staffing needs to be available to maintain service delivery within agreed levels. The analysis and extrapolation of historic demand data in combination with known events, planned shift allocations etc enables the support organisation to determine when bottlenecks are likely to be experienced.

25.5.4 Product/Service Configuration Tools

At the heart of every sales automation toolset is a product configurator. These applications enable an organisation to model the products which may be sold, their available options and the relationships, exclusions and dependencies between these options. For example, widget x comes in 3 sizes and the y series adapter is only available for 2 of them, selecting the y series adapter precludes the selection of the z series flange bracket option etc. The sales configurator ensures that people ordering widget x only make valid selections that conform to the available options compatibility matrix for the product. Such a tool would be invaluable in the modelling of services and their optional characteristics.

25.5.5 Campaign Management

Marketing automation tools enable marketeers to define outbound communication programmes as part of an ongoing campaign to raise awareness, spark interest, create demand or maintain mindshare. The recipients of the content are tracked through the system (usually via click through updates when the recipients visit URLs included within the messages), as are any responses and follow up enquiries received. The purpose of such a system is to determine the effectiveness of the messaging from the marketing function and the level of interest generated by their content. This functionality would be very useful to enable problem management teams to gain an understanding of the effectiveness of proactive educational/informational messages that they broadcast to subsets of the user community and to potentially show the relationship between such campaigns and reductions in incidents etc.

25.6 Extending the Scope of ITSM to Incorporate Additional Areas

IT teams implementing ITSM processes are often overly focused on end user impacting services and don't take the time to extend the scope of their activities into other IT areas which service the internal IT function. This is a terrible waste, as ITSM principles can have significant benefits and synergies when combined with other ITSM disciplines.

- Security management
- Storage management
- Routine operations

Security Management and ITSM

No topic is hotter within IT than security. It seems that every senior manager is endowed with a healthy dose of paranoia regarding viruses, data theft,

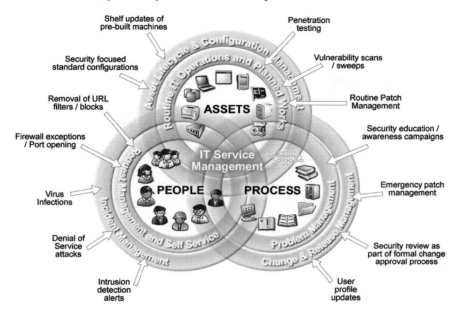

Fig. 25.2. Balanced process model with Security Management

malicious network intrusions etc. This has enabled the security tools market to grow exponentially in recent times. The security market is awash with thousands of niche solutions serving the needs of specific security issues. And yet there is very little joined up thinking to link these security applications together and to embed them within the day to day operational procedures of the business. All too often, security projects are knee jerk reactions to external events that deliver short term peace of mind but fail to sustain long term confidence. The above diagram shows how some of the common security processes and tasks could be integrated within an ITSM framework to ensure that they are delivered consistently and appropriately.

Storage Management and ITSM

The volume of data produced by business is increasing at a phenomenal rate. In 1999, I worked on my first terra byte database – at the time this was considered to be a very large system. Today, disk prices are such that storage space is cheap. So cheap in fact that it is largely an irrelevance. This has meant that old school storage management has evolved into something else – today's challenge isn't about finding room to keep the stuff, its about finding the time necessary to back up the stuff that changed today ... Added to backup time lags, the need to be able to search and retrieve data quickly is now more of a challenge. ITSM processes can dramatically improve the way in which routine and non-routine storage management tasks are managed and implemented.

Routine IT Operations and ITSM

The IT operations team are the people that work at the coal face of the IT industry. In often inhospitable conditions (well machine rooms tend to be noisy, cold and loaded with tripping hazards – a far cry from the advertisements within the trade press where they are gleaming showcases of new technology), they attempt to put the policies of IT management into practice by working unsociable hours, using less than adequate resources and manual script based tools. Despite all this, they manage to get the job done in the main. However, it is an unquestionable fact (because every analyst for the past decade has repeated it) that 80 % of all incidents are directly attributable to poorly managed change. As a significant proportion of changes are implemented/deployed as part of the IT Operations workload it therefore makes sense to begin managing this "routine" work with the same level of attention and control as other changes within the IT environment.

25.7 Business Intelligence Moves Beyond Basic Statistics and Embraces SPC

Until IT begins to make real use of the mountain of meaningless data it generates it will be destined to flounder in its own mess. Data without meaningful analysis is worthless. Analysis helps identify patterns and trends. Patterns can be modelled. Models can be tested to prove ones hypothesis. A proven hypothesis can be used to extrapolate historical data forwards. Forward predictions combined with statistically valid probability weightings provide usable management information. Information is the basis of all intelligent decision making. Statistical Process Control (SPC) theory is ready to assist IT with the ongoing proactive management of linear flow based systems with statistical fluctuations. All IT processes can be modelled as linear flows. All IT processes fluctuate. SPC can be used to proactively manage IT performance fluctuations in a pragmatic and valid manner. SPC can help avoid knee jerk reactions to statistical blips and provide focus so that underlying systemic issues are identified and addressed.

25.8 Reactive Capabilities become Proactive and then pre-emptive

"What gift do you think a good servant has that separates them from the others? It's the gift of anticipation. And I'm a good servant. I'm better than good. I'm the best. I'm the perfect servant. I know when they'll be hungry and the food is ready. I know when they'll be tired and the bed is turned down. I know it before they know it themselves."

Mrs Wilson, Gosford Park, 2001

The IT Service Management system of the future will be an omni-present entity with real time analytical capabilities enabling it to make intelligent value based judgements in accordance with the predefined business policies and objectives. With luck, such a system will reduce the level of manual intervention (tinkering) needed to maintain the IT environment and will free up resources to extend the reach of IT further still, allowing the profession to at last become a valued and trusted member of the business community in its own right.

Depending upon industry sector, IT Service Management (ITSM) costs account for between 65 %–80 % of all IT expenditure. That's currently the equivalent of almost $300 billion per year worldwide (which is more than the GDP of Norway). Almost more than three quarters of every IT budget is spent keeping the application lights burning and the wheels of the IT machine turning. Most of this money goes on labour costs. There are more jobs within ITSM and related areas than in any other field within computing. And yet given this prevalence it is bizarre that so little is known about it. This book attempts redress the balance slightly by giving an honest unbiased view of the discipline, its objectives, major processes, and their benefits and shortcomings.

IT is the single most pervasive discipline within the business world today. It touches and affects everything. Irrespective of their particular market sector and expertise, organisations are completely reliant upon IT to enable them to get on with the business of doing business...Managing and mitigating IT risk is critical to the survival of every business. Success is an optional extra! Proactive IT Service Management can be thought of as risk management for IT – Can you afford to ignore it?

List of Figures

Index

Printing: Krips bv, Meppel
Binding: Stürtz, Würzburg